e-RPG

Building Web Applications with RPG

Bradley V. Stone

MIDRANGE COMPUTING
IIR PUBLICATIONS INC.

e-RPG

BUILDING WEB APPLICATIONS WITH RPG

First Edition

First Printing—February 2000

© 2000 Midrange Computing
ISBN: 1-58347-008-5

Midrange Computing
5650 El Camino Real, Suite 225
Carlsbad, CA 92008
www.midrangecomputing.com

V4R4

To my wife, Cindy,
who supported me through the many hours
of putting this book together.

CONTENTS

INTRODUCTION xv
    The Old Standard · xvi
    The New Standard · xvi
        A Whole New Ball Game · · · · · · · · · · · · · · · · · xvii
    e-RPG · xviii

Chapter 1:   AN INTRODUCTION TO HTML 1
    The World Wide Web Lingo · · · · · · · · · · · · · · · · · · · 1
        Hyperlink · 2
        Webmaster · 3
        HTML · 4
        Static Web Pages · 4
        Dynamic Web Pages · · · · · · · · · · · · · · · · · · · 6
    HTML Structures and Tags · · · · · · · · · · · · · · · · · · · 7
        HTML Is to the Web as DDS Is to AS/400 Screens · · · · · · 8
        The Basics of HTML Tags · · · · · · · · · · · · · · · · 9
        Header Tags · 10
        Body Tags · 11
        Heading + Body = Web Page · · · · · · · · · · · · · · · 13

Formatting Your HTML Output with Tables · · · · · · · · · · · · 14
    Using Tables to Align Fields · · · · · · · · · · · · · · · · 15
    Using Tables to Report Data · · · · · · · · · · · · · · · · 17
HTML – The Basic Structure of e-business· · · · · · · · · · · · · 19

Chapter 2:   JAVASCRIPT 21
JavaScript—What's It for? · 21
A JavaScript History Lesson · 22
JavaScript at Work · 23
    JavaScript Cookies · 24
    Field Validation · 25
    Window Relocation or Creation · · · · · · · · · · · · · · · 25
Piecing JavaScript Together· 26
    Variables· 26
    Operators · 27
    Constructs · 28
JavaScript: Objects, Properties, Methods, and Events · · · · · · · 29
    Objects and Properties· 30
    Methods · 31
    Events · 31
JavaScript Examples · 32
    Using JavaScript to Write HTML · · · · · · · · · · · · · · 33
    Using JavaScript to Redirect a Browser· · · · · · · · · · · · 33
    Using JavaScript to Interactively Validate Field Data · · · · · 34
    JavaScript, Cookies, and a Shopping Basket · · · · · · · · · 37
    A JavaScript Quoting System · · · · · · · · · · · · · · · · 42
More Information on JavaScript · · · · · · · · · · · · · · · · · · 44

Chapter 3:   COMMON GATEWAY INTERFACE PROGRAMMING 45
Everything Needs an Interface · · · · · · · · · · · · · · · · · · · 46
    Been Shopping? · 47
    Been e-Shopping? · 47
CGI—Not a Programming Language · · · · · · · · · · · · · · · · 48
    CGI Used as an Interpreter · · · · · · · · · · · · · · · · · · 48
CGI Programming on the AS/400· · · · · · · · · · · · · · · · · · 49
Input and Output with CGI · 50
    A BASIC History · 50
    AS/400 CGI Programming · · · · · · · · · · · · · · · · · · 51
AS/400 CGI Programming Setup · · · · · · · · · · · · · · · · · · 52
    HTTP Configuration Setup for CGI Programming · · · · · · 53
    Service Program Needed for CGI Programming · · · · · · · 54

CGI Program Creation · 55
User Profiles QTMHHTTP and QTMHHTP1 · · · · · · · · 58
AS/400 CGI Programming Considerations · · · · · · · · · · · · 58
A CGI Job's Library List · · · · · · · · · · · · · · · · · · 59
Keep an Eye on Your CGI · · · · · · · · · · · · · · · · · · 60
Access Logs · 61
CGI is Just around the Corner · · · · · · · · · · · · · · · · · 62

Chapter 4:   **THE AS/400 HTTP SERVER** 63
How the HTTP Server Works · · · · · · · · · · · · · · · · · · 64
Configuring the AS/400 HTTP Server · · · · · · · · · · · · · · 66
HTTP Server Commands · · · · · · · · · · · · · · · · · · 66
HTTP Server Configuration · · · · · · · · · · · · · · · · · · · 68
Creating an HTTP Server Configuration · · · · · · · · · · · 68
Configuration Directives · · · · · · · · · · · · · · · · · · 72
HTTP Server Instance · 84
Creating an HTTP Server Instance · · · · · · · · · · · · · · 85
A Closer Look at the Provided HTTP Server Instances · · · · · 87
Putting an Instance and Configuration Together · · · · · · · · · · 89
A Final Note on HTTP Server Instances · · · · · · · · · · · · · 91
The Port Directive · 91
Virtual Hosts · 92
Authority for IFS Objects · · · · · · · · · · · · · · · · · · · 93
The Display Authority (DSPAUT) Command · · · · · · · · · 94
The Change Authority (CHGAUT) Command · · · · · · · · · 95
The Work with Authority (WRKAUT) Command · · · · · · · 96
The AS/400: Web Serving Potential · · · · · · · · · · · · · · · 97

Chapter 5:   **HTTP APIs** 99
Where the APIs Are Found and How They Are Used · · · · · · · 100
HTTP APIs: A Closer Look · · · · · · · · · · · · · · · · · · · 102
QtmhWrStout – Write Standard Output · · · · · · · · · · · 102
QtmhRdStin – Read Standard Input · · · · · · · · · · · · · 105
QtmhGetEnv – Get Environment Variable · · · · · · · · · · 108
QthmCvtDB – Convert to DB · · · · · · · · · · · · · · · · 112
Getting the APIs Ready to Use · · · · · · · · · · · · · · · · · 116
Copy the QTMHCGI Service Program · · · · · · · · · · · · 116
Create a Binding Directory · · · · · · · · · · · · · · · · · 116
Add QTMHCGI to Your Binding Directory · · · · · · · · · · 117
Wagons, East! · 117

Chapter 6: YOUR FIRST E-RPG PROGRAM 119
e-RPG: A New Term for a New Era · · · · · · · · · · · · · · · 120
e-RPG Says, "Hello World" · · · · · · · · · · · · · · · · · · 122
The Hello World e-RPG Program · · · · · · · · · · · · · · 123
e-RPG's Basic Necessities · · · · · · · · · · · · · · · · 125
Compiling and Running Your
Hello World e-RPG Program · · · · · · · · · · · · · · 127
Viewing the HTML Source · · · · · · · · · · · · · · · 129
e-RPG and Dynamic Output · · · · · · · · · · · · · · · · · 130
Relate e-RPG to RPG · · · · · · · · · · · · · · · · · · 130
A Dynamic e-RPG Example · · · · · · · · · · · · · · · · 132
What about Displaying Numeric Data? · · · · · · · · · · · 135
Using BIFs to Convert Numeric Data to Character Data · · · 136
Applying the %EDITC and %EDITW BIFs
to the Customer Report · · · · · · · · · · · · · · · · 137
Modularizing APIs for Ease of Use · · · · · · · · · · · · · · 140
The #WrStout Subprocedure · · · · · · · · · · · · · · · 140
Is e-RPG in Your Future? · · · · · · · · · · · · · · · · · · 144

Chapter 7: READING INPUT FROM A BROWSER 145
HTML's Input Tools · 146
Query String Input vs. Standard Input · · · · · · · · · · · · 148
Query String Input · · · · · · · · · · · · · · · · · · · 148
Standard Input · 149
Using Query String Input · · · · · · · · · · · · · · · · · · 150
Static Query String Input · · · · · · · · · · · · · · · · 150
Dynamic Query String Input · · · · · · · · · · · · · · · 152
Reading Query String Input with e-RPG · · · · · · · · · · 156
Using Standard Input · 160
Standard Input in HTML · · · · · · · · · · · · · · · · · 160
Reading Standard Input with e-RPG · · · · · · · · · · · · 162
Read On · 163

Chapter 8: PUTTING HTML, JAVASCRIPT, AND RPG TOGETHER 165
BVS-Computers · 166
Signing in to BVS-Computers · · · · · · · · · · · · · · · 166
Go Shopping at BVS-Computers · · · · · · · · · · · · · · 169
Set-up for BVS-Computers · · · · · · · · · · · · · · · · · · 175
HTTP Configuration · · · · · · · · · · · · · · · · · · · 175
Physical Files · 177
External Data Structure · · · · · · · · · · · · · · · · · 177

e-RPG Programs · 178
The HTML File · 180
The Future of BVS-Computers · · · · · · · · · · · · · · · · · 180

Chapter 9: **HTTP SERVICE PROGRAMS** 183
Standard HTTP Subprocedures · · · · · · · · · · · · · · · · · · 184
The #WrStout Subprocedure · · · · · · · · · · · · · · · · · 185
The #GetEnv Subprocedure · · · · · · · · · · · · · · · · · 186
The #RdStin Subprocedure · · · · · · · · · · · · · · · · · 188
The #CvtDb Subprocedure · · · · · · · · · · · · · · · · · 190
HTML Subprocedures · 193
Create Hyperlink (#Link) · · · · · · · · · · · · · · · · 193
Create MailTo: Hyperlink (#MailTo) · · · · · · · · · · 195
Return Bold Text (#Bold) · · · · · · · · · · · · · · · · 196
Return Italics Text (#Italics) · · · · · · · · · · · · · · 197
Return Centered Text (#Center) · · · · · · · · · · · · · 197
Return Input Field (#Input) · · · · · · · · · · · · · · · 198
Write Source Member (#WrtSrcMbr) · · · · · · · · · · · 201
Miscellaneous Subprocedures · · · · · · · · · · · · · · · · · 202
Convert Character to Numeric (#CtoN) · · · · · · · · · · 203
Replace Characters (#Replace) · · · · · · · · · · · · · · 204
Service Programs · 207
Service Programs:
Your Secret Weapon for e-RPG Programming · · · · · · · · 208

Chapter 10: **E-RPG TIPS AND TECHNIQUES** 209
Debugging e-RPG Programs · · · · · · · · · · · · · · · · · · 209
Server Side Includes (SSIs) · · · · · · · · · · · · · · · · · 213
Paging · 217
Paging with a Sequential File · · · · · · · · · · · · · · 218
Paging with Keyed Files · · · · · · · · · · · · · · · · · 219
Selecting and Sequencing with Dynamic OPNQRYF · · · · · · · 224
The Web Page · 225
The e-RPG Program · · · · · · · · · · · · · · · · · · · 227
Why OPNQRYF? · 234
Old Dog, New Tricks · 235

AFTERWORD 237
HTML · 238
JavaScript · 238
Common Gateway Interface (CGI) Programming · · · · · · · · · 238

The AS/400 HTTP Server · 239
HTTP APIs· 239
Using RPG for CGI Applications · · · · · · · · · · · · · · · · · · 239
Get Started! · 240

APPENDIX A · 241
HTML Error Messages · 242
HTML References · 243

APPENDIX B · 245
Source for Cookie Basket · 245
Source for BVS-Reprints · 249
JavaScript References · 255

APPENDIX C · 257
Common Gateway Interface (CGI) References · · · · · · · · · · 259

APPENDIX D · 261
Accessing the AS/400 Tasks Page· · · · · · · · · · · · · · · · · 261
Important HTTP Configuration Directives · · · · · · · · · · · · 262
HTTP Configuration Examples · · · · · · · · · · · · · · · · · · 262
    Default HTTP Configuration (V4R4M0) · · · · · · · · · · 262
    Sample of Basic HTTP Configuration · · · · · · · · · · · · 267
Granting Authority to Files in the IFS · · · · · · · · · · · · · · 268
AS/400 HTTP Configuration References · · · · · · · · · · · · · 268

APPENDIX E · 269
HTTP API Parameter Definitions · · · · · · · · · · · · · · · · · 269
HTTP API References · 271

APPENDIX F · 273
Index.html · 273
Invoice Header (INVHDRPF) · · · · · · · · · · · · · · · · · · · 274
Invoice Detail (INVDETPF) · 274
Invoice Detail Logical (INVDET1LF) · · · · · · · · · · · · · · · 275
Item File (ITEMPF) · 275
User File (USERPF) · 275
Sign-In e-RPG Program (SIGNIN) · · · · · · · · · · · · · · · · 276
Display Items e-RPG Program (ITEMS) · · · · · · · · · · · · · 279
Buy Item e-RPG Program (BUYITEM) · · · · · · · · · · · · · 283
Remove Item e-RPG Program (RMVITEM) · · · · · · · · · · · 288
Check-Out e-RPG Program (CHECKOUT) · · · · · · · · · · · 292

Invoice and Ship Order e-RPG Program (INVSHIP) · · · · · · · · · 297
HTTP Configuration · 300

APPENDIX G · 301
HTTP Service Programs · 301
  Write Standard Output (#WrStout) · · · · · · · · · · · · · 302
  Get Environment Variable (#GetEnv) · · · · · · · · · · · · · 302
  Read Standard Input (#RdStin) · · · · · · · · · · · · · · · 303
  Convert to Database (#CvtDB) · · · · · · · · · · · · · · · 304
HTML Subprocedures · 305
  Create Hyperlink (#Link) · · · · · · · · · · · · · · · · · 305
  Create MailTo: Hyperlink (#MailTo) · · · · · · · · · · · · 306
  Return Bold Text (#Bold) · · · · · · · · · · · · · · · · · 306
  Return Italics Text (#Italics) · · · · · · · · · · · · · · · 307
  Return Centered Text (#Center) · · · · · · · · · · · · · · 307
  Return Input Field (#Input) · · · · · · · · · · · · · · · · 308
  Write Source Member (#WrtSrcMbr) · · · · · · · · · · · · 309
Miscellaneous Subprocedures · · · · · · · · · · · · · · · · · · · 310
  Convert Character to Numeric (#CtoN) · · · · · · · · · · · 310
  Replace Characters (#Replace)· · · · · · · · · · · · · · · 312

APPENDIX H · 315
List Items (ITEMLIST) · 315
  Item Master File (ITEMSPF) · · · · · · · · · · · · · · · · 315
  Item Master Logical File (ITEMS1LF) · · · · · · · · · · · · 316
  Item Listing Modules (F.ITEMLIST) · · · · · · · · · · · · · 316
  Item Listing e-RPG Program (ITEMLIST) · · · · · · · · · · 318
BVS-Cars · 320
  BVS-Cars HTML Starting Page (bvscars.html) · · · · · · · · 320
  Car Database (CARSPF)· · · · · · · · · · · · · · · · · · · 321
  External Data Structure for LISTCARS (LISTCARSDS) · · · · 321
  List Cars Subprocedures (F.LISTCARS)· · · · · · · · · · · · 322
  List Cars e-RPG Program (s)· · · · · · · · · · · · · · · · 323

APPENDIX I · 331

INDEX · 333

INTRODUCTION

The term e-business describes a new way of doing business. It's also part of a revolution. Just as the Industrial Revolution modernized manufacturing and production, today the technological revolution is changing the way we do business. A big part of the technological revolution includes doing business on the Internet.

In the past, the Internet has been a place for people to gather information. Online resources such as Usenet, Internet discussion forums, search engines, and Web browsers allowed users to retrieve or discuss interesting information.

Now, the Internet is a place to do business. It is estimated that by the year 2001, billions of dollars will be spent buying merchandise and services on the Web. People already purchase items such as books, cars, and stocks over the Web. The revenue from Web-based sales comprise, on average, 10 percent of a supplier's income. And companies also are using the Internet and intranets to conduct business in hundreds of other ways—from dealer support to customer inquiries to internal reporting. This is what makes e-business so important for you and your company.

THE OLD STANDARD

In the beginning, most companies embraced e-business technology foreign to AS/400 programmers. Companies created new divisions in their Information Technology departments devoted solely to this new technology. These new departments set up non-AS/400-based servers to distribute e-mail, provide Web access, and allow file sharing. AS/400 programmers lucky enough to have e-mail and Web browsing capabilities, soon discovered a new avenue of communication and information retrieval. Taking advantage of such services as newsgroups, discussion forums, and mailing lists, AS/400 programmers accessed the minds of colleagues and individuals to share operations and programming information about the AS/400. Through this initial contact, they experienced a small portion of the power of the Internet.

As the Internet grew and e-business started to take shape, new applications such as Web-based order forms and electronic customer service sites started to emerge. Programs once run using tried-and-true green-screen applications were suddenly being ported to other systems to support these early ventures into Web-based business. Data was usually retrieved from a separate Web server and transferred to the AS/400 for processing. If the team that developed and maintained the original order-entry system was included in the development of these new Web-based applications, the transition was ideally seamless. If they were not, most users' first experiences with e-business most likely weren't pleasant.

Although years of thoughtful work may have been put into developing a company's system, sometimes, in the rush to get connected, oversights and cut corners occurred. When Web-based systems were developed for the same purpose as existing AS/400 systems, duplication of data processes became a problem. Processes that should have been included in the front-end system were omitted, and data had to be reprocessed on the AS/400. Because Web development and AS/400 application development were traditionally viewed as separate endeavors, it was not easy to iron out these discrepancies.

THE NEW STANDARD

If I told you that today you can create and provide fully functional e-business solutions using just your AS/400 and the RPG programming language, would you call me crazy?

For years, the AS/400 has been running multibillion-dollar businesses as well as mom-and-pop stores. When the Internet came onto the scene, it hit hard and fast. Suddenly, businesses required functionality that the AS/400 did not provide. Recognizing the innate potential of the AS/400 to evolve to meet the needs of its users, IBM acted quickly to close this gap in resources.

Since the release of OS/400 V342M0 and V347M0, the AS/400 can act as a Web server, not just a green-screen application server or a database server. In addition, you can solely use RPG to write programs to aid in your Web solutions. This is just the solution for which AS/400 programmers were waiting.

A Whole New Ball Game

You've depended on the AS/400 throughout the years to be a reliable machine that gets business functions done. As the AS/400 has become more powerful, more functional, and most important, more affordable, you can expand your horizons and apply that same trusted architecture to your e-business solutions. The AS/400 can now be a mail server, a file transfer protocol (FTP) server, a file server and, most important, a Web server. (Contrary to popular opinion, getting the Web server running—not programming Web applications—is the most challenging obstacle you will face. It's important to get your AS/400 programmers trained in Hypertext Transfer Protocol (HTTP) server functions before you begin the transition to AS/400-based e-business.)

You may have heard the terms HTML, CGI, Perl, Java, and JavaScript used to describe Web programming, and you may have wondered how your development staff was going to master all these new languages. What if I were to tell you that to use the AS/400 as a Web server, your programmers need only learn one: Hypertext Markup Language (HTML)?

HTML is the basic language needed to make the AS/400 a successful e-business machine. And HTML isn't even a programming language; it's a markup language that is easy to learn and easy to use. If you are wondering how HTML will perform all the functions needed for your Web-based business venture, the answer is sitting in the QRPGLESRC source physical file on your AS/400 right now.

E-RPG

E-RPG is a new term for a new era for the AS/400. RPG, or even COBOL (common business-oriented language), can be used to produce Web interfaces for your company. And the great thing is that there is only a small learning curve, if any. To produce applications on the Web, you really only need to modify your current applications.

Programs that take orders and produce reports can be modified to run as Web applications and still use RPG. When you think about it, there isn't any real procedural difference between a green-screen order-entry system, and a Web-based order-entry system. The only significant difference is the user interface.

The same holds true for reports. The process used to gather the information to produce the report will be the same whether it is printed on green-bar paper or displayed on a Web page.

The purpose of this book is to provide the knowledge needed for your AS/400 staff to start developing e-business solutions for your company using your trustworthy machine. It will take you through the basics of HTML programming to JavaScript programming, through the setup of the HTTP server, and finally e-RPG programming techniques.

It will be a great asset if someone on your development team understands how Web applications work, even if you use the AS/400 for a small portion of your Web business. When you are dealing with other programmers who are developing the front-end Web systems on another platform, you will have someone who understands the terminology and can speak with them.

e-RPG will help you put the ball back in your court when developing e-business solutions by using the power and stability of the AS/400 to enhance your company's exposure and profitability with the resources that you already have available to you.

Now let's get started!

1

AN INTRODUCTION TO HTML

Of the millions of Web pages available on the Internet, there is one ingredient common to all of them. The language used to display the information—whether it is text, graphics, sound bytes, or even streaming video—is Hypertext Markup Language or HTML.

HTML is the foundation of the World Wide Web (WWW). Whenever you use your browser to view a page on the WWW, you can bet that there is HTML in one form or another running behind the scenes to produce the output you see. HTML is a simple way to create documents that are platform independent.

Because HTML plays such an important role for e-business, this chapter introduces you to the concept of both static and dynamic Web pages as well as to the basic structures and tags used to create either type of HTML Web pages. For those new to the WWW, a few terms will be discussed first.

THE WORLD WIDE WEB LINGO

Knowing the lingo of the WWW is a good starting point to building Web pages. These days, the WWW is such a significant part of our lives that terms are being used and created faster than most of us can keep up. You might be exposed to the terms defined here in everyday life, at work, or even in this book.

In any industry there are terms that are specific to that industry. Sometimes these terms make sense and other times they don't—even if they are explained. Also, when you ask for a definition of the terms, there are some people who know what the terms mean but can't explain them to a person who is new to the industry. The common terms that follow are defined so anyone can understand them.

Hyperlink

A hyperlink is one of the most-used devices when developing a Web page. Hyperlinks connect one Web page to another. These pages can be located on the same Web server machine or on machines that are hundreds or thousands of miles apart.

A hyperlink can take the form of either text or a graphic. Hyperlink text is usually underlined and a different color than the rest of the text on the page. A common color you will see for a hyperlink is blue, but depending on how the page is created, a hyperlink can be one of many colors, fonts, or styles.

A hyperlink graphic is used in place of text. The graphic usually does a sufficient job of explaining where this hyperlink will take you even if the graphic doesn't contain any text. A good example of a graphic hyperlink is a picture of an envelope or mailbox. This usually tells the users that, if they click on this graphic, they will be able to e-mail someone associated with the Web page for more information.

When you move your cursor around on a page and the cursor changes to a different icon, usually a pointing hand, you've found a hyperlink. You can "click here" to go to another page that might include more information on the subject material, or the hyperlink may simply link you to a related page.

There is one type of hyperlink that will not take you to another Web page. This is known as a Mail To hyperlink. When this type of hyperlink is clicked, it usually starts your e-mail program and automatically fills in the To address. The text for this type of hyperlink will usually be something like "send me e-mail!" or "contact us." This is a handy hyperlink to encourage feedback from visitors to your Web site or to provide customer service.

A hyperlink can be related to a menu option on the AS/400. When a user selects a certain menu option, the program that is associated with that menu option is executed. This program can display information on the screen or start a job that produces a report. In the same sense, a hyperlink can display another static page or display report information based on selected criteria or input by the user.

Webmaster

The *Webmaster* is an individual who manages a Web site. The Webmaster plays one of the most important roles in the organization as it relates to Web-based material and setting up and monitoring the machines that run Web sites.

The Webmaster develops pages, makes them available to the public, maintains the Web server machine, monitors the traffic to the Web site, and performs any other work needed to keep the site in tip-top shape.

The term Webmaster, although singular, can be a reference to more than one person. It's easier to have a single reference than multiple references when dealing with support for a Web page. A Mail To hyperlink to the site's Webmaster can be compared to a single phone number that someone would use to get in touch with technical support. If you had 15 people who were in charge of Web development, it would be confusing to list all 15 e-mail addresses on your Web page. Using a single Webmaster contact will make it easier for the user, and allow the mail to be routed to the appropriate person or persons.

Don't be afraid to let the Webmaster know if you encountered a problem on their site. That's what they are there for, and most of them actually enjoy getting messages that report problems. Most Webmasters take pride in their work and are eager to fix even the smallest of problems, such as typographical errors.

For the same reason that software companies have technical support and help-desk personnel, Internet sites have a Webmaster to handle technical problems. The Webmaster can be compared to the AS/400 system operator. Believe it or not, all the fun involved in surfing the Web actually includes people in the background who must maintain and upgrade the pages.

HTML

HTML is a language that is used to display Web pages on your browser. HTML is an interpreted language (which means that no compiler is necessary). The data is interpreted as it is encountered and displayed on your browser in a format that is understood by the users.

HTML really isn't even a programming language. It's more of a document-processing language similar to those used to create word-processing documents. Although you never see the commands that allow you to type text in bold or italics using your word processor, you know that there must be something happening in the background to tell your computer to display the text as bold or italics. This is essentially the main purpose of HTML.

HTML can be compared with DDS specs that are used to display screens on the AS/400. In order for you to change the style of text on a screen using DDS, you must use keywords that change the attributes of that text, whether you are changing the color or displaying the text as bold or underlined. HTML includes text that is usually surrounded by tags to tell the browser what font, color, or style to use to display designated text.

Static Web Pages

The term *static* means something that is characterized by a lack of movement, animation, or progression. This means that the Web page doesn't change very often, and when it does it is though some sort of human intervention.

Static Web pages are created by an HTML programmer, uploaded to a Web server (published), and viewed when you surf the Web. These pages change when the Webmaster of the site changes the HTML code of the page, which changes the content of the page, and then uploads the updated HTML source to the Web server. The next time you view that particular Web page, you are viewing a new edition of that page.

Static Web pages are used for the most part as a starting point or as informational pages. For example, the first page of a Web site usually contains a menu system. This menu includes a set of hyperlinks to other pages. Because the menu doesn't change often, this page can be created as a static document and published to the Web.

If you were to relate a static Web page to something that already exists and is in use on the AS/400, menus would be a good example. When you create menus on the AS/400, they are usually created with Screen Design Aid (SDA). You place text on the menu that tells the user the option. This information is for the user. Behind that text (and what developers are concerned with) are the programs that are executed when the user selects a specific option. In a menu-type static Web page, the hyperlink text would be the same as the menu text, and the hyperlink would be equivalent to the command executed when a menu option is taken.

Figure 1.1 contains a simple menu, created on an AS/400, which is used to direct the user around the AS/400 system. Figure 1.2 contains the AS/400 menu's HTML counterpart using hyperlinks instead of menu options.

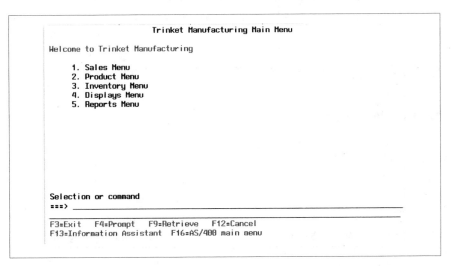

Figure 1.1: AS/400 menu example.

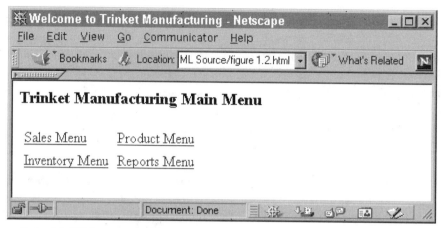

Figure 1.2: HTML menu example.

One difference between an AS/400 menu and an HTML menu is the lack of option numbers in the HTML menu. The user clicks on the menu option instead of entering a number.

Another difference between an AS/400 menu and an HTML menu is the separate options for Display Menu and Reports Menu in the AS/400 menu. On the HTML menu, there is only one option for Reports Menu. With HTML, the printing is done by using the browser's Print option. This feature saves the programmer from writing similar programs for display and reporting, and also saves paper because the users select only the information that they want to print.

Dynamic Web Pages

The term *dynamic* means something that is marked by continuous use, productive activity, or change. This is the opposite of static. So, instead of a Web page that doesn't change often, a dynamic Web page is a page that changes continuously.

Dynamic Web pages are created by Common Gateway Interface (CGI) programs. It is important to remember that CGI is not a programming language itself, but a method of programming. In the AS/400 world, *subfile programs* are programs written in RPG or COBOL that display a list of information to the user. The description *subfile program* in no way tells us in what language the program is written.

In the same way that a subfile program can be written in RPG or COBOL on the AS/400, a CGI program can be written in languages such as Visual Basic, Java, Perl, RPG, or COBOL. In the Internet world, CGI programs are programs that dynamically create a Web page.

Dynamic Web pages are used on the Internet to show real-time information to a user. The CGI program, when executed, writes the HTML code on the fly, displaying a Web page that could be different each time it is viewed. The information displayed on a dynamic Web page is built using data that resides on your server machine. If this data changes, the information displayed on the Web page changes, making the process dynamic.

A good example of a dynamic Web page is a page that tracks a package from its shipping point to its destination. When the package is shipped, it is assigned a tracking number that follows the package everywhere it goes. As the package is scanned at different locations, the shipper's data is updated. At the same time this data is updated, the Web page that displays the tracking information is updated because the Web page uses live data to display information.

Dynamic displays themselves are not a new concept by any means. Each time you write a display, subfile, or report program, you are writing a program that produces a dynamic display or report. Take an inventory display, for example. When you first come to the screen, you see that item number WIDGET has a quantity of 100. Meanwhile, someone in the warehouse is shipping 25 of item WIDGET out the door, deducting this quantity from inventory. Once the amount on-hand in your inventory file is updated, the information that gets displayed to the user is updated. The same would hold true if you had a CGI program that wrote the information to a Web browser, instead of an RPG program that displayed the inventory information for an item on a terminal.

HTML STRUCTURES AND TAGS

This section introduces you to the various commands, known as *tags*, used in HTML programming. Once you've reviewed the HTML tags discussed here, it is a good idea to experiment with them to see what they do. As with most learning processes, actually doing the work is when you will learn the most. When you see the results of your HTML code, it will all come together.

The tags discussed in this section are by no means all-inclusive, but they will provide you with the basics. Tutorials are available on the Internet should you desire to take your HTML code to the extreme. If you understand the basic tags discussed here, you will accomplish what some HTML programmers sometimes forget: the purpose of a Web site is to provide information first and foremost. Adding graphics and pretty designs can come later.

HTML Is to the Web as DDS Is to AS/400 Screens

The first display screen you created using DDS might have seemed tedious at first, but once you were comfortable with it, it became a breeze. After you were able to program display screens on your own, you probably were introduced to the AS/400s Screen Design Aid (SDA). SDA is a What-You-See-Is-What-You-Get (WYSIWYG) AS/400 screen development tool that makes creating display screens simple.

Being able to build screens without SDA gives you the power to know what you can do with field attributes while in SDA. This gives you the capability to fine tune your screens outside of SDA.

Developing Web pages in HTML is the same as building display screens, although I suggest taking the opposite approach to learning HTML. Instead of learning all the HTML structures and tags needed at once, create a page with a WYSIWYG Web-page developer and then study the source generated to see what HTML tags were used. Also, when you encounter a page while surfing the Internet that has something interesting in it, use your browser's View Source option to see what technique was used to create it.

If you are new to HTML programming, I suggest you take it slowly. Don't start with a page that contains graphics, tables, multiple text formats, and hyperlinks. Instead, start small. Create a page that contains text and one or two hyperlinks. Slowly add more features such as graphics or tables. Carefully view the HTML source until you understand what each tag does.

To get started, let's take a look at some of the basics of HTML tags and the more general tags used in HTML programming.

The Basics of HTML Tags

HTML tags are used in Web page creation as delimiters that a browser uses to parse data. Tags usually include a beginning and ending label that surrounds the data. The tags can be used to change the font, color, or style of the information. Tags also are used to create tables and hyperlinks and to display images in your document.

Figure 1.3 shows how to use a generic tag that is for example only. As far as I know, there isn't an HTML tag with the name TAG.

```
<TAG>The data goes in between the beginning and ending tags.</TAG>
```

Figure 1.3: An example of how an HTML tag surrounds data.

Notice that a couple of items are constant with most HTML tags. First, the tag itself is enclosed in the Less Than (<) and Greater Than (>) characters. Second, the ending tag includes a slash (/) before the actual tag. This tells the browser that this is the end of the tag section.

Although ending tags are not always necessary, I believe it is important to use them "just in case." Because there are cases where ending tags are mandatory, you should learn to use them now, so that you will code your HTML correctly in the future. Always using end tags is a good habit. (Remember how you felt when you started working on an RPG program only to find the original programmer didn't qualify the END statements?) Qualifying END statements (i.e. ENDIF, ENDDO, and ENDSL) makes reading RPG code much easier. It is the same with HTML end tags.

The first and most important tag is the <HTML> tag. This tag encloses the entire document and lets the browser know that the document it is displaying is HTML. Figure 1.4 shows how the <HTML> tag is used.

```
<HTML>
All the other HTML code goes between these tags.
</HTML>
```

Figure 1.4: The all-inclusive <HTML> tag.

9

The <HTML> tag is an all-inclusive tag that surrounds all of the HTML text included in the document. Other tags are used to separate different sections of the document as well.

Header Tags

Now that you know what the basic structure of a tag is, let's review some of the basic tags and when to use them. HTML pages can be broken into two sections. The first section is known as the header section. This would be the equivalent to a screen or report heading. The tags used most often in the header section are <HEAD> and <TITLE>. These tags are described in Table 1.1.

Table 1.1: Header Tags.

Tag	Action	Example
HEAD	Tells the browser that the header section follows.	<HEAD>Heading HTML</HEAD>
TITLE	Defines the document's title. This text appears in the status bar.	<TITLE>This text will appear in the status bar of the browser</TITLE>

Table 1.1 contains real examples except for the <HEAD> tag. That's because the <HEAD> tag is used as an inclusive tag. It does nothing more than tell the browser that the information between the beginning and ending tags is header information. The <HEAD> tag is similar to the <HTML> tag that tells the browser that the information included in this document is of type HTML. Figure 1.5 shows an example of HTML code that uses all these header tags.

```
<HTML>
<HEAD>
<TITLE>This text will appear in the status bar of the
browser</TITLE>
</HEAD>
</HTML>
```

Figure 1.5: Example HTML source using basic header tags.

Figure 1.6 shows what the browser output will be from the HTML code shown in Figure 1.5.

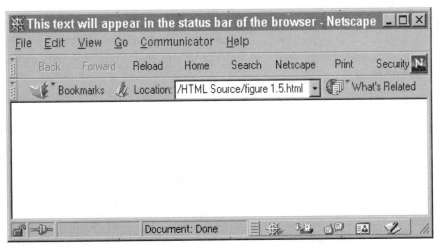

Figure 1.6: Output from HTML source in Figure 1.5.

In Figure 1.6, notice that the status bar of the browser reads the same as the text between the <TITLE> tags. Nothing else is displayed on the browser by the two tags used. For displaying information on the browser, you place information in the body of the document.

Body Tags

The <BODY> tags in an HTML document can be compared to the detail lines found on an AS/400 screen or report. The body of an HTML document follows the head and includes the meat-and-potatoes of the information you want to output to the user. The <BODY> tags enclose the entire body section of the document, as is shown in Figure 1.7.

```
<HTML>
<HEAD>
Heading HTML Code
</HEAD>
<BODY>
All of the code for the body of the HTML document goes here.
</BODY>
</HTML>
```

Figure 1.7: The <BODY> tag encloses the information within the body of the HTML document.

11

Table 1.2 shows a few of the more common tags used the in the body of an HTML document and gives an explanation of what function each tag performs. These tags are used more often in e-RPG programs that produce reports and display information.

Table 1.2: Body Tags.		
Tag	**Action**	**Example**
A	Anchor – used to create a hyperlink	<A href="http://www.mypage.com">Click Here for my Homepage!</A>
CENTER	Centers text	<CENTER>This text is centered</CENTER>
BOLD	Displays text as bold	<BOLD>This text is **BOLD**</BOLD>
TABLE	Table data	<TABLE> *Table Data* </TABLE>
TR	Table row data	<TR>*Table Row Data*</TR>
TD	Table cell data	<TD>*Table Cell Data*</TD>
H*n*	Header text	<H1>This is Header 1 Text</H1>
FORM	Form	<FORM>*Form Data*</FORM>
TEXTAREA	Scrollable textarea input	<TEXTAREA name=comments rows=5 cols=50></TEXTAREA>
INPUT	Input field	<INPUT type=text name=email size=30>
BR	Line break	

The last two tags in Table 1.2 are different from the rest. The <INPUT> and <BR> tags have no ending tags.

For more complete information on HTML and tags, you can read the vast amount of information available for free on the Internet or pick up a book on HTML. This book simply introduces the tags you will see most often and explains how tags are used to produce an HTML document.

Heading + Body = Web Page

Now that we've reviewed the basic steps to create a Web page, you can combine the steps to make a Web page that uses all of the examples. With this process, the flow and use of these tags will be self-evident after careful examination.

This sample Web page simply displays information. It contains fields that can be filled in on screen, but nothing will happen because there is no processing program to read the data. Also, I have left out the TABLE, TR, and TD tags for this example. The e-RPG section of this book reviews how to process these fields. For now, focus on how tags work. Figure 1.8 contains the HTML code for the first real HTML example.

```
<HTML>
<HEAD>
<TITLE>e-RPG:  Our first HTML Example</TITLE>
</HEAD>
<BODY>
<H1>Heading 1 Goes Here</H1>
<H2>This is Heading 2.  Smaller than Heading 1</H2>
<BOLD>Please fill out the following form.  Feel free to leave a
comment in the comment box as well.  Press the SUBMIT button
when you are done. <BOLD>
<BR>
<FORM>
   Name:<INPUT type=text name=yourname size=50>
<BR>
E-Mail:<INPUT type=text name=email size=30>
<BR><BR>
Comment Box
<BR>
<TEXTAREA name=comments rows=5 cols=50></TEXTAREA>
<BR>
<INPUT type=button value="Submit">
</FORM>
<CENTER>
<A href="mailto:stone@midrangecomputing.com">Send me mail!</A>
</CENTER>
</BODY>
</HTML>
```

Figure 1.8: The HTML code for our example, using the tags discussed in this chapter.

Figure 1.9 shows what the final product looks like when the source in Figure 1.8 is viewed from a browser.

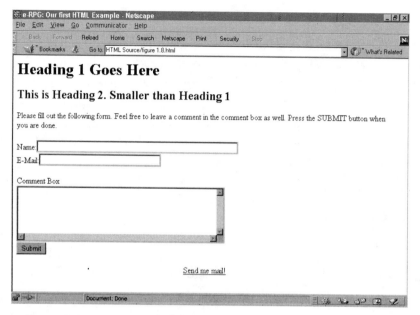

Figure 1.9: Browser output from Figure 1.8.

Chances are that if you're an avid Web surfer, you've seen a form similar to the one shown in Figure 1.9. While this example shows you how easy it is to create the form, processing the information requires a little more work. Chapter 6 covers e-RPG programming.

FORMATTING YOUR HTML OUTPUT WITH TABLES

Tables may be the most used tags in the Web programming world. The uses for tables is endless when it comes to formatting a Web page.

If you have ever done any HTML programming, you know that sometimes it's hard to align text next to a graphic: When you insert the graphic, it acts as one character on the line. But, you know you've seen Web pages that appear to have an entire paragraph next to or surrounding a graphic, similar to how words wrap around a photograph in a newspaper article. This is done with tables.

Another use for tables is in displaying data in columns and rows, as is commonly seen in reports. Using tables with rows and columns to display this data makes it easier to read.

Using Tables to Align Fields

Examine the HTML code shown in Figure 1.10 and the corresponding Web page it creates as shown in Figure 1.11. Notice how the input fields for Name and Mother's Maiden Name don't look right. This is because they aren't aligned.

```
<HTML>
<HEAD>
<TITLE>Unaligned Input</TITLE>
</HEAD>
<BODY>
<FORM>
Name:<INPUT type=text name=yourname size=50>
<BR>
Mother's Maiden Name:<INPUT type=text name=mommaiden size=30>
</FORM>
</BODY>
</HTML>
```

Figure 1.10: A bad example of formatting input fields.

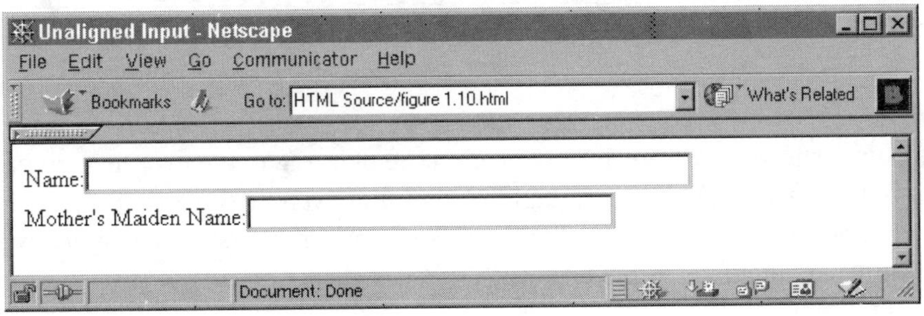

Figure 1.11: Output from Figure 1.11.

When you use a table to align these fields, the outcome will be much more pleasing to the eye. Examine Figures 1.12 and 1.13, which use a table to align the data shown in Figure 1.10.

```
<HTML>
<HEAD>
<TITLE>Aligned Input</TITLE>
</HEAD>
<BODY>
<FORM>
<TABLE>
<TR><TD>Name:</TD>
<TD><INPUT type=text name=yourname size=50></TD></TR>
<TR><TD>Mother's Maiden Name:</TD>
<TD><INPUT type=text name=mommaiden size=30></TD></TR>
</TABLE>
</FORM>
</BODY>
</HTML>
```

Figure 1.12: An example of using tables to format input fields.

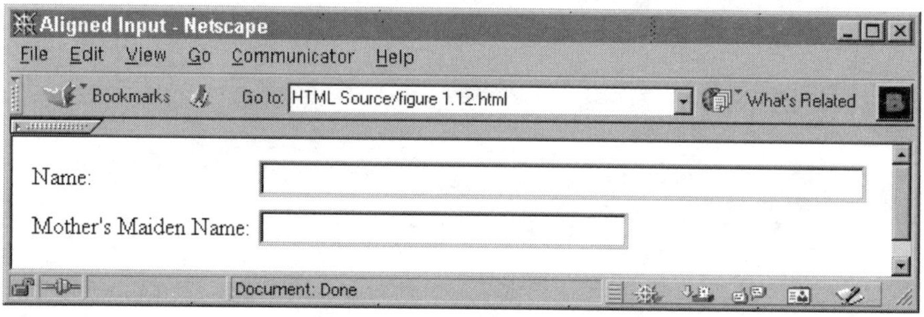

Figure 1.13: Output from Figure 1.12.

The output shown in Figure 1.13 is much more pleasing to the eye. In Web page design, there are many tools available. Sometimes even the little things like lining up input fields make all the difference between a successful page and a page that someone might not come back to.

Using HTML and WYSIWYG page development tools, rather than Screen Design Aids (SDA), makes it simple to create attractive, eye-pleasing Web pages.

Using Tables to Report Data

You can see how tables can help you design forms for a Web page, but let's look at how to use tables to format output data.

Most of us are familiar with subfiles on the AS/400. Subfiles contain neatly formatted detail data (much like a report does). Through our programming careers, one thing seems to remain constant: there will always be a header section followed by repeating detail data. There's just no getting away from that fact.

HTML can be used much the same as subfiles are used to produce easy-to-read output.

Let's take for example an inventory file, such as an item file. This file may contain an item number, a description of the item, and a quantity on hand. You already know how to run a report on this item file, and also how to write a subfile program to display this data on an AS/400 screen. But, how do you display this data in HTML format? Our good friend, the table, pulls through again.

The actual programming required to create the HTML for such tables is discussed in chapter 6. For now, let's focus on how you use the <TABLE> HTML tags to format output to a browser. Table 1.3 shows the data to be output to the browser.

Table 1.3: Item File Data.		
Item Number	**Item Description**	**Quantity On-Hand**
FF1LB	One Pound Bag of French Fries	60
QPHAMPAT	Quarter Pound Hamburger Pattie	1,050
BUN12	Twelve Pack of Buns	42
BUNSS12	Twelve Pack Sesame Seed Buns	15

Transferring the data from Table 1.3 into an HTML table should be rather easy because the data is already in a table as it is displayed on the page. It is a good example of how the <TABLE> HTML tags work. There are really only three tags to remember:

1. <TABLE></TABLE> These tags surround the entire table.

2. <TR></TR> These tags surround a row of data and are included inside the TABLE tags.

3. <TD></TD> These tags surround a cell of data in a row and are included inside the TR tags.

Figure 1.14 contains the HTML code for the Web page that will display the item inventory data on a Web browser.

```
<HTML>
<HEAD>
<TITLE>Juicy Burgers 'r' Us</TITLE>
</HEAD>
<BODY>
<TABLE border="1">
<TR><TD>Item Number</TD>
<TD>Description</TD>
<TD align="right">On-Hand</TD></TR>
<TR><TD>FF1LB</TD>
<TD>One pound bag of french fries</TD>
<TD align="right">60</TD></TR>
<TR><TD>QPHAMPAT</TD>
<TD>Quarter Pound Hamburger Pattie</TD>
<TD align="right">1050</TD></TR>
<TR><TD>BUN12</TD>
<TD>Twelve Pack of Buns</TD>
<TD align="right">42</TD></TR>
<TR><TD>BUN12SS</TD>
<TD>Twelve Pack Sesame Seed Buns</TD>
<TD align="right">15</TD></TR>
</TABLE>
</BODY>
</HTML>
```

Figure 1.14: HTML code to display inventory data using a table.

Examining Figure 1.14, you will see that I have surrounded the entire table with the <TABLE></TABLE> tags. Next, I have surrounded each row of data with the <TR></TR> tags. Lastly, I surround each table cell located in each row with the <TD></TD> tags. The only other thing to note is the align="right" keyword on some of the <TD> tags. This is simply a keyword that tells the browser that the data in this cell should be aligned to the right. This keyword is used on numeric data so that these particular cells will contain data that is aligned to the right. Figure 1.15 is the output for the HTML code shown in Figure 1.14.

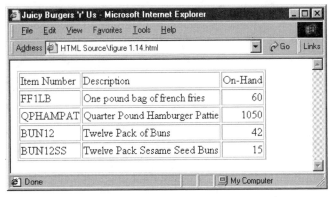

Figure 1.15: Output from Figure 1.14 uses a table to align data.

As you can see in Figure 1.15, the data in the On-Hand column is aligned to the right the same as it would appear on a subfile or report produced on the AS/400.

Tables are real workhorses of Web page design. Using tables to align text fields and, more important, to present data in tabular, row-and-column format are only two uses for tables. You will find other uses as you report data on your Web pages.

HTML – THE BASIC STRUCTURE OF E-BUSINESS

Before you can start writing programs that create Web pages, you must first understand the basics of HTML. If you can't create HTML pages and if you aren't familiar with the basic tags and structures, you won't be able to use the Web as a powerful tool for e-business.

Although this chapter touched on the basics of HTML, it is by no means a complete resource for HTML. There are plenty of sources on the Web that include well-written tutorials and step-by-step guides. This chapter was meant as an introduction to HTML, as well as to the HTML tags used later in this book.

If you are still unsure of your HTML coding abilities, please take the time to practice creating pages similar to those examples shown in this chapter and in other resources. Practice until you are familiar with the use of all HTML tags explained in this chapter. After all, practice makes perfect!

2

JAVASCRIPT

When you research and develop your e-business strategy, you will no
doubt run across another programming language known as JavaScript.
JavaScript is another powerful tool in the arsenal of the e-business programmer.
Don't let the name scare you. JavaScript isn't directly related to Java. The only
thing JavaScript and Java have in common is their names. If it weren't for the
huge Java programming surge, JavaScript wouldn't be called JavaScript. A brief
history of JavaScript will be covered later in this chapter. Let's first look at the
uses for JavaScript.

JAVASCRIPT—WHAT'S IT FOR?

JavaScript can be used in Web pages to perform many functions that otherwise
would require a Common Gateway Interface (CGI) program to perform on the
server side.

JavaScript runs on the client's machine, and it is as easy to add to a Web page as
it is to add HTML commands. JavaScript also is included as part of your HTML

document. The JavaScript source can be located between the <HTML> beginning and ending tags along with the rest of the HTML source.

JavaScript makes pages more interactive and user friendly without the use of server side programs. JavaScript can be used to redirect your browser's window, open a new window, auto-fill fields on a form, even interactively verify input from a browser, among many other things.

JavaScript is helpful in almost all of these cases, and there is much more that JavaScript can do besides these tasks. Once you learn the basics of JavaScript and feel comfortable using it, you will find many design uses for it.

A JavaScript History Lesson

JavaScript is not Java, is in no way directly related to Java, and is not nearly as complex a programming language as Java is. In fact, Java Script is not really a programming language at all.

JavaScript is, in fact, a scripting language that has an interesting history. JavaScript was developed by Netscape to interact with its server software called LiveWire. At the time of its development, it was named LiveScript. LiveScript was developed to aid in the server-side administration of LiveWire and to enhance the presentation of client-side HTML.

The developers of Java partnered with Netscape and renamed LiveScript JavaScript. It's been confusing ever since. JavaScript gained a lot of its notoriety by implementing the word *Java* into its name, but because Java is a difficult language to master, many programmers were apprehensive about using something that sounded like it might include Java programming.

JavaScript code is embedded in HTML code and is an interpreted language. This means you do not compile and make objects for JavaScript. When the JavaScript code is read it is run, similar to OCL from the System/36 days, or the BASIC programming language.

This short history on JavaScript should ease your mind and let you know that there is a difference between the increasingly popular Java programming language and the scripting language JavaScript.

It is entirely possible to create Web pages without using JavaScript at all, or using only JavaScript. By experimenting with JavaScript, you can save time developing your Web site and make it more interactive and user friendly.

JavaScript at Work

If you think you have never seen or used JavaScript, you're probably wrong. Chances are you have used it on the Web pages you visit—without even knowing it. If you've ever visited a site that asks you to provide information such as your name or e-mail address, and then returned to that page to find the fields were filled in automatically, you've most likely seen JavaScript at work.

JavaScript also is used with online forms or surveys where the user can enter information. If you've ever had a dialog box appear on screen notifying you that a certain field is required when you tried to skip that field, such as a telephone number, you've seen JavaScript at work.

JavaScript also can be used to display how many times you've visited a page. For example, you visit a Web page and fill in your name when a dialog box appears. The page then displays the following message:

"Hello, Brad. You have been to this page one time."

If you leave this page, continue surfing, and return to the page, you might see the following message on screen.

"Hello, Brad. You have been to this page two times."

How did it know how many times you had visited the page? Again, JavaScript at work.

You may be familiar with or heard some of the terms related to JavaScript programming. One of the most recognized and powerful JavaScript tools is called a *cookie*.

JavaScript Cookies

Cookies are files that store bits of information on the client-side machine. In other words, when you visit a site that uses cookies, the site uses JavaScript to place this file on your machine as you browse the page. Cookies usually have expiration dates that are set by the Web programmer. They may be set to expire in a week, or much longer. It depends on the use of the cookie for the particular application.

When HTML programmers use cookies, they are trying to save you keystrokes and time. Cookies help make visiting a Web page a pleasant experience.

Some people are afraid of cookies, but there isn't a reason to be. Cookies are, for the most part, harmless. They are stored in a central specific directory on your machine so that they are contained and cannot affect any of your other system files or programs. It is virtually impossible for a cookie to damage or hurt your machine, so unless you're really paranoid, don't be alarmed when your browser asks if you want to accept a cookie from a site you are visiting. However, you will only see this warning if your browser is set up to ask you if you want to accept cookies or not.

After you return to the page that created the cookie, the cookie is then read using more JavaScript and the information stored in the cookie is used to automatically load information back to your browser or to perform another specific task.

JavaScript cookies are one way that shopping cart technology is used on the Web. Cookies allow you to visit a site, fill your shopping cart, and leave without checking out. When you return a day, a week, or two weeks later, your shopping cart still contains the items that you left there. You can either check out or add or remove items from your shopping cart.

Shopping carts are probably the best use for cookies on the Web today. There are other ways to store this information, but it would require users to enter something, such as an order number, the next time they return to get their shopping cart back in the state they left it. With cookies, this harmless information can be stored on your machine for later use. An example of using JavaScript and cookies as a shopping basket can be found later in this chapter.

The bottom line with cookies is this: don't be scared to accept them, and if the application permits, be sure to include them in the Web pages you design.

Field Validation

JavaScript also can be used to perform interactive validation of fields that appear on a form. When a user completes a form on a Web site, instead of running a program and displaying a new page to show any errors, JavaScript can be used to perform this validation without leaving the current page.

This process can be performed either when the user leaves the current field or submits the entire form for processing. It depends on how you want to set up your site.

This type of validation makes your pages more user friendly and executes more quickly than a server-side program. Even the execution of fairly complex JavaScript functions is seemingly instantaneous.

Checking field data interactively, as opposed to displaying another page containing errors, eliminates the chance of losing information that is already entered on the form since you don't leave the page on which you are entering the information. Sometimes users, especially newer users, aren't familiar with the Back button on their browser, which returns them to the previous page. If the user doesn't leave the actual page until things are entered correctly, there is little chance of confusion on their part. They won't feel frustrated or threatened by the complexity of your site.

Window Relocation or Creation

There will be times when you want to redirect a user to another page or create a separate window for the user to enter information, such as a user ID and password.

Using JavaScript is an easy way to redirect pages or create new windows. For example, when a user leaves your page, you can use JavaScript to open a small informational window that displays the message, "Thank you for visiting."

Reading information from a browser's form fields with JavaScript makes passing variables to a CGI program easier. If the data is not sensitive, this is a perfectly acceptable way to do this. Because you are already using JavaScript to validate the data, why not use JavaScript to pass the data to the next processing CGI program? This technique is discussed later in this chapter and in chapter 7.

PIECING JAVASCRIPT TOGETHER

JavaScript consists of many of the same elements that are included in other programming languages. Most of us are familiar with the programming language RPG. RPG contains elements such as fields, either file or user-defined; operators such as ADD, EVAL, and LOOKUP; and constructs such as IF, DO, and WHEN.

JavaScript also contains variables, operators, and constructs that make up the basis of the language. They are very similar to other languages such as C or Java, but easier to use. Let's take a closer look at each of these constructs.

Variables

Variables in JavaScript are the same as variables in other programming languages. Fields that are defined in HTML forms contain properties that can be accessed by JavaScript as variables. These properties can be used and manipulated as any other variable in your JavaScript. For example, a text field on a form has a property of Value that contains the value of the field. The Value property can be used to retrieve or change the value of the field. Another property is Length and it contains the length of the field. This property can be used to access the length of a particular field, but cannot be changed in your JavaScript.

The variables used in JavaScript are program- or user-created objects that store data. JavaScript variables can either be global or local to the function in which they are declared. User-defined variables in JavaScript are very similar to variables used in RPG on the D-Specs. These are variables that the user creates to hold information, whether it is character, numeric, or boolean.

Operators

JavaScript operators are similar to those found in languages such as C, Java, or Pascal. Operators are used to assign values to variables or to test certain conditions in your program. Table 2.1 contains some of the more common operators used in JavaScript.

Table 2.1: Common JavaScript Operators.

Operator	Action	Example
>, <	Greater Than, Less Than conditional operators	If (number1 > number2)
==	Equal To conditional operator	If (number1 == number2)
!=	Not Equal To conditional operator	If (number1 != number2)
&&	AND conditional operator	If (number1 == number2) && (number1 > number3)
||	OR conditional operator	If (number1 > number2) || (number1 == number3)
++	Increment a numeric variable	number++
=	Variable assignment	Text = "Hello!"
+,-,*,/	Add, Subtract, Multiply, and Divide mathematical operators	number1 = (number2 + number3) number1 = (number2 – number3) number1 = (number2 * number3) number1 = (number2 / number3)

There are a couple of gotchas that you must watch out for when using JavaScript operators. The first, and most important, will be familiar to you if you have done any C or JavaScript programming.

Do not confuse the Assignment (=) and Equal To (==) conditional operators. It is important to remember that when you are testing a condition, (is the value of field a equal to the value of field b?), to use two subsequent equal signs. If you do not, it will treat the statement as an assignment even if it exists within a conditional statement. This usually ends up with the condition always returning a "true" value.

The second item to watch out for is the use of parentheses to express precedence within an expression. This holds true for both conditional testing and mathematical expressions. For example, coding:

```
if (variable1 = 1) && (variable2 = 2) || (variable3 = 3)
```

will not be treated the same as:

```
if (variable1 = 1) && ((variable2 = 2) || (variable3 = 3))
```

In the same way, the following mathematical expressions will be treated differently as well, and in most cases, they will produce two different values.

```
variable1 = variable2 * variable3 + variable4
variable1 = variable2 * (variable3 + variable4)
```

In JavaScript, if you use parentheses incorrectly or omit them, trying to find why your script isn't working will be very tiresome. If you don't understand Boolean logic and operational precedence, now may be a good time to brush up on the common rules of precedence.

Constructs

Constructs are used to perform operations such as *testing* and *looping*. Constructs are fairly equal across most programming languages today and the constructs used in JavaScript are very similar in form and function to those used in RPG or COBOL. Table 2.2 shows some of the basic constructs used by JavaScript.

Table 2.2: Common JavaScript Constructs.

Construct	Action	Example
If	Test a condition	If (number1 > number2)
For	Looping	For (x=0; x<100; x++)
While	Conditional looping	While (x > 100)

Constructs are usually contained within the delimiters that JavaScript uses. In programming, a delimiter specifies the beginning, or more important, the end of an expression. COBOL programmers will be familiar with using a period (.) as a delimiter. Other languages, including JavaScript, use a semicolon (;) as a delimiter of single-line expressions. Other delimiters are used to group a set of expressions, such as an IF or DO construct.

The delimiters used to contain a set of instructions or a construct are the so-called curly brackets {} or braces. Figure 2.1 shows an example of how these braces are used to contain a set of instructions within a construct.

```
if (selectedyear == currentyear) {
    totalsales = 0;
    while (x < 12) {
        totalsales = (total sales + monthlysales[x];
        x++;
    }
}
```

Figure 2.1: Using curly brackets to contain instructions.

Figure 2.1 not only shows how to use the brackets as delimiters, but it shows how most JavaScript programmers indent their source to make it more readable. Figure 2.1 contains two examples of using brackets to act as delimiters of a construct. The first construct is the IF statement. Next, a WHILE statement is used. Because the WHILE statement is executed only if the IF statement is found true, it is included inside the brackets that contain the statements inside the IF construct. Similarly, all of the statements that we want to execute multiple times inside the WHILE construct are included between the curly brackets following the WHILE instruction.

You also will notice that single lines are followed by the semicolon delimiter. Although this delimiter is not always needed, it is good practice to always use them, even if they aren't required.

JavaScript: Objects, Properties, Methods, and Events

JavaScript contains some terms that should be understood before you start programming. Because these terms are used so frequently in JavaScript programming, you may want to make a cheat sheet to remind you of their definitions and uses as you begin your JavaScript programming project. (There also are numerous Web sites that feature JavaScript tutorials; check them out.)

Objects and Properties

In our midrange world, we are used to thinking of objects as anything that resides on the AS/400. If we were to apply this concept to JavaScript, an object would be anything that is on a Web page, as well as the Web page itself. If you can point at it, it's an object. Images, tables, buttons, and links are all objects.

Each object has certain properties that describe the object. A document is an example of an object. The background color of the document would be an example of a property. Object properties are normally referenced in the following form.

```
object.property
```

Therefore, the document and background color object property would be listed as:

```
document.bgcolor
```

The *document* represents the document, and *bgcolor* represents the background color property of that document. So, if we wanted to set the background color of our document to red, we would specify the following:

```
document.bgcolor="red"
```

As you can imagine, there are enough document and property combinations to fill a book. Instead of explaining all of the document properties, I direct you to a wealth of information on NetScape's JavaScript developer's Web page

```
http://developer.netscape.com/tech/javascript/index.html
```

This page contains everything you want to know about objects, properties, methods, and events. It's a great reference when you're looking for the right way to perform a certain JavaScript function.

If you need more, or very specific information, use your favorite search engine to search for JavaScript tutorials. Most sites contain links to other sites so that you will eventually find the information you need.

Methods

Methods are exactly what they sound like. They are things that you can do on a page. Each object has a set of methods assigned to it. The document object has a write method that will write to that document.

```
document.write("Hello World")
```

This example will write the text "Hello World" to the browser.

As I mentioned before, you can create Web pages without any JavaScript, or you can create Web pages using only JavaScript. To perform the latter, you would use the document.write method to write HTML to your page. The text used in the document.write method doesn't have to be plain text. It can contain HTML code, which will be written to the page when the particular line of JavaScript code is executed. There is really no benefit to creating your Web pages this way, but it is always nice to know that it can be done.

As with properties, there are simply too many combinations of objects and methods to review, so I suggest referencing the Netscape JavaScript developer's page mentioned earlier.

Events

Events are used in JavaScript to execute a set of instructions, usually in the form of a user-created function. Events are usually included in objects such as forms or buttons. The events themselves are usually self-explanatory. A list of events includes the following:

- onClick – This event occurs when a user clicks on a particular object on the document.

- onMouseOver– This event occurs when the mouse pointer is dragged over a particular object on the document.

- onMouseOut – This event occurs when the mouse pointer is dragged away from a particular object on the document.

- onFocus – This event occurs when the cursor is placed in a certain object, such as a text input field, on a document.

- onBlur – This event occurs when the cursor leaves a certain object, such as a text input field, on a document.

- onLoad – This event occurs when a document is first loaded onto the browser.

- onUnload – This event occurs when the user exits the document, either by closing the browser or opening another Web page.

Each of these events will appear in different spots on your Web page. The onClick will appear most often with a button. When the button is pressed, the JavaScript function indicated will be executed. The onLoad event will most often appear in the <BODY> tag of your document. When the page is loaded, the JavaScript function in the <BODY> tag will be executed, similar to the initialization subroutine (*INZSR) of an RPG program.

Again, I encourage you to visit Netscape's JavaScript Developer's Web site for more detailed information on this subject as well as for additional examples.

JavaScript Examples

JavaScript can be placed anywhere within the HTML code of your Web page. The only rule regarding placement of JavaScript is that it must exist between the HTML tags <SCRIPT></SCRIPT>. These tags tell the browser that a scripting language follows.

JavaScript can exist as direct commands or as functions. Functions are similar to subroutines in RPG. They are an easy way to create a modular format for your code. If you find that you are performing the same thing over and over again, creating a subroutine, or function, is a good way to minimize coding.

JavaScript can be executed from one of many events that can be coded into your HTML.

Using JavaScript to Write HTML

The first and most basic example of JavaScript is to use it to output HTML to the browser. Although this is not an entirely useful example, it will get you used to using the <SCRIPT> tags. (You could simply write the HTML code into the document without JavaScript. The well-rounded Web programmer however, should know how to use either method.)

Figure 2.2 includes HTML code that will write "Hello World" to the browser using JavaScript.

```
<html>
<script language="JavaScript">
document.write("Hello World");
</script>
</html>
```

Figure 2.2: JavaScript that writes "Hello World" to the browser.

In Figure 2.2, notice how the <SCRIPT> tags are used. They simply enclose the JavaScript source that we are using. The document.write statement means "write this to the browser."

Using JavaScript to Redirect a Browser

A more useful example of using JavaScript is to redirect the browser. Let's assume that our Web page only includes a button. This button is labeled Click Here to go to Midrange Computing. When the user clicks on the button, the browser is automatically directed to Midrange Computing's Web site, just as the button promises. Figure 2.3 contains the code to perform this simple, yet amazing, feat.

```
<html>
<script language="JavaScript">
function gotoMC() {
    window.location="http://www.midrangecomputing.com";
}
</script>
<input type="button"
       value="Click Here to go to Midrange Computing"
       onClick="gotoMC();">
</html>
```

Figure 2.3: JavaScript that redirects a browser.

As you examine Figure 2.3, you will see that I have added a few new techniques, such as using a JavaScript function. The function is named gotoMC()", and lo-cated within the <SCRIPT> tags. When this function is executed, the state-ment window.location is processed which causes the location being viewed to change to the value within quotes following this statement.

Another important piece to this puzzle is the onClick event specified for the but-ton. This event tells the browser what JavaScript function to execute when the button is clicked.

Using JavaScript to Interactively Validate Field Data

Web pages that ask the user to fill in data and don't include interactive error checking can be annoying. The user is taken to a page and informed that the in-formation provided was incorrect. The user is then asked to use the browser's Back button to return to the previous page and correct the information. This would be similar to developing a green-screen application that displays each er-ror, such as Invalid Customer Number, on another screen and asks the user to press F12 to return to order entry. It's not fun for the user of the application and it's not fun to program.

JavaScript can be used to display dialog boxes for errors that are processed be-fore the actual page action takes place. Figure 2.4 shows the code for a simple field validation routine.

```
<html>
<head>
<script language="JavaScript">
function IsBlank(value) {
    for (var x = value.length - 1; x >= 0; x-) {
        if ((value.charAt(x) != " ") && (value.charAt(x) != "")) {
            return false;
        }
    }
    return true;
}
function ValidateForm(form) {

    if ((IsBlank(form.username.value)) ||
        (IsBlank(form.email.value))) {
        alert("Please fill in both name and email address");
    }
    else {
        alert("Thank you, " + form.username.value + ".");
    }
}
</script>
</head>
<body>
<form>
  Name: <input type=text name=username size=30><BR>
  E-Mail: <input type=text name=email size=30><BR>
<input type=button name="button1" value="Submit" on-
Click="ValidateForm(this.form);">
</form>
</body>
</html>
```

Figure 2.4: JavaScript example for field validation.

The example in Figure 2.4 contains two different functions. The first function is named IsBlank(). This function receives a value and tests to make sure the field is not blank. This is similar to testing values in RPG against the special value of *BLANK or *BLANKS. JavaScript doesn't contain special values like this, so this is a good example that you can use JavaScript to create your own functions very easily. Another important tidbit to note is that JavaScript views a null value (""), a blank ("b"), and two blanks ("bb") as different values. This is why a loop is needed to test the entire field.

The second function is named ValidateForm() and receives a form in as a parameter. It then checks the two values in the form, user name and e-mail address, to make sure that values for both of the fields have been entered. If they were, a message saying "Thank you" followed by the user name is displayed in a dialog box. If either or both of the fields are blank, an error message is displayed informing the user to enter both user name and password.

Figure 2.5 shows what this page looks like in a Web browser.

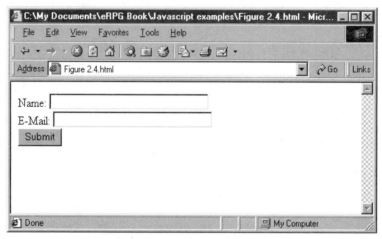

Figure 2.5: The entry screen created by the source in Figure 2.4.

Figure 2.6 shows the error message being displayed when either field is left blank.

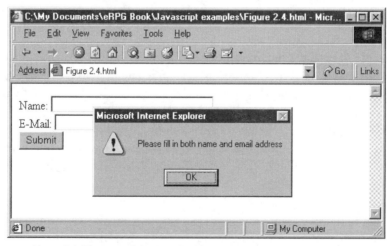

Figure 2.6: The error dialog box displayed when either entry field is left blank.

Because the dialog box is used to display the errors, processing time is much quicker (almost instantaneous), and the user doesn't leave the current page. To some users, especially those new to surfing, this type of error display message will be more familiar to them, and they won't feel that they've lost their spot, as they would if another page were displayed showing the errors.

JavaScript, Cookies, and a Shopping Basket

In order to use cookies on your Web site, you'll need a few ingredients. The first ingredient is a heavy dose of JavaScript. Using JavaScript, you can create the rest of the ingredients. You will need to create functions that write cookie data, re-trieve cookie data, and delete a cookie. I have compiled some simple JavaScript functions to perform these tasks, as shown in Figure 2.7.

```
<script language="javascript">
<!- begin script

function WriteCookie(name,value,expireTime,expireTimeFormat) {
    function WriteCookie(name,value,expireDays) {
    var expire = new Date();
    expire.setTime (expire.getTime() + (expireDays * 24 * 3500000));
    document.cookie = name + "=" + escape(value) +
                    "; expires=" + expire.toGMTString() ;
}

function GetCookie(name) {
  var value = name + "=";
  var i = 0;
  while (i < document.cookie.length) {
    var j = (i + value.length);
    if (document.cookie.substring(i,j) == value) {
      var len = document.cookie.indexOf(";",j);
          if (len == -1)
          len = document.cookie.length;
          return unescape(document.cookie.substring(j, len));
    }
    i = document.cookie.indexOf(" ", i) + 1;
    if (i == 0) break;
  }
  return null;
}

function DeleteCookie(name) {
var expire = new Date();
    expire.setTime(expire.getTime() - 2 * 86400001);  //2 days ago
    document.cookie = name + "=*; expires=" + expire.toGMTString();
```

Figure 2.7: JavaScript code to write, retrieve, and delete a cookie (part 1 of 2).

```
}
// end script ->
</script>
```

Figure 2.7: JavaScript code to write, retrieve, and delete a cookie (part 2 of 2).

The first function, WriteCookie(), accepts three parameters. The first parameter is the name of the cookie. The second is the data to be stored in that cookie. The last parameter contains a value representing the number of days that you want the cookie to be available. This is then translated into a date that is stored in the cookie as a cookie expiration date. The name, data, and expiration date are then written to the cookie using the document.cookie method.

The second function, GetCookie(), accepts only one parameter. This parameter is the name of the cookie that you wish to retrieve. This function parses the data out from the cookie, and returns it to the caller.

The last function, DeleteCookie(), accepts a cookie name as a parameter. It then deletes the cookie specified in the parameter. It does this by setting the expiration date to two days before the current date. Doing this causes the cookie to expire, thus removing it from the system.

All three of these functions are generic enough so that you can use them in almost any JavaScript that you write in which you choose to use cookies. Using only these three functions, you are able to store one piece of data that you can retrieve from the client at a later date. There are cases, however, where you will want to store more than one piece of data.

Multiple Cookies and Multiple Elements

Cookies can be used on your site as a shopping basket, as mentioned earlier. With the three functions provided in Figure 2.6, you might wonder how this is possible since the cookie really only stores one piece of information. Cookies are used to store shopping basket information in two ways. First, instead of one piece of data being stored in a cookie, we can store multiple elements in the data, separating each of these elements by a delimiter.

An example of storing multiple elements of data in a cookie is when a list of item numbers is included in a cookie. You wouldn't want to limit the user to only selecting one item, so you construct a string that contains an item number followed by a delimiter, followed by another item number and delimiter, and so on. The string would look similar to the example:

```
Item1`Item2`Item3`…
```

This string is a pseudo-array. In order to process the elements in this string, the data is parsed out, using the delimiter, into an array where the program can deal with it in a simpler fashion. After the data is manipulated, the array elements are then placed back into a delimited string and written to a cookie.

Another way to store multiple sets of information is by using more than one cookie. In your shopping basket application, you will no doubt want to store quantity information as well as item information. The quantity information can be stored in a similar fashion, so that the position of the quantity in the structure corresponds to the correct item number.

To demonstrate the processes of using multiple cookies that hold multiple values, I have created a sample program, called CookieBasket using both JavaScript and HTML. Included in Figure 2.8 is the partial source for this example. The JavaScript functions have been left out so that you can view the example without having to worry about how the JavaScript works. The full source for this example can be found in appendix B.

```
<HTML>
<HEAD>
<TITLE>Cookie Basket</TITLE>
</HEAD>
<BODY>
<script language="javascript">
// Note:  See appendix B for full Cookie Basket source
</script>
Click on the item you wish to add to your shopping basket.<BR>
<TABLE border="1"><TR>
<TD><a href="#" onClick="AddItem('Jackhammer');">Jackhammer</a></TD>
```

Figure 2.8: JavaScript source for CookieBasket, a shopping basket that stores item numbers and quantities in separate cookies (part 1 of 2).

```
<TD><a href="#" onClick="AddItem('PickAxe');">PickAxe</a></TD></TR>
<TR><TD><a href="#" onClick="AddItem('Shovel');">Shovel</a></TD>
<TD><a href="#" onClick="AddItem('Auger');">Auger</a></TD></TR>
<TR><TD><a href="#" onClick="AddItem('Wheelbarrow');">Wheelbarrow</a></TD>
<TD><a href="#" onClick="AddItem('Crowbar');">Crowbar</a></TD></TR>
</TABLE>
<form>
<input type="button" value="Clear Basket" on-
Click="DeleteAllCookies();">
<input type="button" value="View Basket" onClick="DisplayBasket();"><BR>
</form>
</BODY>
</HTML>
```

Figure 2.8: JavaScript source for CookieBasket, a shopping basket that stores item numbers and quantities in separate cookies (part 2 of 2).

The sample shown in Figure 2.8 displays a list of items on the browser. This screen is shown in Figure 2.9. When a user clicks on an item, a message is displayed in a dialog box telling the user the item they selected has been added to the shopping basket, as shown in Figure 2.10. This item is then placed into the shopping cart by first retrieving the item cookie data. This data is then placed into an array. The item selected is then checked against existing items in the array. If the item already exists in the array, the corresponding quantity element is incremented. If the selected item doesn't exist in the item array, a new element is written to the array and a quantity of one is added as an element to the quantity array. These two arrays are then placed back into a delimited string of data and written as cookies.

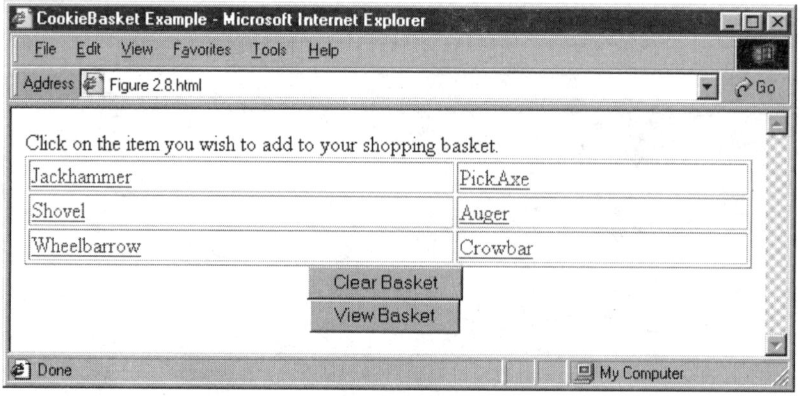

Figure 2.9: Initial screen from the CookieBasket example.

Figure 2.10: Dialogue box that is displayed when a user clicks on an item.

The CookieBasket.html sample also contains two buttons. The first button, Clear Basket, will empty the shopping basket of all its items by deleting the item and quantity cookies. The second button, View Basket, will display a table listing the items and quantities currently in the shopping basket. An example is shown in Figure 2.11.

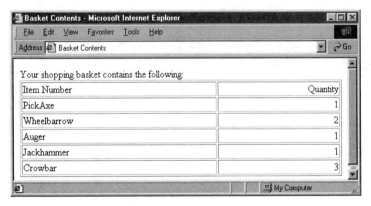

Figure 2.11: A view of the shopping basket contents.

In today's world of e-business, people are finding new ways to do all sorts of things. Shopping basket technology has really taken off because of its important role in online shopping. Although there are many ways to create a shopping basket, the CookieBasket.html sample shown here is one that requires no server programming to store information. All of the processing and data storage is done on the client's machine, which not only makes the process run faster, but takes the burden of storing the shopping basket contents off of your server machine.

A JavaScript Quoting System

JavaScript can provide a dynamic quoting system, another important feature, for your Web site. When users visit your site, they are most likely ready to buy. They want instant quotes. If they get to your site and find that a quote can be mailed to them within two or three working days, they will lose interest quickly. If they find your competitor can give them an on-site quote, without having to call your sales department or speak with anyone, they will most likely choose them over you.

Pricing information on a Web site is really not as difficult as it might seem. If you have some sort of pricing structure set up that can be keyed into a table, that table can be transferred to the Web and loaded into an array for use on your site. The example used in this section is a company that produces reprints of articles. The customer is able to select the paper weight, number of pages, number of copies, and the shipping method. The choices will affect the final price. Figure 2.12 shows the Web page for BVS-Reprints.

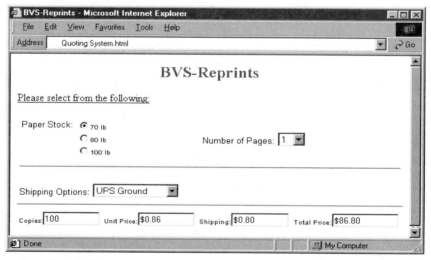

Figure 2.12: BVS-Reprints allows the user to get a quote online.

When a user changes any of the fields on the screen in Figure 2.12, the values that are displayed for Unit Price, Shipping, and Total Price will change accordingly. The Total Price will always display the total price that this quoting system generates.

The most complicated portion of the BVS-Reprints example is the way that the arrays are used to hold the data. A two-dimensional array is used to store the copies/number of pages data. To create a two-dimensional array, you must first create a single array. Next, you read through the array, setting the value of each element to an array. Figure 2.13 shows snippets of code for this example.

```
pageArr = new Array(1,6,12);
qtyArr = new Array(25,50,75,100,250,500);
priceArr = new Array(pageArr.length);
for (i=0; i < priceArr.length; i++) {

    priceArr[i] = new Array(qtyArr.length)
}
```

Figure 2.13: Creating a two-dimensional array in JavaScript.

PageArr is an array that holds the limits for the number of pages in a reprint. QtyArr is an array that holds the value boundaries for the number of reprints ordered. PriceArr is the final array that will become two-dimensional and hold the pricing data, as if it were in a table. When initializing the size of priceArr, notice the length property of the pageArr array. Next, loop through the priceArr setting each element as another array with the number of elements that are in the qtyArr array. You could hard-code the sizes, but using this method requires less work should you have to add or remove any pricing structures.

Finally, after setting up the arrays, load them with data. Figure 2.14 shows a simple way to load a two-dimensional array with data.

```
priceArr[0][0] = 2.0232
priceArr[1][0] = 4.3424
priceArr[2][0] = 6.2376
priceArr[0][1] = 1.2646
priceArr[1][1] = 3.4642
priceArr[2][1] = 4.6012
priceArr[0][2] = 0.9980
priceArr[1][2] = 3.2164
priceArr[2][2] = 4.2551...
```

Figure 2.14: Loading a two-dimensional array with data.

The example in Figure 2.14 doesn't load the entire array, but it does load the first few elements. The rest is simply repeating the process for each element of the table.

The table is then used to figure the prices to display on the screen. Each time a user changes a value on screen, a JavaScript function named `figurePrice()` is called. This function uses the values on the display to determine which indexes in the `priceArr` array to use to figure the price. Then, everything is computed and displayed to the user.

The method used to figure the shipping cost of an item is taken a step further. The shipping price is figured using a three-dimensional table. The first dimension of this table is used to store the shipping type, Ground, 2nd Day Air, or Overnight. The second is used to store the number of pages in the reprint job. The more pages, the more weight, and the higher the shipping cost. The third dimension is used to store the paper weight. Again, this affects the weight of the shipment, therefore altering the shipping cost.

Because this is a rather complicated example, I have provided the complete source in appendix B and on the included CD-ROM. Experiment with the page for a while. After you have experimented with it, and understand what it is doing on the outside, take a look at the source itself. This example provides many pieces that can also be used in other JavaScript ventures that you may create.

MORE INFORMATION ON JAVASCRIPT

This chapter included the basics about JavaScript to get you going. It is in no way intended to be your only resource for JavaScript. I encourage you to try writing some JavaScript and also to surf the Web for endless tutorials and examples on JavaScript. You'll quickly discover just how easy and effective JavaScript can be in your e-business solutions.

There are also many discussion forums available where you can post your questions for experienced JavaScript programmers to answer. Before you post, though, be sure to read the Frequently Asked Questions (FAQ) document.

JavaScript can be very helpful when creating pages for e-business, so start writing some scripts and practicing your new JavaScript skills!

3

COMMON GATEWAY
INTERFACE PROGRAMMING

For a user to interact with a Web page, a method must exist to pass information between the browser and the machine that is displaying and processing the Web page.

Common Gateway Interface (CGI) programming is a method used to process data sent between a Web server and a client. A Web server is a machine that processes the Web requests sent from the client. The client is the Web browser that is used to retrieve information from the server.

(CGI is not a programming language. This will be discussed more in detail later, but I wanted to clear this up before going any further.)

When you go to your favorite Web site by typing www.myfavoritesite.com into your browser's location bar, you are accessing a machine over the Internet. This machine is a Web server. The client is you. Or, more specifically, your Web browser. Clients communicate with servers in many applications. One example with which you might be familiar and can relate to is when you use a terminal or terminal emulation package on your AS/400 to enter an order or write an RPG program.

In this example, the AS/400 is the server and your terminal or emulation package is the client. The interface between the client and server is the software package that is running. You enter information into the client; this information is processed by the server by using programs included in the software package. The software package could be thought of as a CGI application, as it is a *common gateway* between you and the server machine.

EVERYTHING NEEDS AN INTERFACE

To accomplish the tasks that we set out to do every day, and that our company relies on us to perform as computer programmers, we need some sort of interface between the information on our machine and the user. Whether the interface is human or mechanical, these interfaces help us achieve our goals smoothly and efficiently.

We use human and machine interfaces every day. Banking is a perfect example. An ATM machine is a mechanical or electronic interface that allows us to deposit or withdraw money from our bank account. A bank teller is a sort of human interface that allows us to do exactly the same thing. The difference between the two is that the ATM is a machine, and the teller is a human, yet both perform the same function.

Shopping is yet another example. We can go to a bookstore, browse the titles, and purchase books. The bookstore may also have an online shopping page that allows us to search for and purchase books. Each interface performs the same function, and there are advantages to using each type of interface. Searching for a book on a Web page usually takes much less time than searching through the store, but we might receive better customer service dealing with a human than with a machine.

To expand on this idea, let's take a look at the way the Internet is used for shopping online.

Been Shopping?

A good example of an everyday activity that uses many interfaces is grocery shopping. When you go to the supermarket, your goal is to fill your shelves with food items that you have run out of, or soon will. You write down your needs on a list (or enter them into a Palm Pilot), and drive to the store. When you arrive, you enter the store and begin shopping.

As you shop, you pick out the items you need and place them in your cart. You continue this cycle until you have picked up everything on your list.

The last thing you need to do is pay for the items. You place the items on the conveyer in a check-out line and the cashier rings them up and places them into a bag. You then pay for the items and return home.

The experience of shopping contains many examples of interfaces used to accomplish a goal. First, to get to the store, you used an interface in the form of your car. This interface helped you reach a location where you could pick up groceries. Then you use an interface, in the form of a shopping list (or your hip Palm Pilot), to store the information you wish to remember. Once there, you view this information and refer to it frequently.

While shopping, the next interface you used is a shopping cart. The shopping cart allows you to store items conveniently before you are ready to pay for them. Just imagine if you had to carry all the items in your arms, or buy items one at a time.

Last, the cashier rings up your items. The cashier is also an interface that allows you to pay for the items you first set out to get, thus accomplishing your goal of replenishing your cupboards.

Been e-Shopping?

All of the interfaces involved in shopping in a supermarket are in a different form when shopping on the Internet, except for maybe the shopping list, which you still use in a similar fashion. The vehicle that gets you to the e-Store is your Web browser. The shopping basket is a virtual container, usually in the form of a database on the server machine. And the checkout cashier is a program that calculates your total purchase and charges your credit card with the amount.

CGI programs perform all of these tasks while you are shopping on the Internet. They allow you to interface with the store and accomplish your goals in the same way that the tools used in conventional shopping do.

Hopefully this comparison and contrast gives you an idea of what CGI programming is used for. With this basic understanding, we can learn what CGI is, and what it is not.

CGI—Not a Programming Language

You probably are noticing a recurring theme: CGI is not a programming language. There is no such thing as a CGI compiler or interpreter, and there is no programming language named CGI.

CGI is an interface between a Web server and a client in the same sense that an executable (EXE) on your PC is an interface between you and the data located on your machine. There is no EXE programming language, but EXE programs can be created from one of many languages available today.

Think of CGI as a translator between the Web server and the client.

CGI Used as an Interpreter

Let's say one day you decide to fly to Spain. Before you go, you are clever enough to realize that you don't know a word of the Spanish language, except for maybe *gracias*. You decide to hire someone to act as an interpreter on your trip. This person is fluent in both English and Spanish.

When you arrive in Spain, you are suddenly bombarded with people speaking at you in a language that you do not understand. Luckily for you, you brought an interpreter. The interpreter translates the messages to you in plain English. You respond by telling the interpreter the words with which you want to reply. The interpreter then tells your new Spanish friends your words by translating English into Spanish. You are having a conversation with someone who doesn't know your language, and whose language you don't know. How is this possible? A translator, or in other words, a common language interface, makes this possible.

CGI programs act in the same was as the interpreter. These programs take information from a Web server and put it into a form that you can use in your programs. Also, when you wish to respond, a CGI program will take your information and put it into a form that the Web server can use.

The interpreter that you take to Spain could be one of many races, ages, sexes, or religious affiliations. You could take a 78-year-old male German Christian, or you could take a 23-year-old female Yugoslavian atheist. While these examples may seem far-fetched, they are effective in explaining that the interpreter you choose to use for your CGI programming could be one of many different languages or systems. You could choose to use one or more of the following for your CGI programming needs:

- Visual Basic
- Java
- C
- Perl
- Net.Data
- Lotus Notes
- Cold Fusion
- RPG
- COBOL

Any one of these programming languages or systems would be suited for the job of a CGI application. Some of them can be used on the AS/400, others cannot.

CGI PROGRAMMING ON THE AS/400

The previous section explained what CGI is, and what it is not. Because we are working with the AS/400 (and since this book is entitled e-RPG), it would be safe to assume that we are able to use RPG, a language with which most of us are very familiar.

CGI programming on the AS/400, thanks to Application Program Interfaces (APIs) supplied by IBM, can be performed with COBOL, RPG, or any other Integrated Language Environment (ILE) language available on your AS/400. This is great news to us green-screen folks. Not only do we get to try something new, but when the IT manager is asked to produce an e-business solution for your company, you can reply confidently, "We can do it with RPG!" You might get a few raised eyebrows, but if you get the chance, you will open up a whole new world of possibilities for your AS/400 programming team.

What exactly does this mean to you as an RPG programmer? It means that if you have felt left behind in the e-business world, no longer do you have to hear from your PC programming counterparts, "You can only do green-screen programming." Now you can prove them wrong and write fully functional, robust applications on the AS/400. And when someone asks you what language you are using for the CGI portion of the application, you can proudly respond, "That's RPG, my friend!"

INPUT AND OUTPUT WITH CGI

Every usable application requires two things. First, we need a way to input data into a system. Second, we need a way to output information to the user. It is usually more complicated than that, but for this chapter I don't want to get too deeply into these processes. Programming examples will be included in later chapters of this book. For now, let's focus on the basics of how CGI programs are used to read and write information from and to a browser.

A BASIC History

I like to think back to the first programming language I learned, BASIC. The machine I used was a TRS-80 Color Computer. I had asked for an Atari, but one day, this other computer arrived that plugged into the TV. It had the ability to play games, which were limited. Because of this, I started writing my own games and in the process taught myself the BASIC programming language.

This language was simple, yet powerful enough to last for years as one of the top programming languages not only for production applications, but for teaching programming basics as well.

If you were like me, and played with BASIC as a youngster, you probably remember the first program you wrote that included input as well as output. It was no doubt something similar the following:

```
10 INPUT "WHAT IS YOUR NAME?": INPUT N$
20 PRINT "HELLO, ": PRINT N$
```

The output was as follows:

```
WHAT IS YOUR NAME?
?BRAD
HELLO, BRAD
Ok
```

You had discovered input and output with BASIC. The program asked you for your name, and then displayed whatever you entered on the screen. You were on your way to writing truly intricate user interface programs that would impress your friends, parents, and the local computer guru at Radio Shack.

This simple input program can be viewed as a CGI program in a sense because the program was an interface between you, the user, and the computer itself. Once the information you entered on the screen was read in, what you did with it from there was up to you.

AS/400 CGI Programming

Even if my story about my BASIC programming experience bored you, made you laugh, or even brought back memories of visiting the Radio Shack guru that you'd rather forget, it is an example of how we all learned to make a computer interface with a user.

Today, as AS/400 programmers, we now have a very powerful machine compared to the TRS-80s or VIC-20s on which some of us started programming. We are using the AS/400 to provide business solutions for our company. These solutions involve programs that use the business rules established by the company to (hopefully) make employee's jobs easier. Either way, these applications use both input and output, usually in the form of green-screens and reports.

Now that the world has accepted the Internet as a valid and profitable method of doing business, we must learn a new method of using input and output. The new applications must be used on a Web browser, something some of us may not be familiar with.

As we explained in chapter 1, output to a browser is accomplished using Hypertext Markup Language (HTML). HTML is a standard set of instructions that is interpreted by a browser and displayed as text to the visitor of the Web page. HTML can exist in a static file or can be written dynamically using APIs available on the AS/400. Writing dynamic data to the browser is known as writing to *standard output*.

Reading input from a browser is performed using APIs that are available to our programs through a service program on the AS/400. Data can be read from input fields on the browser, or even passed as parameters in the URL. Both of these methods are discussed in detail in later chapters of this book.

To perform the operations for input and output to a browser, there is some setup involved. The next section explains what is needed to provide this functionality.

AS/400 CGI PROGRAMMING SETUP

To configure your AS/400 to function as a Web server that can run CGI programs, there are a few key elements that you need to remember. The most important is that you must have TCP/IP configured correctly on your machine. This book does not cover the configuration of TCP/IP on the AS/400, but there are plenty of resources available. Configuring TCP/IP is a procedure that should be performed by your AS/400 system administrator.

After you have TCP/IP configured and installed, there are three more important things to keep in mind when setting up your AS/400 to perform CGI functions. The first is telling it where your CGI programs are located. This is done by adding *directives*, or statements that tell the AS/400 certain things about your machine, to an HTTP configuration setup.

The next step is to copy a *service program* into the library that will function as your CGI programming library. This service program comes installed on your machine and contains subprocedures that allow you to perform input, output, and other functions when working with CGI programs.

The last piece of the puzzle is the creation of a CGI program. When you create a CGI program that reads input from or produces output to a browser, you must compile your programs and reference the service program mentioned in the previous step. This involves a couple of keywords that you may not be familiar with unless you have done some programming in the Integrated Language Environment (ILE) on the AS/400.

A general overview of these topics is presented here. They are each covered in more detail in later chapters of this book. This general overview will give you an idea of what to expect later in this book as regards to CGI programming on the AS/400.

HTTP Configuration Setup for CGI Programming

An HTTP configuration is a list of statements, or directives as they are known, that tells the AS/400 Web server what it can and cannot do, what files it can and cannot access, as well as a host of other functions. For CGI programming, there are a few mandatory directives needed to let your AS/400 process CGI programs.

Enable

The first of these directives is the Enable directive. The Enable directive allows you to specify what methods are valid on your server. There are two methods used for the majority of CGI program processing.

- Get – Used to retrieve information from the URL. These values are known as *query string environment variables*. They follow the URL and are preceded by a question mark (?).

- Post – Used to request that the server accept the entity sent with the request. This is usually used when submitting information from a form, thus making the values of that form available to the processing program.

The Enable directive is specified as follows:

```
enable method_name
```

The keyword METHOD_NAME is substituted for the method you want to enable. The default rule for methods is disabled, so if you do not specifically specify the Enable directive for a method, that method is disabled.

Exec

The Exec directive is used to specify to the AS/400 the location of executable programs, most often CGI programs. CGI programs that are written in RPG or COBOL, or any other AS/400 program, must reside in the QSYS portion of the Integrated File System (IFS). In other words, if it's a program that you created on the AS/400, it has to reside in a library, not in a folder or a directory.

The Exec directive is specified as follows.

```
exec /qsys.lib/as400_library_name.lib/*
```

The library specified in place of AS400_LIBRARY_NAME will be the library that you will use to store your CGI programs. For example, I call my CGI library AS400CGI. This library contains all of my CGI program objects.

If you do not specify an Exec directive in your HTTP configuration, the AS/400 will not know what to do when a request is made to execute a particular CGI program.

The Exec directive is covered in more detail in chapter 4.

Service Program Needed for CGI Programming

The AS/400 ships with a service program that allows you to perform CGI functions that interact with a Web browser. This service program contains subprocedures that allow you to write data to and read input from a Web browser. The name of the service program is QTMHCGI, and it is located in library QTCP.

One of the first steps when setting up your AS/400 to run CGI applications is to create a library to hold the CGI programs. The next step should be to make a copy of the service program QTMHCGI from library QTCP into the library that will hold your CGI programs. On my system, the library that contains my CGI programs is named AS400CGI, so this is the library to which I copy QTMHCGI. Use the following command:

```
CRTDUPOBJ OBJ(QTMHCGI) FROMLIB(QTCP) OBJTYPE(*SRVPGM) TOLIB(AS400CGI)
```

This command creates a duplicate of the QTMHCGI service program and places it into your CGI library. One of the main reasons for doing this is so that you do not have to provide access to the QTCP system library. Doing so could cause a security risk.

The subprocedures included in the service program, as well as their functions are described in detail in chapter 5.

CGI Program Creation

Because you need to reference the subprocedures in the service program QTMHCGI, creating your CGI programs requires a step to bind these subprocedures into your program. This process will be something new to you if this is your first experience with ILE. If you have created programs previously, this step should be familiar.

When you write a CGI program, you use the Call Bound Procedure (CALLB) op-code to call the subprocedures included in the QTMHCGI service program. In order for your program to see these procedures, you must specify that you want to bind the service program with your CGI program. There are two ways of accomplishing this task.

CRTPGM and the Service Program Parameter

The first way to bind your CGI application with the modules available in the QTMHCGI service program is to use the CRTPGM command. To use this program, you must already have a module (type *MOD) or a service program (type *SRVPGM) created that contains the main processing of your CGI application.

You are probably used to creating your RPG programs with the Create Bound RPG (CRTBNDRPG) command. Using this first method, you replace this command with the Create Module (CRTMOD) command. If we had a CGI program named RPGCGI, we would create it with the following command:

```
CRTMOD MOD(RPGCGI) SRCFILE(QRPGLESRC) MBR(RPGCGI)
```

If this command completed normally, we would have a module named RPGCGI. Because QTMHCGI already exists as a service program, the next step is to use the CRTPGM command to bind these two objects into an executable program. This is done as follows:

```
CRTPGM PGM(RPGCGI) MOD(RPGCGI) SRVPGM(QTMHCGI)
```

During the creation of the program RPGCGI, the AS/400 will bind the module object, named RPGCGI, with the service program QTMHCGI and create a program. The references to the subprocedures, which exist in QTMHCGI, will be resolved at this time. This method is known as *bind by reference*.

CRTBNDRPG and a Binding Directory

An easier way to accomplish the binding of your program and the CGI subprocedures is to use a binding directory. A binding directory is a list of objects, modules, or service programs referenced at compile time to resolve calls made to any external subprocedure.

Using a binding directory, we can use the CRTBNDRPG command when compiling CGI programs. I find this method easier because the program is created in one step, as compared to the method described above.

The first thing we need to do is create a binding directory. This is a simple step. The binding directory can be placed in any library, but I like to place it in the same library in which my CGI programs exist. To create a binding directory, use the Create Binding Directory (CRTBNDDIR) command:

```
CRTBNDDIR BNDDIR(AS400CGI/CGIBNDDIR)
```

This creates a binding directory named CGIBNDDIR in library AS400CGI.

Once we have a binding directory, we want to add a binding directory entry. The only entry we need to add right away is the reference to the QTMHCGI service program that should already exist in our CGI library. To add an entry to the binding directory, use the Add Binding Directory Entry (ADDBNDDIRE) command as follows:

```
ADDBNDDIRE BNDDIR(AS400CGI/CGIBNDDIR) OBJ((AS400CGI/QTMHCGI))
```

This command adds a reference to the QTMHCGI service program so that when we create our CGI applications, we only need to supply the name of the binding directory to the CRTBNDRPG command.

A binding directory works in a similar fashion to a library list. When we specify a binding directory on our CRTBNDRPG command, any references made to external subprocedures are checked using the entries provided in the binding directory specified on the CRTBNDRPG command. Using this method means that if you have more than one module or service program to bind together, you don't need to specify them all in the CRTBNDRPG command. You only need to reference the binding directory that contains the names of the modules or service programs that you are using.

To use the binding directory parameter on the CRTBNDRPG command, use the following command:

```
CRTBNDRPG PGM(AS400CGI/RPGCGI) SRCFILE(*LIBL/QRPGLESRC) +
DFTACTGRP(*NO) BNDDIR(AS400CGI/CGIBNDDIR)
```

We are creating a program named RPGCGI in this example. We reference the binding directory CGIBNDDIR, which contains an entry to resolve the references made to the subprocedures in service program QTMHCGI.

When specifying a binding directory on the CRTBNDRPG command, notice that you must specify that the default activation group is not used (DFTACTGRP (*NO)).

If you are unfamiliar with activation groups and how they work, I recommend reading the RPG Reference manual.

As you get deeper into CGI programming, you might find that you want to create other service programs that perform various functions. Chapter 9 includes a set of such service programs. Each time you create a new service program, you can add it to your binding directory so that creating your CGI programs will not require a lot of work. I recommend this method for creating CGI programs, and I believe that you will find it easier to use as well.

User Profiles QTMHHTTP and QTMHHTP1

There are two user profiles that exist on your machine and are needed to allow your AS/400 to act as a Web server. These two user profiles are used for two different functions.

- QTMHHTTP – This user profile is used when accessing documents that exist on the AS/400. This user profile must have authority to any objects that are served. If documents will be served from the QDLS file system, this user profile must have a directory entry.

- QTMHHTP1 – This user profile is used to serve CGI programs. This user profile must have authority to any object that it uses.

These two user profiles are used for serving Internet documents and for running CGI programs. They are only used for the HTTP server jobs. The only modification that should be done on these user profiles is to give them authority to objects that will be needed for Web processing. This includes programs, files, and documents located in the IFS.

AS/400 CGI PROGRAMMING CONSIDERATIONS

When developing CGI programs on the AS/400, there are a few things that you should keep in mind. These are peculiarities that I ran across while writing CGI applications. You might run across them—and others—too.

A CGI Job's Library List

The libraries available to your CGI programs are those specified on the system library list as well as the library that you specify on the Exec directive of the HTTP configuration.

CGI programs and other Web serving functions run in the QHTTPSVR subsystem. The jobs that run the Web applications are known as Batch Interactive (BCI) jobs. These jobs run using the user profiles QTMHHTTP and QTMHHTP1. These user profiles are defined to use the IBM default job description QDFTJOBD. Even if you change the job description associated with the user profiles to specify a different initial library list, these jobs will still only use libraries defined in the system libraries and the library defined on the Exec directive of the HTTP configuration.

If you want the programs to access other programs or data files, they either need to be in a library that is specified on the system library list or the library in which your CGI programs reside. This is unfortunate, but it is necessary for security reasons. Because anyone can access your system using these Web pages, you risk possible havoc if access to production libraries is possible.

I have found a way around this problem by manipulating the job's library list inside the CGI program itself. You can use the Add Library List Entry (ADDLIBLE) or Remove Library List Entry (RMVLIBLE) using the QCMDEXEC API, which calls a CL program to execute the commands, or you could write your own service programs to push and pop libraries from the library list.

When I need to access a data file that is not available, I define the file in my RPG programs as user open (USROPN). Just before I want to perform an operation on the file, such as a READ or CHAIN, I add the library in which the file resides to my library list, using a set of library list subprocedures. Next, I open the file and perform an input and/or output operation. When I am done, I close the file and remove the library from my library list. This narrows the window of opportunity for potential hackers.

(As a note, IBM does not recommend this procedure unless you make sure you remove any libraries from the job's library list as soon as you are complete.

Again, this is for security reasons. I personally have not run across any problems with manipulating the job's library list. I do, however, make it a habit to remove libraries from the job's library list after I am done using them.)

I have included in appendix C a set of subprocedures that will allow you to manipulate the CGI job's library list easily. This set of subprocedures is a small set of functions. For a complete list of subprocedures, refer to my article, "Library Operations Through Service Programs," in the February 1999 issue of *Midrange Computing*.

Keep an Eye on Your CGI

There will be times while you are developing applications that you will run into problems. As with any AS/400 program, there is a potential that jobs will error out and have a status of Message Wait (MSGW). You might not realize this until you receive a timeout error from your browser, or if it seems like a CGI program is taking longer than usual to complete.

I like to keep an eye on my CGI program jobs, especially when testing. To do this, use the Work with Active Jobs (WRKACTJOB) command. In running server jobs, the name of the instance will be the name of the job. Using this job name as a qualifier on the WRKACTJOB command allows you to watch only those jobs that you are concerned with.

For example, let's assume you are running a server instance named DEFAULT. This would mean that the server jobs running this instance would also be named DEFAULT. If you entered the command:

```
WRKACTJOB JOB(DEFAULT)
```

You would see only the jobs running for this particular instance. From there, you can look at the jobs for any MSGW status. Looking at the error or job log for this job is the same as dealing with any other job. Simply perform a Display Job (option 5) and view the job log. Use option 7 to view error messages if the job is in a MSGW state.

Access Logs

The AS/400 has the ability to create an access log that can be used to report access and errors that occur on your AS/400 that relate to the Web server.

Access logs, by default, are not created. To create them you need to specify a directive in the HTTP configuration. The directive used is AccessLog and would look like the following:

```
AccessLog Log_File_Name
```

The Log_File_Name should be replaced with the name of the file in which you want to store the access logs. The file will be created, if it does not already exist, in the library QUSRSYS. Every day, a new member will be created in this file and access to your Web server will be logged. The name of each member will be in the format QCYYMMDD. The member names will always start with Q. The C will be replaced with a century code. YY will be replaced with a two digit year, MM will be replaced with the month, and DD will be replaced with the day.

Should you want to store the access log in a more common format, you can do this using the LogFormat directive:

```
LogFormat DDS | Common
```

If the LogFormat directive is not specified, and the AccessLog directive is used, this directive defaults to DDS and the logs will be stored in DDS format. If the Common log format is specified, the log information will be stored in a format similar to that found on other Web serving machines.

I find it easiest to store the access logs in the root system of the IFS in common format. This way I can use one of the many products available that can report Web use on the logs produced by the AS/400. I usually create a directory named Logs on the root system of the IFS. I then split it into subdirectories for each server instance that I am running. Then, I specify this location for my access logs using the AccessLog directive and I specify Common on the LogFormat directive. The use of these directives is as follows:

```
AccessLog /Logs/DEFAULT/
LogFormat Common
```

This stores my access logs in the /Logs/DEFAULT/ directory of the IFS in the Common format. If you have a program that can produce reports from a common log format (there are many available), you could point the program at this directory, or map a drive to this directory, so that the program could access this data.

CGI IS JUST AROUND THE CORNER

I am sure you will find, as I did, that the AS/400 has come a long way in its ability to adapt to an ever-changing industry. The ability to serve Web pages and, more important, to use CGI programming, makes it very powerful. Using languages such as RPG or COBOL to perform these CGI tasks also saves time.

This chapter provided a general overview of the processes involved in CGI programming as a whole, and also as it pertains to the AS/400. The chapters to come dive deeper into the configuration and programming of the AS/400 to function as a Web server. Read on to discover the new world available to the AS/400.

4

THE AS/400 HTTP SERVER

HyperText Transport Protocol (HTTP) is a communications protocol used mainly to serve Web pages. HTTP is the link that allows communication between a client, usually someone surfing the Web, and a server. The server is the machine that holds most of the data requested by the client. When you key in your favorite Web address in your browser, you are actually accessing data in the form of Hypertext Markup Language (HTML), stored on the server machine.

HTTP servers run on a variety of different machines, such as mainframes, PCs, or AS/400s. With the implementation of the HTTP server in V3R2 and V3R7, IBM opened up a whole new area of functionality for the AS/400. What was once known as an applications machine with fairly plain text interfaces now performs as a fully functional HTTP server as well. This facelift has given the AS/400 a new set of possibilities and clientele for the midrange market. The stability of the AS/400 makes it an almost perfect HTTP server.

This chapter is meant to give you a head start on getting your AS/400 set up as an HTTP server. It will cover how the AS/400 HTTP server works, and provide instructions on setting up HTTP server configurations and instances that make serving Web pages and Common Gateway Interface (CGI) programs possible. You will find a summary of this information in appendix D.

HOW THE HTTP SERVER WORKS

The AS/400's HTTP server works in much the same way as other machines that function as HTTP servers. The client machine requests a specific server using a Uniform Resource Locator (URL). The URL is the string of characters (www.myhomepage.com) that you type into your browser. The steps taken to process a URL request are as follows:

1. The client machine makes a request using a URL.

2. If the connection is successful, the server processes the request made by the client. The request is the name of the file that you are accessing.

3. If the request is successful, the server sends a response to the client and the connection is closed.

The same basic steps are used by most HTTP servers. If you watch the status bar at the bottom of most browsers, you can actually see these steps taking place.

When the connection is made, if no port number is specified implicitly in the URL, port 80 is automatically used. This is true for most HTTP servers today. Different requests to a machine for specific functions use default ports that are recognized as standards. For example, Post Office Protocol (POP) requests are made to port 110, Simple Mail Transfer Protocol (SMTP) requests are made to port 25, and HTTP requests are made to port 80.

If this seems confusing, here is a simple way to think of the World Wide Web. Imagine that all the server machines on the Internet are simply hard drives available to your machine. The only difference is that these are, in most cases, read only hard

---

e-Tip

The default port number for serving HTTP requests on most machines is 80. If the port number is not implicitly defined on the server address, the port number defaults to 80.

drives, so you can only retrieve information from them. When you make a URL request, you tell your computer to access a file from one of these hard drives. The URL specifies the drive name, path, and the document (such as `index.html`) of the file you want to retrieve.

Imagine you are making a request to view a grocery list that you have stored as a document on a hard drive local to your machine. You would access it using a path and document name similar to the following example.

```
C:\My Documents\GroceryLists\Jan102001.doc
```

This request would open up the document `Jan102001.doc` that is located in the `\My Documents\GroceryLists` path on your hard drive named C:.

Now, imagine that this grocery list resides on the Internet. To access it, you also give a path. Instead specifying C: as the drive followed by the path and the document name, you specify HTTP:// followed by the path and the document name. This is known as the URL.

```
HTTP://www.groceries.com/GroceryList.html
```

The only other difference between these examples is the file type. The file in the first example is a normal document and viewed with a product such as Microsoft Word. The file in the second example is a Hypertext Markup Language (HTML) document and is viewed with a browser such as Netscape's Communicator or Microsoft's Internet Explorer.

Storing documents on a Web server can serve many functions. Let's assume you have just returned from a vacation to Florida, and you wish to show pictures of your trip to your friends and family. You could print multiple copies of the prints and mail them, but this would require time, in the form of addressing all of the envelopes, and money, in the form of stamps and reprints.

Your next option is to scan the pictures in and e-mail them to your friends and family. This again will take time, not so much in the form of scanning in the pictures, but in the time it will take to e-mail the images.

One more option is to take the scanned images and place them on your Web site. Next, you inform your friends and family of the URL where the pictures are located. They can then open their browser and view the pictures online. This saves times, keeps the images in one location, and allows them to view the pictures when they want.

The same holds true for documents that you would use for business. You could post information such as release notes, bug fixes, contact information, and company profiles all in one central location. Accessing the data is convenient for the user and makes your maintenance of the information easy as well. If something changes in one of the documents, you change the information on your Web page instead of sending the changes to each and every person that has interest in it.

There are many more uses for an HTTP server, as you will discover as you proceed in setting up your AS/400 as a server. Let's focus now on the steps to set up your AS/400 as an HTTP server.

CONFIGURING THE AS/400 HTTP SERVER

The AS/400 HTTP server will require a little bit of work to get it up and running. The HTTP server must be configured to allow documents to be accessed, programs to be run, and graphics to be displayed. Before you can begin using the HTTP server set up, you must first have TCP/IP configured on your machine. If you are unsure if you have TCP/IP configured on your machine, consult with your AS/400 or network administrator.

HTTP Server Commands

The HTTP server has many commands that allow you to customize the settings for your HTTP server. The configuration commands you will use most often are listed below.

1. Configure TCP/IP HTTP (CFGTCPHTTP) – This command takes you to a menu that lists the options you can perform to configure your HTTP server.

2. Change HTTP Attributes (CHGHTTPA) – This command allows you to change attributes associated with the HTTP server, such as whether or not to autostart the server and how many server jobs to start. Both a minimum and a maximum number of jobs can be specified.

3. Work with HTTP Configuration (WRKHTTPCFG) – This command allows you to add, change, remove, configure, or restore an HTTP configuration setting.

4. Start TCP/IP HTTP Server (STRTCPSVR SERVER(*HTTP)) – This command allows you to start all HTTP server instances, one HTTP server instance, or restart a server instance.

5. End TCP/IP HTTP Server (ENDDTCPSVR SERVER(*HTTP)) – This command allows you to end one or all of the HTTP server instances.

One other place that allows you to work with your HTTP configuration is the AS/400 Tasks Web page. This page can be accessed by using a browser and entering the domain name or IP address of your AS/400 into the URL and specifying either port 2001 or 2010.

The AS/400 Tasks page is used to create and configure both HTTP server instances and HTTP configurations. For now, both of these options must be performed using the AS/400 Tasks page. This page also can be used to perform many of the functions that are available through the AS/400 command line as mentioned earlier in this chapter. You might find one of these interfaces more convenient to work with, but you will need to use both of them to configure and create your HTTP server.

The AS/400 Task page will be discussed in more detail later, under setting up HTTP configurations and server instances.

When configuring your HTTP server, there are two important terms that you should understand. The HTTP Server Configuration and HTTP Server Instance are two items that work hand in hand, and you can't run your HTTP server without them being created and configured on your machine.

HTTP SERVER CONFIGURATION

The HTTP Server Configuration is a file that resides on your system and tells the server what clients making requests to your machine can and can't do. It also provides important mapping, security, and execution rules. Each of these rules exists as a separate line in the HTTP Server Configuration, and is known as a *directive*.

An HTTP configuration is used to define the dos and don'ts associated with a specific HTTP server instance. An HTTP server instance is covered later in this chapter.

> **e-Definition**
>
> A directive is a command in the HTTP configuration that tells the HTTP server what can and cannot be done as well as other rules specific to the HTTP instance the configuration is assigned to.

Creating an HTTP Server Configuration

To create an HTTP Server Configuration, use the IBM HTTP Server Configuration page that shipped on your AS/400. Unfortunately, at the time this book went to print, there are no actual AS/400 commands that can be used to create an HTTP Server Configuration, and you must perform this type of HTTP configuration through your browser.

To access the IBM HTTP Server Configuration page, you must first start your Administration server instance. I will describe what an instance is later in this chapter, but for now, use the following command:

```
STRTCPSVR SERVER(*HTTP) HTTPSVR(*ADMIN)
```

Next, open your browser and enter the following URL, replacing your.as400.ipaddress with the IP address or server name of your AS/400.

```
http://your.as400.ipaddress:2001
```

If you wish to use a Secure Sockets Layer (SSL) connection while accessing this information, you can substitute the port number 2001 with 2010. When starting out, I suggest using port 2001.

After you enter this URL, you will be prompted for a user ID and password. Enter either your user ID and password or the user ID and password of a user, set up on your AS/400, who has authority to perform system operator functions. Consult your system administrator if you need help.

The next screen you see is your AS/400 Tasks page. It will look similar to the screen shown in Figure 4.1. Click on the IBM HTTP Server for AS/400 link to access the HTTP Configuration Page.

Figure 4.1: The AS/400 Tasks page.

Once you click on the IBM HTTP Server for AS/400 link, you will be linked to a page that will allow you to configure your HTTP server. We want to create an HTTP configuration, so click on the Configuration and Administration link located in the list of links on the left side of the page.

On the Configuration and Administration page, you will see a list of links. Click on the Configurations link and you will be given a list of options. Your browser should look similar to Figure 4.2.

Figure 4.2: The browser after selecting the Configuration link.

Figure 4.3: Creating configuration MYCONFIG using the CONFIG configuration as a template.

Next, click on the Create Configuration link. You will then be given an option to create a configuration from a blank template, or to create one using an existing configuration. The AS/400 usually comes supplied with a default configuration that is named CONFIG. This configuration is a good reference for all the available directives and how to use them for your specific release level. You might want to start by creating your configuration using the CONFIG configuration as a template. Figure 4.3 shows how I created a configuration named MYCONFIG using the IBM-supplied CONFIG configuration as a template.

Click on the Apply button and the system will take care of the rest. Your browser should display a message telling you if the configuration was created success-fully, or if there was an error. Figure 4.4 shows the screen after the creation of the configuration MYCONFIG was successful.

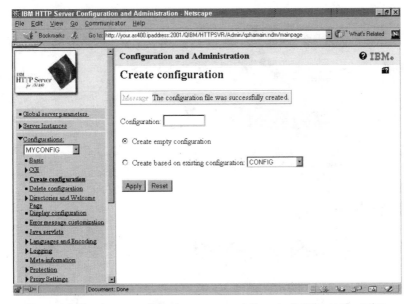

Figure 4.4: Your browser will display a message telling you that the configuration was created successfully.

Once you have created an HTTP Server Configuration, you can start entering configuration directives.

Configuration Directives

There are so many directives available to you when setting up an HTTP configuration file, that these directives and their explanations could fill a book.

In my experience, though, I have found five main directives that you will use most often when configuring your HTTP server. These directives are Map, Pass, Exec, Fail, and Redirect. The directive names do a good job of explaining what each directive doew, but they are explained in detail.

Table 4.1 lists these directives as well as a short description of the functions.

Table 4.1: Important HTTP Configuration Directives.

Directive	Action	Example
Map	Maps a directory or file to another location.	Map /cgi-bin/* /QSYS.LIB/AS400CGI.LIB/*
Exec	Allows access to executable programs in a particular library.	Exec /QSYS.LIB/AS400CGI.LIB/*
Pass	Allows the client to access a particular directory or library on your HTTP Server.	Pass /HTML/* or Pass /QSYS.LIB/AS400CGI.LIB/*
Fail	Refuses access to a particular directory or library on your HTTP Server.	Fail /Private/* or Fail /QSYS.LIB/APDATA.LIB/*
Redirect	Redirects the client to a new location.	Redirect /oldpages/* http://www.newpage.com
Welcome	Specifies the file to access when no file is specified in the URL.	Welcome index.html

Other directives and how they are used can be found in one of the many sources provided by IBM. There is also a default configuration file set up on your machine when you receive it. This file contains a list of almost every directive as well as a description of what each does. This default configuration file is named CONFIG. You can view this configuration file by using the Work with HTTP Configuration (WRKHTTPCFG) command:

```
WRKHTTPCFG CFG(CONFIG)
```

If you haven't changed the command defaults for the WRKHTTPCFG command, you don't even need to specify a configuration file. CONFIG is the default for this command.

Glancing through this configuration file will give you a good idea of what each directive does. Also, with every new release there seems to be a few more directives available, so be sure to view the release notes dealing with the HTTP server when installing a new version of the operating system.

Let's review the five configuration directives in detail.

The Map Directive

The Map directive is used to specify a template for requests, and map those requests to a different location. In other words, you supply a template and a replacement value for that template. If the incoming request matches your template, it will be substituted with the second value you specify on the command.

The Map directive is specified in the following context.

```
Map request_template new_template
```

The request_template value is the string that will be incoming from the request URL. The new_template value is the string you want to substitute for the request_template. If you've used any type of find-and-replace option in a word processor, or even Program Development Manager (PDM) on the AS/400, you can think of a Map directive as the same type of option.

The request template is case sensitive, and the new template path is only case sensitive in directories that are case sensitive, such as the root system of the Integrated File System (IFS) or the QDLS folder structure.

The Map directive is useful for hiding the actual directory structure of your server machine from the user accessing a certain URL or for simply rerouting requests to a particular directory to another directory. An example of using the Map directive is:

```
Map /home/* /Intranet/homepages/*
```

When the user enters a URL with the path /home/ into the location bar of the browser, this Map directive tells the HTTP server to look in the location /Intranet/homepages/ for the document requested. If you have a document named index.html in the directory of /Intranet/homepages/, the user would enter the following URL to access this document, assuming that this Map directive is in place:

```
http://www.myas400.com/home/index.html
```

When the server sees the request for the /home/ directory, it checks the HTTP configuration for any Map directives that match the request. It sees the Map directive specified previously and knows that it should look in the actual directory of /Intranet/homepages/ for the requested document, not in the /home/ directory. In this example, the /home/ directory does not need to exist on your machine. Only the actual directory where the request is routed to must exist on your machine.

Another reason for using Map directives is because the AS/400 file system differs from other file systems such as UNIX or Microsoft NT. If you could not map requests, anything that resided in the QSYS.LIB portion of the IFS would look awkward to the user. The URL would have to be similar to the following example:

```
http://www.myas400.com/QSYS.LIB/HTMLLIB.LIB/HTML.FILE/INDEX.MBR
```

This request would access the member INDEX in the file HTML in the library HTMLLIB. Luckily, though, we have a directory structure in the root file system of the IFS, as well as the shared folder (QDLS) system to store documents in.

If you plan on doing any CGI programming, it should be noted that CGI programs can only exist in the QSYS.LIB file structure of the IFS. This is where we usually place RPG, CL, and COBOL programs. Using the Map directive, we can make requests to CGI programs a little more standard. For example, we could use the following Map directive for CGI programs that exist in a library named AS400CGI.

```
Map /cgi-bin/* /QSYS.LIB/AS400CGI.LIB/*
```

The first objective of this directive is to hide the file structure from the person accessing the URL. The second objective is to map a more standard directory name to the library on the AS/400 that contains our CGI programs. In a way, this Map directive hides the fact that the server machine is in fact an AS/400. When the user types in the path /cgi-bin/ in the location bar of the browser, the HTTP server knows to map this location to the library AS400CGI on the AS/400.

The cgi-bin library is a common directory name used to store CGI programs on most Web server machines. On the AS/400, a CGI program can be written in RPG or COBOL. If the user wanted to access one of these CGI programs, and the previous Map directive was used, the following URL would be used:

```
http://www.myas400.com/cgi-bin/CGIPGM.PGM
```

If we did not specify the Map directive, the user would have to use the URL below.

```
http://www.myas400.com/QSYS.LIB/AS400CGI.LIB/CGIPGM.PGM
```

Using this URL is a dead giveaway of the machine type that the HTTP server is running on. This could be used to the advantage of someone wanting to sabotage your machine. The AS/400 is a secure machine, but no machine is invincible. Using the Map directive to hide the directory structure is one way to secure your machine.

Another important item to note is that the extension of .PGM is used in the URL to access the CGI program. On the AS/400, you'll recognize this as the object type. This could be another giveaway of what type of machine is being used as the HTTP server. Because of this, the following Map directive can be specified so that the .PGM extension does not need to be specified.

```
Map /cgi-bin/* /QSYS.LIB/AS400CGI.LIB/*.PGM
```

This Map directive will automatically place the extension of .PGM onto any request to the /cgi-bin/ directory. So, to access a CGI program, the user would specify the following URL:

```
http://www.myas400.com/cgi-bin/CGIPGM
```

This not only gives a more standard look to the URL, but it also doesn't give any clues to the user as to what type of system the HTTP server is running on.

As you will see in the following sections describing the Exec and Pass directives, the Map directive is not always needed to redirect requests. Even so, it is good to know what the Map directive does, because you may find a use for it in the future, or you might simply want to keep your mapping and other directives separate.

The Exec Directive

The Exec directive tells the HTTP server that any requests made that match the template should be treated as executable programs. The AS/400 allows only executable programs to reside in an actual library, otherwise known as the QSYS structure of the IFS. This means that your CGI programs must be in a library, and not in a directory, a folder, or the root portion of the IFS.

Once an Exec directive is met, the request is not checked against any other template directives in the configuration file.

The Exec directive is specified in the following context.

```
Exec [request_template] program_path
```

The request_template value is the string that will be incoming from the request URL. The program_path is the location of the programs that can be executed as

CGI programs. Only the program path is needed for this directive, as any mapping can be performed with the Map directive.

The request template is case sensitive, and the program path is case sensitive only in directories that are case sensitive, such as the root system of the IFS or the QDLS folder structure.

An example of a command Exec directive reads as follows:

```
Exec /QSYS.LIB/AS400CGI.LIB/*
```

This directive tells the HTTP server that if a request is made to this path, it should be treated as an executable program.

You might be thinking to yourself that the user doesn't type in the actual library structure in the URL because of the Map directive, so how does this work?

The Map and Pass directives can be used in conjunction with each other.

```
Map   /cgi-bin/* /QSYS.LIB/AS400CGI.LIB/*.PGM
Exec /QSYS.LIB/AS400CGI.LIB/*
```

Using both the Map and Exec directives together allows us to use the standard CGI naming directory for requests to our server for CGI programs.

To further explain this concept, assume that the following URL was used:

```
http://www.myas400.com/cgi-bin/CGIPGM
```

First, the Map directive is reached. The system using this Map directive says, "I see you are requesting a document in the directory '/CGI-BIN/'. You have this mapped to the location '/QSYS.LIB/AS400CGI.LIB/' and since you used the '*.PGM' wildcard, I understand that you're looking for the document '/QSYS.LIB/AS400 CGI.LIB/CGIPGM.PGM'."

Second, the Exec directive is reached. It just so happens that the request matches the Exec directive as well. The system says, "I see that you have specified that any documents requested from the '/QSYS.LIB/AS400CGI.LIB/' structure should be treated as executable programs."

The system then tries to find the program named CGIPGM in library AS400CGI and attempts to execute it. Any other template checking is omitted after an Exec directive template is matched, as in this example.

As stated earlier, the Map and Exec directives could actually be combined into one Exec directive, allowing the elimination of the Map directive. You might find it easier to specify a request template on your Exec directives simply to cut down on the number of directives in your configuration file. Then again, you might find it easier to have directives that only perform one operation each. How you do this is entirely up to you.

An example of specifying a request template on an Exec directive would be similar to the following:

```
Exec /cgi-bin/* /QSYS.LIB/AS400CGI.LIB/*.PGM
```

This single Exec directive replaces the Map and Exec directives that I used earlier in this section. It performs exactly the same as would the two separate directives.

It may be a good idea to start using Map and Exec directives separately until you get the hang of what they do, but it's up to you. Either way will perform the same. The only advantage to using mapping on the Exec directive is to eliminate a Map directive, possibly making the configuration easier to follow.

The Pass Directive

The Pass directive is one of the more powerful directives you will use. This directive tells the server what folders and documents that a user can access from the browser. This is a great security feature. Instead of telling the system what directories and documents people can't access, it tells them which ones they can access.

Think of the Pass directive as the traffic cop for your Web server. If a user requests a document (excluding a CGI request, which is handled by the Exec directive) that does not fit any Pass directive you have specified, they will receive an error stating that they are trying to request a document that is forbidden.

Once a Pass directive is met, the request is not checked against any other template directives in the configuration file.

The Pass directive is specified in the following context:

```
Pass [request_template] file_path
```

The `request_template` value is the string that will be incoming from the request URL. The `file_path` is the location on your server that you are granting access to for the request of documents or other files, such as images. Only the file path is needed for this directive, as any mapping can be performed with the Map directive.

The request template is case sensitive, and the file path is case sensitive only in directories that are case sensitive, such as the root system of the IFS or the QDLS folder structure.

A sample Map and Pass directive combination would look like the following:

```
Map /home/* /Intranet/homepages/*
Pass /Intranet/homepages/*
```

The Map directive reroutes any requests to the /home/ directory to the /Intranet/homepages/ directory. The HTTP server then gets a request for a document in the /Intranet/homepages/ directory, it checks the Pass directives to make sure that this request is allowable. It acts as a security guard and bounces all illegal requests. For example, enter the following request:

```
http://www.myas400.com/home/index.html
```

The HTTP server knows first to map the /home/ directory to the actual directory of /Intranet/homepages/ from the Map directive. Second, it sees that you are allowing requests from the /Intranet/homepages/ directory from the Pass directive, and allows the request to complete.

But, enter the following URL:

```
http://www.myas400.com/Intranet/index.html
```

The request will be rejected. First, the Map directive is ignored because the directory requested of /Intranet/ isn't included as a path on any Map directives in the HTTP configuration file. Second, there is no Pass directive saying that a user can access documents inside the /Intranet/ directory.

As with the Exec directive, the Map and Pass directives can be combined into one Pass directive. For example, the following Pass directive would do the same as the Map and Pass directive combination shown earlier:

```
Pass /home/* /Intranet/homepages/*
```

Again, it is up to you to decide how you want to use these directives.

Never use a Pass directive that is too generic and that will give access to more than you intend. For example, using the following Pass directive would be considered very dangerous:

```
Pass /*
```

This generic Pass directive allows access to virtually every object on the machine. It might seem tempting to use this directive, but I strongly encourage you to never use it.

e-Tip: Never use a generic Pass /* directive because it will allow access to your entire AS/400 file structure.

The Fail Directive

The Fail directive is used to reject any incoming requests that match the template specified. This directive is useful for denying access to any documents that can be accessed because of a following Pass directive.

The Fail directive is specified in the following context.

```
Fail request_template
```

The `request_template` value is the path or file that you wish to deny access to. This template can contain a wildcard (*) as a value, or simply specify a single document that you wish to protect. The request template is case sensitive.

Let's assume that you have a Pass directive that allows access to the directory /webpages/. For some reason, you decide to place a document named salaries.html into this directory, and you do not want anyone to be able to access to it. The following would be your Fail and Pass directives to accomplish this.

```
Fail /webpages/salaries.html
Pass /webpages/*
```

It is important to understand that if these directives were reversed, the Fail directive would have no affect because once the incoming template matches a Pass directive, no other request template checking is performed.

The example given may seem a little out there, but it is simply an example of when someone could use the Fail directive. I myself have found no reason to use it. If you specify your Pass directives explicitly enough, you should have no need for the Fail directive.

The Redirect Directive

The Redirect directive is used to reroute requests to another server. This can be useful if a Web page or CGI application that once resided on your Web server moved to another machine.

The Redirect directive is specified in the following context:

```
Redirect request_template URL
```

The `request_template` value is the path or file that you wish to use to reroute a request to another server. This template can contain a wildcard (*) as a value, or simply specify a single document that you wish to protect. The request template is case sensitive. The URL value contains the URL of the server that you want to reroute the requests to.

Let's assume for this example that on your server you used to have some documents that users could access to view potential problems concerning Year 2000. You stored these documents in the directory /Intranet/Y2k/. One day you are surfing the Web and you discover that someone else has a page similar in content to yours, but much easier to read and follow. You decide that you want your users to view this page instead of your page that resides on your server. To do this, specify the following:

```
Redirect /Intranet/Y2K/* http://www.newy2kpage.com
```

After you add this directive and stop and restart your HTTP server instance, if a user requests a document in your /Intranet/Y2k/ directory, the user will be redirected to the new page specified on the Redirect directive.

The Welcome Directive

The Welcome directive is used to specify a default file to display if no file is specified in the URL. For example, when a user simply enters http://www.yourpage.com into the browser, there is no file specified. In this case, the Welcome directive would be used to determine which file to display.

The Welcome directive is specified in the following context:

```
Welcome file_name
```

The `file_name` value is replaced with the name of a file that should be viewed as a default. Most Webmasters set this value up as `index.html`, `index.htm`, `default.html`, or `default.htm`.

Other Considerations for using Directives

While all the directives mentioned in the previous section are important, in my experience of configuring the HTTP server to perform the basic functions, only the Map, Exec, and Pass directives are required.

I suggest using explicit Pass directives because the Fail directive is case sensitive. For example, examine the following Fail directive:

```
Fail /securedocs/currentsalaries.html
```

You would assume that this directive would not allow a user to request the document `currentsalaries.html` in your `securedocs` directory. But, if the user enters the following URL, the document will be accessed:

```
http://youras400.com/securdocs/CuRrEnTsAlArIeS.htm
```

You will notice that all the user had to do was change the case of any letter of the document and the Fail directive would not apply. This is because the Fail directive is case sensitive.

> **e-Tip** Consider using explicit Pass directives instead of generic Pass directives and explicit Fail directives.

The order you use the directive in also makes a difference. Always use the Pass directive as the last directive in the group. Once the HTTP server reaches a Pass directive all other rules, such as Map or Exec are terminated. For this reason, I suggest always using directives in the following order:

1. Map
2. Exec
3. Pass

This will ensure that your Map and Exec directives are not ignored as they are located and that they will be processed before any Pass directive that you specify.

---

e-Tip: Always specify directives in the following order: Map, Exec, and then Pass.

One final consideration concerns changes you make to your configuration file. Any changes made will not take affect until you stop and restart the server. Some directives will take effect if you specify *RESTART on the SRTTCPSVR command, but I generally stop the server and restart it after I am sure all of the jobs for the particular instance have ended.

HTTP SERVER INSTANCE

An HTTP Server Instance is a set of server jobs that process incoming requests. One job, the Batch (BCH) job, is the actual HTTP server job. The other jobs are known as Batch Immediate (BCI) jobs. These jobs handle incoming requests to the server. The number of BCH jobs that will be running depends on the values that you specified for your CHGHTTPA command. The default allows five jobs to run, which should be plenty to handle multiple incoming requests.

In the same way that interactive jobs run in the QINTER subsystem and batch jobs run in the QBATCH subsystem, the HTTP Server Instance jobs run in the QHTTPSVR subsystem on most machines. HTTP Server Instances can be configured to autostart when they are created. This means after you perform an IPL, your HTTP Server Instances will automatically start so that people can begin accessing documents from your AS/400 again. HTTP Server Instances can also be started using the Start TCP Server (STRTCPSVR) command, specifying *HTTP as the server to start and specifying the instance to start. HTTP Server Instances can be ended using the End TCP Server (ENDTCPSVR) command, specifying *HTTP as the server and specifying the instance to end.

One word of warning when using the ENDTCPSVR command is to be absolutely sure to explicitly specify to end the *HTTP server when this is the result that you desire. The default for this command on most machine is *ALL. This will end all TCP/IP servers and could cause havoc for any user or anything else connected to your machine using TCP/IP.

Every HTTP Server Instance that is active on your machine uses a particular HTTP Server Configuration. Each instance can use its own configuration, or two or more instances can use the same configuration. The configuration tells the HTTP Server Instance which documents can be accessed or which documents are off-limits. The configuration that a specific HTTP Server Instance uses is set up when an HTTP Server Instance is created.

Creating an HTTP Server Instance

Creating an HTTP Server Instance is similar to creating an HTTP Server Configuration. The AS/400 Tasks page is accessed first. Enter the following URL to access the AS/400 Tasks page:

```
http://your.as400.ipaddress:2001
```

After this page is accessed, you will see a page similar to Figure 4.1. Click on the IBM HTTP Server for AS/400 link, the same link used for creating or configuring an HTTP configuration.

After you have clicked on the IBM HTTP Server for AS/400 link, you will be on the page that allows you to configure your HTTP server. We want to create a server instance, so click on the Configuration and Administration link.

e-Tip

Be sure to explicitly specify the server 'HTTP on the ENDDTCPSVR command when ending server instances.

If you recall the previous section on creating an HTTP configuration, we followed the Configurations link. In this case, click on the Server Instances link. After you do, you will see a page similar to that shown in Figure 4.5.

Figure 4.5: HTTP Configuration page after clicking on Server Instances.

As you can see, all the options for working with HTTP Server Instances are available after clicking on the Server Instances link. Our goal is to create a server instance, so click on the Create Server Instance link. After you do, you will see a page similar to that shown in Figure 4.6.

Figure 4.6: Create an HTTP Server Instance page.

Notice that there are two parameters to fill in. The first is the name of the HTTP Server Instance that you wish to create. The second is the name of the configuration to use when you start this HTTP Server Instance. In the previous section on creating an HTTP configuration, I created a configuration named MYCONFIG. This is the configuration that I will select to use. I am going to name my server instance MYSI. After these parameters are entered, simply click on the Create button. If your instance is created, you should see a message stating that your server instance was successfully created.

You should now be able to go in and change the attributes of your server instance using the same configuration page that you used to create the server instance. Instead of using the Create Server Instance link, you can click on one of the other links to delete, change, or work with a server instance.

A Closer Look at the Provided HTTP Server Instances

Your AS/400 usually comes with two HTTP Server Instances already set up to use. The first HTTP Server Instance is used mainly for administration tasks and is known as the Administration HTTP server instance. This server should be running only when you are performing administrative tasks. If this instance is set to autostart, I suggest that this be changed immediately. Changes to the ADMIN instance can be made in the same location where changes are made to other server instances.

The second server instance included on your machine is known as the Default HTTP server instance. This instance can be used to begin using your AS/400 as an HTTP server. This instance uses the configuration file named CONFIG that comes preloaded as well.

The *ADMIN HTTP Server Instance

In the previous section about setting up a configuration, we touched briefly on the Administration (*ADMIN) server instance. To start the Administration instance, issue the following command:

```
STRTCPSVR SERVER(*HTTP) HTTPSVR(*ADMIN)
```

This instance must be running for you to access the AS/400 Tasks page on your AS/400. The parameter *ADMIN is a special value used for this HTTP Server Instance.

If you view your system's active jobs, you will see at least four jobs running with the name ADMIN. This is your *ADMIN HTTP Server Instance in action. If this server is running, you can use the AS/400 Tasks page to perform a variety of options on your machine.

The DEFAULT HTTP Server Instance

Your system also comes loaded with an instance that can be used as a template or for serving as a default server instance. This HTTP Server Instance is usually called the DEFAULT HTTP Server Instance.

To start the DEFAULT HTTP Server Instance, the following command is used:

```
STRTCPSVR SERVER(*HTTP) HTTPSVR(DEFAULT)
```

If you view your system's active jobs, under the QHTTPSVR subsystem you should see at least four jobs running named DEFAULT. If this is your first time using the HTTP server on your AS/400, you should be able to open a browser and enter the IP address or DNS name of your AS/400 and view a sample home page that is provided by IBM. This sample home page will resemble the one shown in Figure 4.7.

The sample home page provided by IBM is by no means anything spectacular. It is just there to provide an example of how an HTTP Server Instance works together with an HTTP Server Configuration. The DEFAULT HTTP Server Instance uses a default configuration named CONFIG. If you look at the directives in the CONFIG configuration, you will see mainly Pass directives that point the browser to a specific path and an HTML file that IBM includes.

e-Tip:

To check if a particular server instance is active, issue the command:

```
WRKACTJOB JOB(instance)
```

Replace instance with the name of the server instance you want to check. If you see jobs listed, the instance is active. If not, the instance is not running.

Figure 4.7: Sample home page provided by IBM.

PUTTING AN INSTANCE AND CONFIGURATION TOGETHER

We have seen how to create a configuration, and how to create a server instance and assign a configuration. If you looked at the default configuration file CONFIG that is used by the default server instance DEFAULT, you probably noticed that the path used on the Pass directive is quite long and cumbersome. This section will focus on creating your own instance and configuration for your own use.

To get started, I suggest creating your own instance and configuration using the CONFIG configuration as a template. Next, create a directory on your AS/400 that you plan on letting users access. To create a directory, use the following command:

```
CRTDIR DIR(/directoryname)
```

This command creates a directory in the root of the Integrated File System (IFS) with the name you specify. For the examples that follow, I will use the directory name MyHTML.

Next, you need to allow users to access this directory. Edit the configuration you created using the Work with HTTP Configuration (WRKHTTPCFG) command, specifying the name of your configuration. You will find two IBM-supplied Pass directives that were copied from the CONFIG configuration. Remove one Pass directive and change the other to read as follows:

```
Pass /MyHTML/*
```

Exit the configuration and start your server instance. To make sure that your instance will not conflict with any other instances running, for example the DEFAULT server instance, issue the following commands.

```
ENDTCPSVR SERVER(*HTTP) HTTPSVR(*ALL)
STRTCPSVR SERVER(*HTTP) HTTPSVR(MYSI)
```

Remember, I created an instance named MYSI, so be sure to substitute the name of your server instance if it is different. Also, before issuing the STRTCPSVR command, view your active jobs and make sure that all jobs in the QHTTPSVR subsystem have ended first.

Next, check to make sure the instance is active. Use the Work with Active Jobs command to do this. Either display all the jobs running in the QHTTPSVR subsystem, or specify the instance in the job name parameter of the WRKACTJOB command.

Once you are sure the instance is running, create a small HTML file named TEST.HTML and upload it to the directory that you created. Once it is there, go to your browser and enter the following URL:

```
http://your.as400.ipaddress/MyHTML/TEST.HTML
```

If you receive an error, refer to the error index in appendix A. If you see your page, congratulations! You are on your way to using the AS/400 as an excellent Web server.

A FINAL NOTE ON HTTP SERVER INSTANCES

Because the AS/400 can run multiple HTTP Server Instances, there must be something unique about each one of them. Two properties make the server instance unique. The properties are *hostname name* and *port number*.

The Port Directive

The Port directive is used to process data when a request is made to a specific port number. If a port number is not specified in the configuration, port 80 is automatically used for the instance that uses the configuration. You cannot run two different instances using the same port. Usually, if you try to start an instance using the same port as an active instance, the instance will error out and end. A message will be logged into the QSYSOPR message queue and a job log explaining the error will be produced.

Specifying a port number in your configuration will allow you to split up your applications. Running a different server instance for different applications may be a good idea, because the configuration used may have to be set up to allow access to different documents for different users. It is also helpful to set up an instance using a different port for testing your HTML pages and CGI programs so that you don't have to interrupt users.

One last thing to remember is that specific ports are reserved. IBM suggests starting your own ports above 1024. Also, ports 2001 and 2010 are specifically reserved for the AS/400 Tasks page, which we used to set up instances and configurations. Accessing the server with port 1025 would look like this:

```
http://www.myas400.com:1025
```

The port number simply follows a colon after the IP address or domain name of the AS/400 you are requesting documents from. If you didn't specify a port number, this would be the same as specifying port 80, which is the default port.

---

e-Tip: When using a port number other than 80, always use a port number greater than 1024. Also, remember that ports 2001 and 2010 are reserved by IBM.

Virtual Hosts

Virtual hosting is yet another feature to enhance your Web serving needs. Using a virtual host means that you are redirecting requests depending on the host name used in the URL. If you have two host names pointing to the same IP address, they can still be treated separately and use the same instance with little modification to the configuration each instance uses. Examine the following host names:

- *www.myas400.com*
- *www.ourcompany.com*

Assuming both of these requests point at the same IP address, they can be treated differently by specifying a host name after the Map, Exec, and Pass directives. This is an example of using a virtual host. For each of these domains, you can specify a host name following a directive, and they can be routed to different physical locations on your AS/400. Examine the following Pass directives that give an example of using a virtual host:

```
Pass /* /myas400/* www.myas400.com
Pass /* /ourcompany/* www.ourcompany.com
```

Requests coming to the URL www.myas400.com will be automatically routed to the myas400 directory in the IFS. Subsequently, requests made to www.ourcompany.com will be routed to the ourcompany directory in the IFS.

In this case, I am not using separate Map and Pass directives. When, and if, you start using virtual hosts, specifying mapping in the Pass directive will save you a lot of headaches. This is because once a Pass directive is reached and matched, all other processing is stopped, unlike the Map directive, where multiple generic Map directives may cause conflicts.

Using virtual hosts allows small companies who can't justify the purchase of separate machines to use the same machine and share the cost. To the end user, it seems that they are at another location, while in reality they are requesting documents from the same Web serving machine.

AUTHORITY FOR IFS OBJECTS

While using your AS/400 as a Web server, you will soon find that using the root system of the Integrated File System (IFS) is unavoidable. Sure, you can serve all your HTTP documents from members that are located in libraries on your machine, but using the IFS will make updating HTTP documents, JavaScript, and graphics files used on your Web pages much easier.

The root system of the IFS is similar to a network drive or a drive on your PC. It consists of directories, subdirectories, and files. These files may be HTML documents (Web pages), graphic files, or style sheets. Uploading to these directories is a breeze with your favorite FTP program.

If you are using object level security on your AS/400 (a very good idea if you are using it as a Web server on the Internet), then you will need to become familiar with UNIX type authorities. The good thing is you only need to worry about one user profile when it comes to serving documents from the IFS. The authorities used for the IFS root system are listed:

*R – Read

*W – Write

*X – Execute

These three authorities can be used alone, or can be mixed in any combination. For example, *RW, RX, *XW, and *RWX are all valid combinations of these authorities.

The QTMHHTTP user profile must be granted at least Read rights to directories and documents that you are using as part of your Web page. If you do not grant this authority to QTMHHTTP, you will most likely receive the following error:

```
Error 403 - Can't Browse Selected File
```

To begin working with these authorities, I recommend using three commands that are new to the AS/400, and were added because of the IFS.

The Display Authority (DSPAUT) Command

The Display Authority (DSPAUT) command is used to display users and their related authorities to objects, directories, and files that exist in the root portion of the IFS. This command can also be used to display authorities in folders and the QSYS.LIB portion of the IFS. We will focus on the root system.

The DSPAUT command shows what users have authority and which authorities they have. Let's assume you have a directory named /Webpages where you keep all of your Web pages and related files. You can display the authority for the /Webpages directory itself by using the command listed.

```
DSPAUT OBJ('/Webpages')
```

If you want to display the authority for a file or directory located inside the /Webpages directory, for example a file named index.html, you would use the following command:

```
DSPAUT OBJ('/Webpages/index.html')
```

Unfortunately, you can display the authority for only one object at a time. But, you can display a list of files to select from that are located inside a particular directory by using the following command:

```
DSPAUT OBJ('/Webpages/*')
```

This command displays a selection list of all files and directories located within the /Webpages directory. When you select an object, that object's authority is displayed.

The Change Authority (CHGAUT) Command

The Change Authority (CHGAUT) command is used to add or remove certain authorities from either directories or files. Let's assume that you have just created a directory named /Webpages that will contain your Web pages. The first thing you will need to do is grant the user QTMHHTTP at least Read (*R) authority to this directory. You would do this with the following command.

```
CHGAUT OBJ('/Webpages') USER(QTMHHTTP) DTAAUT(*R)
```

Now, the HTTP server jobs running under the user profile QTMHHTTP will be able to access the /Webpages directory.

Now let's assume that you have just uploaded the first Web page into this directory named index.html. You now need to grant at least *R authority to this file so that users can view it. You would do this with the following command:

```
CHGAUT OBJ('/Webpages/index.html') USER(QTMHHTTP) DTAAUT(*R)
```

Users will now have access to the index.html file in the /Webpages directory.

Now, you're convinced that this will work, so you go ahead and build 10 more pages that include graphics and style sheets. You upload all of these objects into the /Webpages directory. You fire up your browser to test them out, but the only page you can view is index.html, the file you granted authority to earlier. You must now grant authority to all the objects you just uploaded. Sound tedious, especially if there are hundreds? Don't fret, the CHGAUT command allows wildcards! Use the following command to grant *R authority to all the objects in the /Webpages directory:

```
CHGAUT OBJ('/Webpages/*') USER(QTMHHTTP) DTAAUT(*R)
```

Now, all of your files will have the proper authority and can be viewed from a browser.

Setting up a file structure like the /Webpages example will make maintaining authority a breeze. Try to keep all of your Web pages in a single directory, and then split them into different sections for different pages. This way you can grant authority first to the directory, and then to all objects within the directory, no matter how many.

The Work with Authority (WRKAUT) Command

The Work with Authority (WRKAUT) command allows you to update authorities to objects in the IFS with an easy-to-use interface. Simply type in the object, directory, or file that you want to work with and a display shows you the users that currently have authority, as well as the authorities they have. See Figure 4.8 for an example of the WRKAUT command.

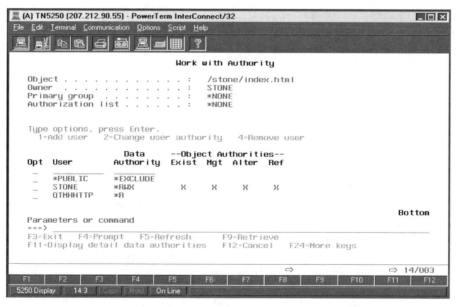

Figure 4.8: The Work With Authority (WRKAUT) display.

The display in Figure 4.8 was accessed using the following command:

```
WRKAUT OBJ('/stone/index.html')
```

You can also use a wildcard with the WRKAUT command to display a list of objects within a directory with the following command:

```
WRKAUT OBJ('/stone/*')
```

This displays a list of directories and files located within the directory named /stone.

THE AS/400: WEB SERVING POTENTIAL

The AS/400 has the potential to be a very stable and powerful Web server if configured correctly. In today's world of e-commerce, stability and speed are the keys. As the AS/400 gets faster and less expensive, using an AS/400 as your Web server is a very viable option that should not be overlooked.

We've all depended on the AS/400 to run our businesses with traditional green-screen applications. Now, we can use the same machine to serve our customers via the World Wide Web with the same stability we expect of the AS/400 for our everyday applications.

5

HTTP APIs

To create Web pages, static or dynamic, in the past one had to rely on a machine other than the AS/400. This meant added cost, added staff, and added complications to e-business solutions. Now that IBM has supplied the tools to the AS/400 community to perform these tasks on a machine that we are already familiar with, the playing field is level. No longer do we have to rely on platforms that don't quite match the AS/400 in stability and performance to provide our e-business solutions.

With the release of V3R2 and V3R7 of the OS/400, IBM supplied a set of Application Program Interfaces (APIs) that make Common Gateway Interface (CGI) programming possible from virtually any language available to the AS/400. These APIs are used to perform functions such as writing to standard output (writing to a browser), reading from standard input (reading from form fields on a browser), and retrieving environment variables.

These APIs might be new to the AS/400, but they are not new to other CGI programming languages such as Perl, a language that has been used extensively for CGI programming in the non-AS/400 world. What the rest of the world has been using for years, now comes to our world, and just in time for a huge boom in the e-business market.

This chapter reviews the most used and most important APIs available to us and gives examples of using them with RPG. These APIs are the backbone of CGI programming on the AS/400 and should not be ignored. Without them, producing e-business applications on the AS/400 would be difficult, if not impossible.

WHERE THE APIs ARE FOUND AND HOW THEY ARE USED

The APIs discussed in this chapter are a perfect example of how the Integrated Language Environment (ILE) can be used to significantly help the AS/400 developer, regardless of programming language choice. I see CGI programming with RPG not only as a way to increase the services available to midrange systems users, but also as a stepping stone into the world of ILE.

The APIs used for HTTP programming are found in a service program named QTMHCGI in library QTCP. Service programs are a portion of ILE that make building applications on the AS/400 nonlanguage-specific. Because of this, modules written in C, such as these APIs, or any other language can be used by RPG programmers without knowledge of the actual programming language. Even if you are writing your applications in COBOL, these APIs can be used as-is in the examples given in RPG throughout this book.

If you were to display the service program QTMHCGI using the Display Service Program (DSPSRVPGM) command, you would see a display similar to the one shown Figure 5.1. The display lists the procedures that can be exported and used from this service program for CGI programming.

```
                        Display Service Program Information
                                                              Display 5 of 10
Service program  . . . . . . . . . . . :   QTMHCGI
  Library  . . . . . . . . . . . . . . :     QTCP
Owner  . . . . . . . . . . . . . . . . :   QSYS
Service program attribute  . . . . . . :
Detail . . . . . . . . . . . . . . . . :   *PROCEXP

                           Procedure Exports:

Procedure Name                                                      ARGOPT
QtmhGetEnv                                                           *NO
QtmhRdStin                                                           *NO
QtmhWrStout                                                          *NO
QtmhCvtDb                                                            *NO
QtmhPutEnv                                                           *NO




                                                                   Bottom
 F3=Exit    F12=Cancel    F17=Top    F18=Bottom

                                           ⇨                ⇨ 01/001
```

Figure 5.1: The procedures included in the QTMHCGI service program.

These APIs are used by calling the procedures from your RPG program. To call them, you use the CALLB op-code, because they are bound procedures. The parameter lists needed for the calls are the same as the normal call that many of us are familiar with. Figure 5.2 contains an example of the RPG code to call one of these APIs.

```
C                    CALLB        'QtmhWrStout'
C                    PARM                        WrtDta
C                    PARM                        WrtDtaLen
C                    PARM                        WPError
```

Figure 5.2: An example of calling an HTTP API using CALLB.

When you create an RPG program that uses these APIs, you will have to reference the QTMHCGI service program in your Create Bound RPG (CRTBNDRPG) or Create Program (CRTPGM) command. You can do this by either specifying the service program on the CRTxxxPGM command or by specifying a binding directory that contains the QTMHCGI service program as an entry. The latter method is preferred and will be discussed later in this chapter.

It is a good idea to make a copy of the QTMHCGI service program and place it into the library that you plan on using as your CGI library. You can rest assured that if any changes are made either from an OS version upgrade or the application of PTFs, your CGI programs will not be affected because a copy of the service programs will be used. To create a copy of the QTMHCGI service program, use the Create Duplicate Object command.

```
CRTDUPOBJ OBJ(QTCP/QTMHCGI) TYPE(*SRVPGM) TOLIB(Your_CGI_Library)
```

This topic is covered later in this chapter.

HTTP APIS: A CLOSER LOOK

Now that you know where the APIs are located and how they are accessed, the following sections detail how they are used to produce e-RPG programs. Each of these APIs performs a specific function that you will find essential in your CGI programming, such as writing information to or reading input from a browser. You will find a summary of these APIs in appendix E.

QtmhWrStout – Write Standard Output

The most important and most used of the HTTP APIs is the QtmhWrStout API. This API is used to write data to standard output, or in other words, write HTML or JavaScript commands to a browser. It makes the browser display the information requested, just as the RPG WRITE op-code writes data to a green-screen or to a printout.

If you are familiar with the use of dynamic screen APIs, this API will most likely cause a slight case of déjà vu. If you are not, don't worry. The API's bark is worse than its bite.

Up until now, the examples given have all been static HTML. Remember that static HTML is created using a text editor or Web page tool and saved as an HTML file. The file is then transferred to the Web server and requested as an HTML document by a user. When it is requested, the browser translates the information and displays the information in a human readable format.

Using the QtmhWrStout API, you create HTML dynamically, or on the fly. The concept is no different than creating a program that displays information on a 5250 terminal. Data is read in from a file, the data is placed into screen fields in a record format, and the screen is written to the terminal using either the WRITE or EXFMT op-code.

The QtmhWrStout API is actually easier to use from a certain point of view. When you call this API, the data that you pass to it is written to the browser at that very moment. Also, there are no display files to worry about, which mean no fields or DDS to create, and there are no worries of level checks. Each time you use this API it's like creating a brand new screen. The difference is that you are using the browser instead of a terminal to relay the information to the user.

QtmhWrStout's Parameters

The QtmhWrStout API, as with most APIs, has a set of required parameters. This is actually the easiest of the HTTP APIs to use, which is good since it is also the most used. Table 5.1 lists the parameters needed for this API. An asterisk is used to define a varying length field.

Table 5.1: QtmhWrStout Required Parameters.		
Parameter	Type(Size) – Use	Description
Data	Char(*) – Input	A varying character field that contains the data, such as HTML code, that is to be written to the browser.
Length of Data	Binary(4) – Input	A binary field that tells the API the length of the data in the *Data* parameter.
Error Parameter	Char(*) – Input/Output	The standard API Error structure.

Data

The first parameter required is a parameter that holds the data that you wish to write to the browser. This field does not have to contain all of the data for an entire Web page. This field usually contains the data for one line of HTML code followed by a new-line character. This API can be called several times, so you can build the HTML page line by line. Don't worry about speed; the user viewing the page will not notice a difference between this and a static HTML file being displayed.

An example of what is contained in the data parameter is as follows:

```
<a href="www.mysite.com">Click Here!</a>\n
```

In this example, the data is HTML code that will produce a hyperlink on the page. The hyperlink will read "Click Here!" and when clicked on, will direct the browser to www.mypage.com. The \n represents a new-line character.

You should note one thing about using this API. In some versions of OS/400, there is a limit of 1,024 characters to the data field and unpredicted results can occur if this limit is breached. I make it a habit to define the size of this field as 1,024 in most cases. This way I know that if I transfer and implement the application to a machine that runs an older version of the operating system, I won't encounter any problems.

Length of Data

The second parameter contains a binary field that holds the size of the data that you are writing to the browser. This field isn't necessarily the size of the field itself, but the size of the field minus any trailing blanks.

I make it a habit to determine the value of this field right before the call to the QtmhWrStout API. I do this either using the CHECKR op-code or the %LEN Built In Function (BIF). Because the %LEN BIF isn't available on all operating systems, when writing production e-RPG programs that could be ported to another AS/400, I usually use CHECKR. Most examples in this book will use the %LEN method for simplicity, but I will show you how both methods work. Figure 5.1 contains sample code for both of these methods.

```
The CHECKR Method:
C          ' '              CHECKR     Data:1024      DataLen
The %len BIF Method:
C                           eval       DataLen = %len(%trim(Data))
```

Figure 5.1: Two ways to figure the length of the Data parameter for the QtmhWrStout API.

Error Parameter

The error parameter is the last required parameter and is standard in most APIs. Because there is nothing unique about this parameter as it pertains to the QtmhWrStout API, I won't discuss it. If you are unfamiliar with this parameter, the examples used in this book will work fine for you without modification.

QtmhRdStin – Read Standard Input

If we can write data to a browser, it is reaonable to assume that we can read data from a browser. As we can WRITE and READ from an AS/400 screen, we can also do both on a Web page by using APIs. Without the ability to read input from a browser, it would be futile to consider using a browser for anything more than sending the user information.

Reading input from a browser is accomplished with the QtmhRdStin API. This API, while used less frequently than the QtmhWrStout API, is a little more involved. This API will only read information that is made available with the POST operation. The POST operation is performed with an HTML form using the AC-TION and METHOD keywords. In addition, a SUBMIT button is used to submit the form. The HTML code resembles the following:

```
<FORM ACTION= "/cgi-bin/CGIPGM" METHOD="POST">
…form fields…
<INPUT TYPE="SUBMIT" VALUE="Click Here">
</FORM>
```

The information following the ACTION keyword tells the browser what to do when the form is processed. In this case, it will call a program named CGIPGM located in the /cgi-bin/ directory. The METHOD keyword tells the browser what method to use. In this case, the POST method is being used. As for the actual submitting of the form, this is done with a button of type SUBMIT. When this button is pressed, the information in the form will be made available to the CGI program for reading from standard input.

The QtmhRdStin API will become familiar to you once you understand when and where it is used. If you've ever come across a Web page where you entered information in text boxes such as your name, phone number, or e-mail address, then no doubt you have used this read-from-standard-input function in one form or another. It's one of those "I always wondered how that worked!" situations.

After you enter your information on the form and press the Submit button, the data you entered is read in by a CGI program using the same methods that the QtmhRdStin API uses. The data is then available to the CGI program in the form of standard input to perform verification, manipulation, or for storage to a file. QtmhRdStin is a very powerful API and used frequently in Web pages that require the user to enter input.

QtmhRdStin's Parameters

The parameters required by QtmhRdStin are displayed in Table 5.2.

Table 5.2: QtmhRdStin Required Parameters.		
Parameter	**Type(Size) – Use**	**Description**
Receiver Variable	Char(*) – Output	The variable name that will hold the data received from the Read Standard Input API.
Length of Receiver Variable	Binary(4) – Input	A binary field that holds the length of the Receiver Variable.
Length of Response Available	Binary(4) – Output	The length of the data read in by the Read Standard Input API.
Error Parameter	Char(*) – Input/Output	The standard API Error structure.

Receiver Variable

The first parameter, the receiver variable, holds the data read in by the QtmhRdStin API. This data will almost always be in the same form: it will contain the names of the fields, followed by an equal sign, and the value of the variable. Each variable/value combination is separated by the ampsersand (&) symbol, as shown in the following example:

```
FirstName=Brad&LastName=Stone
```

The first variable is FirstName, which contains the value "Brad". The second variable is LastName and contains the value "Stone". The ampersand (&) separator separates the two variable/value combinations. Don't start worrying about parsing this data yet; there is an easy way to do this, and it will be covered later in this chapter.

Length of Receiver Variable

The second parameter for the QtmhRdStin API holds a value that you specify to the API. This parameter tells the API how many bytes you expect it to read in for the receiver variable. This is not the length of the variable itself, but the length of the receiver variable minus any trailing blanks.

This parameter has caused problems with many AS/400 Web developers. If you don't use the correct value, your last variable might not be processed. The API may ignore the last parameter, which will cause headaches and frustration while testing and debugging your CGI application.

Th Content Length environment variable should be used for this parameter. The API (QtmhGetEnv) that retrieves this value is covered later in this chapter.

Some people have found that using a dummy variable on their forms will solve the problem of this API not parsing the last variable. A dummy variable tricks the computer into thinking there is one more variable on the form; the dummy variable doesn't get parsed. This is no problem for the developer, because all the important variables are parsed. I do not recommend this method. Use instead the Content Length environment variable. (I mention this method because you will no doubt hear about it if you run into the problem of the "missing last parameter.") Some developers will tell you to use the dummy variable method. IBM, on the other hand, will point out that your are passing incorrect data to the Convert to Database API and that you should use the value returned by the Content Length environment variable. The third parameter will tell you the length of the receiver variable that was retrieved from the QtmhRdStin API. If no data was read from standard input, this value will be zero.

Length of Response Available

The next parameter is the length of the response available and is returned from the QtmhRdStin API. After calling the QtmhRdStin API, this parameter will contain the length of the data read from standard input. If there is no data returned from this API, this value will be zero.

Error Parameter

The last parameter, again, is the standard error parameter needed with most APIs used.

A QtmhRdStin Example

To give you an example of the QtmhRdStin API, let's assume that you just used a form that had you enter your first name (field name of fname) and your phone number (field name of phone). If you were to look at the data after using this API, it would resemble the following string:

```
fname=Bradley&phone=15075551212
```

In this example, fname and phone represent the variable names, and the data following the equal sign is the actual data that is to be assigned to this variable. The ampersand (&) character separates the fields and data. In this case, the data tells us that the first name entered was "Bradley" and the phone number entered was "15075551212".

From this point, you could parse this data yourself, but there is a much easier way to do by using the Convert To DataBase API. Because the Convert To DataBase API is also used with another API that retrieves information, it will be covered last.

QtmhGetEnv – Get Environment Variable

The QtmhGetEnv API is used to retrieve values set by the server for particular environment variables. Environment variables are particular to each user who accesses documents from your Web server. In the same way that each user running an RPG program has specific values in the job's Program Status Data Structure (SDS), the environment variables contain information specific to the user who is accessing your Web server.

For example, some of the values for certain environment variables may be set on way for one person accessing documents, while another person would include different values for certain environment variables. Two users running an RPG program will have different values for the user ID variable available in the SDS. Similarly, two users accessing your Web server will have information specific to the request, such as the requesting IP address. Another good example would be the Web browser type. One user might be using Netscape, and another might be using Internet Explorer. Both of these values could be retrieved as environment variables.

Another use of environment variables, as mentioned earlier, is to retrieve the content length of the standard input variable that is available from a POST operation.

Environment variables also are made available by the GET operation. Instead of passing data with standard input, one can make the data available as an environment variable. This is known as a *query string* environment variable. This is the data that follows the Web address in a URL, as shown in the example.

```
http://www.mypage.com/cgi-bin/mycgi.pgm?FirstName=Brad&LastName=Stone
```

This URL accesses a CGI program named MYCGI. Following this is a question mark (?) and a set of query string environment data. This data may look familiar because the format is similar to that data returned from standard input. The HTML source is similar to the source that performs the POST operation, as shown here:

```
<FORM ACTION= "/cgi-bin/CGIPGM" METHOD="GET">
…form fields…
<INPUT TYPE="SUBMIT" VALUE="Click Here">
</FORM>
```

The only real difference here is the value of the METHOD keyword in the form. Instead of making the data available from standard input when the Submit button is pressed, the data will be available as a query string environment variable, and will also be visible as data following the URL. For this reason, this method should not be used for sensitive data.

QtmhGetEnv's Parameters

Table 5.3 contains the parameters used by the QtmhGetEnv API.

Table 5.3: QtmhGetEnv Required Parameters.		
Parameter	**Type(Size) – Use**	**Description**
Receiver Variable	Char(*) – Output	The variable name that will hold the data received from the Read Standard Input API.
Length of Receiver Variable	Binary(4) – Input	A binary field that holds the length of the Receiver Variable.
Length of Response	Binary(4) – Output	The length of the data read in by the Read Standard Input API.
Request Variable	Char(*) – Input	The name of the environment variable that the request is made for.
Length of Request Variable	Binary(4) – Input	The length of the request variable.
Error Parameter	Char(*) – Input/Output	The standard API error structure.

The parameters of the QtmhGetEnv API are similar to those that are used by the QtmhRdStin API. The only difference is the request and length of request variables used by QtmhGetEnv. The request variable contains the name of the environment variable and the length of request variable holds a value that tells the system the length of the variable you are passing it. This may seem confusing at first if you are unfamiliar with environment variables, but they are described in the following section.

Receiver Variable

The Receiver parameter holds the data returned from the QtmhGetEnv API. It is very similar in format to the data returned from the QtmhRdStin API.

Length of Receiver Variable

The Length of Receiver Variable parameter contains a value specified in your program that tells the API the size of the data to retrieve from the environment variable. This field can be set to the size of the Receiver variable.

Length of Response

The value returned in the Length of Response parameter contains the length of the input data retrieved. If it is unable to determine this value, zero is returned. If the size of the receiver variable is too small, this parameter will contain the actual size needed to perform this request.

Request Variable

The Request Variable parameter contains the name of an environment variable that you want to receive from standard input. For example, if you want to retrieve query string data, this parameter would contain the value "QUERY_STRING".

Length of Request Variable

The Length of Request Variable parameter contains the length of the Request variable specified in the previous parameter.

Error Parameter

The standard Error parameter is required for this API.

Environment Variables used by QtmhGetEnv

Environment variables are used to identify the type of data that you want to retrieve from the current requesting job. While there are a great number of environment variables available to you, I will discuss only the most important ones. Table 5.4 contains a list of the most frequently used environment variables.

Table 5.4: Some of the Environment Variables Used by QtmhGetEnv.

Environment Variable	Variable Name	Description
Request Method	REQUEST_METHOD	The request method that was made. This value will either be "GET" or "POST".
Remote Host	REMOTE_HOST	The host name making the request.
Remote Address	REMOTE_ADDR	The IP address of the host name making the request.
Content Length	CONTENT_LENGTH	The length of the data that is to be processed by a POST method.
Query String	QUERY_STRING	The information following a question mark in a URL, which represents data to be processed by a CGI program.

The Request Method environment variable is rather simple and contains one of two values, either "GET" or "POST", depending on the request method used to access the document.

The Content Length environment variable is most often used to retrieve a value that contains the length of data to be processed, in most cases by the Read Standard Input API.

The Query Sting environment variable is used most often when you are processing data that follows the URL and is preceded by a question mark (?). This data is made available when you use a GET request method. You might have seen this type of data if you pay attention to the location bar of your browser when performing a search on certain sites. The URL usually looks something like the following:

```
http://www.pagename.com/query?search=as400&perpage=10
```

This tells URL to run a program named query. The information following the question mark (?) is the variable names to use and the value of those variables. The variables and data are separated by the ampersand symbol (&). In this case, the data tells us that the variable named search contains the value "as400" and the variable named perpage contains the value of "10". When the QtmhGetEnv API is used to request the Query String environment variables, the data retrieved will be only the data following the question mark. It will resemble the following:

```
search=as400&perpage=10
```

Again, as with the QthmRdStin API, the data is very similar and you are probably already thinking of how you would go about parsing out the data. But, the same Convert to Database API that is provided to parse this type of data can be used for both this API and the QtmhRdStin API.

QthmCvtDB – Convert to DB

Converting the data from the Query String environment variable or the Read Standard Input operations can be tedious on your own. Luckily, IBM supplies an API to do the dirty work for you.

The QtmhCvtDB API is used to convert a string of data received from a CGI program into fields with the same name in a supplied DDS file structure. Even though the data read into the CGI program is all character format, the data will be converted to the type specified in the DDS of the file name provided.

QtmhCvtDB's Parameters

Table 5.5 contains the parameters used by the QtmhCvtDB API.

Table 5.5: QtmhCvtDB Required Parameters.

Parameter	Type(Size) – Use	Description
Database Name	Char(20) – Input	A variable that contains the qualified database name, which contains the field descriptions for conversion. The first 10 characters are the file name and the last 10 characters are the library name.
Input String	Char(*) – Input	The variable name that contains the string received from the Read Standard Input API or the Query String environment variable.
Length of Input String	Binary(4) – Input	A binary field that holds the length of the input string to be parsed.
Response Variable	Char(*) – Output	The variable that contains the structure mapped according to the database file describing the input parameters anticipated by the CGI program.
Length of Response Available	Binary(4) – Input	The total length of the buffer into which the CGI input parameters will be parsed.
Length of Response Variable	Binary(4) – Output	The length of the response. If the response variable is too small to contain the entire response, this parameter will be set to the size that is required to contain the entire response.
Response Code	Binary(4) – Output	A code that contains the status of the operation.
Error Parameter	Char(*) – Input/ Output	The standard API error structure

Don't let the number of parameters throw you off for this API. The API's bark is worse than its bite. Out of all of the parameters listed, only four of them really need explanation. The rest can be figured out before the execution of the API.

Database Name

This parameter is the name of a database file that will be used to determine both the field type and size. The first 10 characters contain the file name, and the second 10 characters contain the library that the file resides in. The database and library name specified here should be in uppercase.

Input String

The second parameter that we need to provide is the input string. You already have this information from one of the other APIs, which you used to read information from a browser. This is the character string that is returned using the QtmhRdStin API or the Query String environment variable obtained using the QtmhGetEnv API specifying QUERY_STRING as the environment variable.

Length of Input String

The next parameter that is required is the length of the input string. This value is the length of the input string minus any trailing blanks.

Response Variable

The response variable is usually a data structure, which is defined externally using the same file specification specified in the database name parameter of this API. After a successful call to this API, the data structure specified on this parameter will contain the values from the input string. Field names in the input string are matched with field names in this data structure. In other words, if part of the input string contains the value:

```
FNAME=Brad
```

then the field in the data structure named FNAME will contain the value "Brad". Case is not an issue with this variable. The variable name in the input string can be upper or lower case, and it will be placed into the correct field of the data structure.

Length of Response Available

The next parameter is the length of the response variable. This field is easily determined by specifying the size of the response variable.

Length of Response Variable

The next parameter contains the actual length of the response returned. If the response variable used is too small to contain all of the response data, this field will contain the value of the size of the response variable needed.

Response Code

The response code parameter is returned and tells you the successfulness of the call to this API. Table 5.6 contains a list of response codes and their meanings.

Table 5.6: Response Codes Returned from the QtmhCvtDB API.	
Response Code	Meaning
0	All fields have been successfully translated according to the database file.
-1	The database file contains one or more fields not specified in the input.
-2	The input contains one or more fields not specified in the database file.
-3	A combination of response codes −1 and −2.
-4	An error occurred during conversion. The data may or may not be usable by your program.
-5	This API was called by a program not running with the HTTP server. The request is ignored.
-6	The request was made while running in Binary (%%BINARY%%) mode. The request is ignored.

If you receive response code 0 or −1, then data was most likely converted without a problem. I have a tendency to define a database file that contains all the valid input parameters used in a particular application. Because not all of the fields are used in every call to this API, I receive a response code of −1. This means that the data I wanted to be converted was successfully converted, but there were fields in my database file that did not exist in the input variable I supplied. All other response codes should be researched.

Error Parameter

Again, the Error parameter is required for this API.

GETTING THE APIS READY TO USE

Now that you have information about what these APIs do, you must set them up so that you can use them in your applications. Here we will explore in more detail what you need to do to make these APIs available to your CGI programs.

Copy the QTMHCGI Service Program

The first thing you need to do is decide what you are going to name the library that will contain your CGI programs. I prefer to call mine AS400CGI. This way there is no question about what the library does.

Next, you should make a copy of the QTMHCGI service program into this library. As mentioned before, this is good practice because if OS upgrades or PTFs change anything in these service programs, your CGI applications will remain unaffected. To copy this service program into your CGI library, use the following command:

```
CRTDUPOBJ OBJ(QTCP/QTMHCGI) TYPE(*SRVPGM) TOLIB(AS400CGI)
```

It is also a good idea to recopy this service program when you update versions of the OS, or from time to time. If you find that things are working smoothly, it might not be a big priority. But, if you find that you are having some problems, after applying PTFs or a new version of the OS, you should recopy this service program into your library to make sure that you are getting the latest version. Also, remember that you should stop and restart the HTTP server so that the HTTP jobs running will use the new version.

Create a Binding Directory

Before you start creating your CGI applications, it would be a good idea to create a general purpose binding directory. The binding directory holds a list of modules and/or service programs. When you compile your RPG program and specify a binding directory on the CRTBNDRPG command, it searches through the list of modules/service programs in the binding directory for any subprocedures used.

I prefer to call this general purpose CGI binding directory CGIBNDDIR. Place the binding directory in the CGI library that you created in the previous section. Use the following command to create a binding directory:

```
CRTBNDDIR BNDDIR(AS400CGI/CGIBNDDIR)
```

Add QTMHCGI to Your Binding Directory

The final setup step is adding the QTMHCGI service program to your binding directory. This service program will be used by most, if not all, of your CGI programs. This is why I refer to this binding directory as a general purpose binding directory.

To add the QTMHCGI service program to your binding directory, use the following command:

```
ADDBNDDIRE BNDDIR(AS400CGI/CGIBNDDIR) BNDDIRE(AS400CGI/QTMHCGI)
```

Once this addition is made to your binding directory, you can specify the binding directory on the CRTxxxPGM command instead of specifying each service program or module individually on the command. More modules and service programs can be added to this binding directory to make the process of creating your programs even easier.

WAGONS, EAST!

Well, we've finally made it through all the information required to start writing CGI programs. It's been a long ride, and it will be all fun from here on out. After learning all the components needed to write CGI programs on my AS/400, I found the rest of the process was rather simple. Because my CGI programs were going to be written in RPG, and because I had used a couple of APIs before this point, I knew that it wasn't going to be very difficult writing these CGI programs.

Using the techniques and APIs described up to this point may seem like a big job, but once you get going you will discover naturally all of these items fit together. There's a logical structure to pretty much everything, and CGI programs are no different.

6

YOUR FIRST E-RPG PROGRAM

RPG has been traditionally used to create programs that report information to the end user either through green-screen applications or printed reports. Over the years, though, RPG has been evolving, and continues to evolve today, to a language that can be used on the AS/400 to perform almost any function that you might require.

RPG stands for Report Program Generator. RPG easily outgrew the meaning of the acronym even before it had the capability to be used as a Web-serving language. With the capability to serve and process Web pages, RPG is even more valuable.

For those who have been using RPG for a while, there may be the temptation to move on to other, supposedly more powerful or functional programming languages. Even IBM has hinted that the well-rounded application developer needs more than just RPG to succeed.

I suspect, however, that for the most part, IBM is probably directing these messages to people outside of the midrange market to lure them in. When they get there, they may in fact realize that RPG is a great companion to whatever other language they are using.

Because the majority of AS/400 programmers use RPG for basic business programming, using RPG for server-side Web programming is a logical choice that should not be overlooked. Sure, there are other options, but some of them have a large learning curve. With RPG, you already know how to report the data; the only thing new to learn is what tools—in the form of supplied APIs—to use to get that data out to the end user.

Almost every RPG programmer went through the torture of learning how to program subfiles with RPG, an often difficult concept to grasp. But, once understood, people found new uses for subfiles and quickly became experts in programming them. The same will hold true for Web programming with RPG. Little by little, you will discover new ways to do things in RPG. Soon you will become an expert, and an even more valuable asset to your company.

E-RPG: A NEW TERM FOR A NEW ERA

With the use of RPG IV, its many Built In Functions (BIFs), and its increased string manipulation capabilities, RPG has come a long way. With the addition of the availability and documentation supplied for the use of Application Program Interfaces (APIs), RPG, a language that most AS/400 programmers use everyday, can be used now for e-commerce with little or no learning curve.

The use of RPG to write Common Gateway Interface (CGI) programs helps you eliminate the need for time- and money-consuming training in other Web programming languages such as Java, Visual Basic, Net.Data, or Perl. It also moves the data serving portion of the business back to the AS/400, where the majority of the data and applications reside.

I like to refer to RPG programs that act as CGI programs as e-RPG programs. This way it will not be confusing, after the initial definition, of what function the program I am speaking of performs. In the remainder of this book, CGI programs written in RPG are referred to as e-RPG programs.

You can think of writing an e-RPG program in the same way as writing a display or report program. The fundamentals are the same. The only difference is the output you are producing and the tools you are using to write the data to the desired medium—in this case a Web browser. To output HTML text (which is your goal) you use a system API to write the output to a browser, rather than an EXCPT or WRITE op-code.

---

e-Definition

An e-RPG program is an RPG program that acts as a Common Gateway Interface (CGI) program.

There is a little more to it than just writing data to the browser. But, the only real difference between writing e-RPG programs and regular RPG programs is the use of APIs instead of regular RPG op-codes. The same tools can be used to select and sort data, such as Open Query File (OPNQRYF) or SQL. Even embedded SQL statements can be used in e-RPG programs. You can use whatever initial record selection method you want. The data you are going to display on the browser comes from the same database as that for your existing display and reports—your AS/400 database.

Using the skills that you and your staff have available will make you the e-stars of your company. RPG programmers will have an upper hand in most cases because they are used to dealing with screen input and report generation. They are comfortable with the processes used to gather and display information requested by the user as well as with the error checking and business rules of their system. Most important, they are familiar and comfortable with the databases that reside on the AS/400 because they are used to working with business critical application software, and not just creating flashy Web pages.

Using e-RPG is discovering a completely new form and function for our tried and true programming language, database, and operating system.

E-RPG SAYS, "HELLO WORLD"

"Hello World." It's the first example given in many different programming languages when dealing with the creation of Web pages or any type of Web programming. If you were to search the Web for tutorials on HTML, Java, or JavaScript, you would most likely see a Hello World application as the first and most basic example of using the language to display text on a browser. I'm not one to break tradition, so this will be our first example as well. To get started, let's go through a quick review of what we will need for this example. See Table 6.1 for a quick reference of the steps needed to get things up and running.

Table 6.1: e-RPG Setup Quick-Reference.		
Step	Action	Command
1	Copy Service Program QTMHCGI into your CGI library.	CRTDUPOBJ OBJ(QTMHCGI) FROMLIB(QTCP) OBJTYPE(*SRVPGM) TOLIB(AS400CGI)
2	Add Service Program QTMHCGI into your CGI Binding Directory in your CGI Library.	ADDBNDDIRE BNDDIR(AS400CGI/CGIBNDDIR) OBJ((AS400CGI/QTMHCGI))
3	Set up HTTP configuration.	WRKHTTPCFG [instance]
4	Start Server Instance.	STRTCPSVR *HTTP [instance]

If you skipped any of the previous chapters that discuss the set up of the HTTP server or HTTP APIs needed to create an e-RPG program, I encourage you to stop now and read these chapters. Understanding these concepts is a prerequisite for any Web serving functions on the AS/400.

> **e-Note:** Throughout this book, references to the library AS400CGI are to the library I have defined to hold my e-RPG programs. You can use the library AS400CGI or specify a different library.

After you have completed the server setup, the first step in writing an e-RPG program to output dynamic HTML to a browser is to decide what you are going to display on the page. It is a good practice to draw out how you want the page to look before proceeding with program development. This will ease the flow of work and limit the times that you must go back in to make modifications to the page.

In this first example, the page layout is as simple as it can get. We are simply going to display the text "Hello World" on the browser.

The Hello World e-RPG Program

To output the text "Hello World" onto a browser, we need only a couple of short lines of HTML code. Refer to Figure 6.1 to review the HTML code needed to produce this output.

```
<HTML>
<BODY>
Hello World
</BODY>
</HTML>
```

Figure 6.1: HTML code needed to produce Hello World.

The first thing that our e-RPG program needs to do is write the HTML header lines that tell the browser that this is a text HTML document. These lines tell the browser what type of document it is displaying.

Next, we write the HTML code from Figure 6.1 to the browser. All text that we are writing to the browser is done using the Write to Standard Output (QtmhWrstout) API. Create this program as you would any other RPG program. Simply open a new source member and enter the code. See Figure 6.2 for the code for e-RPG Hello World program named HELLOW.

```
D WPError          DS
D  EBytesP               1       4B 0 INZ(%size(EData))
D  EBytesA               5       8B 0
D  EMsgID                9      15
D  EReserved            16      16
D  EData                17      56
 *
```

Figure 6.2: e-RPG program HELLOW (part 1 of 2).

```
D HTTPHeader       C                          CONST('Content-type: text/html')
D NewLine          C                          CONST(X'15')
 *
D WrtDta           S               1024
D WrtDtaLen        S                 9B 0
 *
 * Fill variable WrtDta with the HTML text we want to write to the browser
 *
C                      eval        WrtDta = HTTPHeader + NewLine + NewLine +
C                                  '<HTML><BODY>' + NewLine +
C                                  'Hello World' + NewLine +
C                                  '</BODY></HTML>' + NewLine
 *
 * Figure out the length of the HTML text in the WrtDta variable
 *
C                      eval        WrtDtaLen = %len(%trim(WrtDta))
 *
 * Write the data from the WrtDta variable to the browswer
 *
C                      CALLB       'QtmhWrStout'
C                      PARM                    WrtDta
C                      PARM                    WrtDtaLen
C                      PARM                    WPError
 *
C                      eval        *INLR = *ON
```

Figure 6.2: e-RPG program HELLOW (part 2 of 2).

After looking at the code in Figure 6.2, you may think that's a lot of code to display one measly line of text to a browser. Although this may seem to be the case for this example, you should remember that most of the code in this example is only field declarations that set up data structures, constants, and variables, which will be used in almost every e-RPG program that you write.

The average RPG program that produces a report also has elements that need to be set up in order to produce the report—elements such as the file declaration for the output printer file. The same constrains holds true for e-RPG programs. In chapter 9, service programs will be covered and you will find that most of an e-RPG program's set up needs only to be declared in the service program, and not in the e-RPG program itself,thus reducing coding time and application implementation.

Let's take a closer look at the common declarations as well as the components that will be used in virtually every e-RPG program that your write before we compile our HELLOW program.

e-RPG's Basic Necessities

Every e-RPG program requires a few basic necessities that will be included in virtually every e-RPG program you write. In the same sense that an RPG program that produces a subfile requires a declaration of the display file used, e-RPG programs also have components that will be required in order for them to function. The following sections describe these necessities in detail.

The Write to Standard Output (QtmhWrstout) API

To write information to a browser dynamically with an e-RPG program, you must use the Write to Standard Output (QtmhWrStout) API. This API writes the information you send it directly to a browser.

This process is different from making a static HTML page and then uploading it to the server. With a static HTML file, the browser reads the file that has been created, and translates the information to something viewable by the user.

Programs that write dynamic output to a browser write the data line by line to the browser. The data is then interpreted and translated into a viewable format.

The API Error Data Structure

The next basic necessity when writing an e-RPG program (or when using almost any API) is the error data structure. I use the same error data structure, named WPError and shown in Figure 6.2, in nearly all RPG or e-RPG programs that I write using system APIs. Because I call the QtmhWrStout API in this program, I am including this error data structure. If any other APIs that required an error data structure were used in this program, I would use the same data structure for almost all of them.

If you are familiar with using APIs, then the error data structure is nothing new to you. If you are new to using APIs, IBM provides information regarding them in user manuals and online at `http://publib.boulder.ibm.com/cgi-bin/bookmgr/BOOKS/QB3AVC00/2.4.3`.

HTTP Header Information

The next item needed in e-RPG programs is the HTTP header information. In the program in Figure 6.2, this data is usually declared as a constant and named `HTTPHeader`. It can be seen in most e-RPG examples given in this book.

The header information is the first string written to a browser, and it is followed by two new-line characters. The two sequential new-line characters let the browser know that this is the last header record in this document. If more than one header record is used, only the last header record should be followed by two new-line characters.

The text included in the `HTTPHeader` constant tells the browser that the data following is an HTML text document.

> **e-Tip**
>
> Always follow the header section with two new-line characters.

The New-Line Character

The last item needed is the new-line character. The new-line character, defined in Figure 6.2 as a hex constant, tells the browser where a logical end-of line occurs. If you did not include a new-line character, the browser might not be able to interpret what you are telling it to do and try to interpret the HTML string as one long command. The new-line character also makes viewing the source from your browser's View Source option much easier. If you did not include new-line characters, there is a possibility that the browser wouldn't interpret everything correctly, and that the source would be viewed as one continuous line.

When using the new-line character, I like to place the characters in logical locations that break the code up to make it look similar to HTML code (as if I were typing into a text editor). To show an example of how the new-line character works, refer to Figures 6.3 and 6.4. Figure 6.3 shows what the HTML code would look like without the use of new-line characters. Figure 6.4 shows the same code using new-line characters in logical positions. The new-line characters are represented as a \n in the source, but will not actually appear in your source when used.

```
<HTML><HEAD><TITLE>MyPAge</TITLE></HEAD><BODY>Hello World</BODY></HTML>
```

Figure 6.3: HTML code without new-line characters.

By examining Figure 6.3, you can see that the entire Web page is displayed as one line of source. While this specific example will work, using the new-line character to make the code more readable will make your job easier, as well as limit the chance of error. If your page was very large, not using new-line characters would produce errors. Figure 6.4. shows the same source using the new-line character.

```
<HTML>\n
<HEAD>
<TITLE>My Page</TITLE>\n
</HEAD>\n
<BODY>\n
Hello World\n
</BODY>
</HTML>\n
```

Figure 6.4: HTML code with new-line characters included. (New-line characters are de-noted by the characters "\n".)

Although the examples in Figures 6.3 and 6.4 are small, you will soon see the importance of using the new-line characters. It will make your HTML code more readable, especially as your Web page content grows.

Compiling and Running Your Hello World e-RPG Program

Now is the time we've all been waiting for. Let's see just how easy this is! First, we must compile our Hello World program. I named my program HELLOW. If you named yours something different, substitute the name HELLOW with the name of your Hello World e-RPG program in the commands that follow. Also, I am storing my e-RPG programs in a library named AS400CGI. Be sure to use the library name that you created your program in with the following command. To create the program, we will use the following command:

```
CRTBNDRPG PGM(AS400CGI/HELLOW) SRCFILE(*LIBL/QRPGLESRC) +
DFTACTGRP(*NO) BNDDIR(AS400CGI/CGIBNDDIR)
```

As mentioned earlier in this chapter, it is important to remember that when I refer to library AS400CGI, I am referring to the library I have designated to hold my e-RPG programs, binding directories, service programs, and anything else that my e-RPG programs will use. If you named your library something different, be sure to substitute your library when you see AS400CGI in this book.

Be sure to also double check your HTTP configuration and make sure that your HTTP server instance is running. For this example, your HTTP configuration may be one line, as follows:

```
Exec /cgi-bin/* /QSYS.LIB/AS400CGI.LIB/*
```

After you have successfully compiled the HELLOW program, you most likely will want to run it. The first thing to remember with an e-RPG program is that it is not called from a command line, as a conventional RPG program is. It is initiated from a browser by including it in a link. Start your favorite browser and type the following location, making sure to replace youras400.com with the DNS name or the IP address of your AS/400:

```
http://youras400.com/cgi-bin/HELLOW.PGM
```

If you set up your HTTP configuration using the wildcard, *.PGM, to map your CGI directory instead of just a plain wildcard, *, use the following address to access your e-RPG program:

```
http://youras400.com/cgi-bin/HELLOW
```

Your browser should resemble the browser in Figure 6.5. If you received an error, refer to the error index in appendix A and try the request again. If your program worked and your browser displayed the text "Hello World," congratulations! You have just written your first e-RPG program. Give yourself a pat on the back, show your friends, and grab a celebratory can of soda.

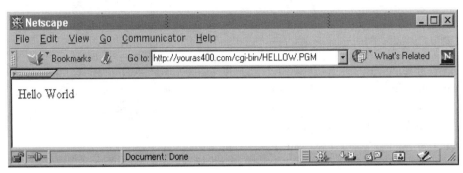

Figure 6.5: Browser output for e-RPG program HELLOW.

Viewing the HTML Source

You might be wondering how this all works. To put it simply, instead of creating a static HTML file to produce the output in Figure 6.5, the e-RPG program HELLOW actually wrote the data directly to the browser. To verify this, use your browser's View Source option. Figure 6.6 shows the output from my browser's View Source option. Depending on the browser you are using, the output will be similar, but not exactly the same as mine.

```
<HTML>
<BODY>
Hello World
</BODY>
</HTML>
```

Figure 6.6: View Source option from HELLOW e-RPG program.

As you can see, the source looks exactly as it would if you were accessing a static HTML file that had been created with any normal text editor or Web page creation tool and accessed from a browser.

You may now be asking yourself, "What does this all mean?" It means you have the ability to use RPG to output any HTML commands, JavaScript, or any other Web-related text that you could write to a static HTML file with a text editor or

Web page creation tool. This is where the word *dynamic* comes into play, and where your imagination takes over.

E-RPG AND DYNAMIC OUTPUT

Now that we know the basics of creating a simple e-RPG program, we are all probably ready to get into the good stuff—actually creating a Web page that performs some sort of function that will be beneficial to our company. We could write examples like the Hello World program all day long, but we would soon grow tired of the plain output.

People want productive, easy-to-access information, such as sales reports and customer service, not just pretty pictures and static text. Since this information no doubt is in constant change, we must output the HTML in a dynamic form.

Relate e-RPG to RPG

If you are still uncomfortable with the idea of using new APIs to produce Web output, don't be. The best thing to do is relate how you would write a normal RPG report program with how you are going to display the information on the Web.

The logic for selecting records will remain constant for both RPG and e-RPG programs. We read through a file looking for records that match the criteria specified, or even use OPNQRYF or SQL to perform the initial selection. In an RPG report program, we simply fill in the fields in our Output Specs or External DDS and perform an EXCEPT or a WRITE on the record format that we are using for our detail line data.

The same holds true for e-RPG programs. The logic for selecting records will be the same. The only thing that changes is how we are going to output the data. Instead of filling the output fields in your O-Specs or external printer file, we place the information between HTML tags. And instead of using the EXCEPT or WRITE op-code, we will write the data to the browser using the Write to Standard Output (QtmhWrStout) API.

e-Tip: Writing programs that output data to a browser will be done the same as programs that output to a screen or report. The only difference is how you output the selected data.

Sometimes, in cases where I am unfamiliar with how to perform a certain function, I find that writing out pseudocode helps. Figure 6.7 includes some easy-to-read pseudocode that may help you understand the process. The only actual code in Figure 6.7 is the HTML tags used to create a table, table rows, and table cells.

```
write <TABLE> HTML tag to browser
read file
repeat while not end of file
   if current record matches our criteria
      write <TR> HTML tag to browser
      clear text field
      repeat for each field to be displayed in a row
         text = text +    + field data + </TD>
      end-repeat
      write text to browser
      write </TR> HTML tag to browser
   end-if
read file
end-repeat
write </TABLE> HTML tag to browser
```

Figure 6.7: Pseudocode to write file data to tables cells and to a browser.

The format of most reports done with e-RPG will have the same basic structure as the pseudocode in Figure 6.7. Again, this same basic structure is used for most reporting programs, so it's not a new concept. Only the format of the data and the process used to report the data are different. In other words, if you can program RPG, you can program e-RPG. Using tables to format the data is an important tip. Remember, you will most likely use tables for a number of things when developing your Web applications, and formatting data is just one of them.

e-Tip: Using HTML tables to output data will ensure that your data is formatted in an easy-to-read columnar format.

A Dynamic e-RPG Example

A common screen included in most software packages is a customer display. This display tells the user information about a customer, such as location and credit status. This first example of a dynamic e-RPG program will display a list of customers who are over their credit limit.

In this example, we will use one data file. The name of the file is CUSTPF. The DDS for this file is shown in Figure 6.8.

```
A              R RCUST                          TEXT('Customer File')
A                CSCST         9S 0             TEXT('Customer Number')
A                CSNAME        30               TEXT('Customer Name')
A                CSADD1        30               TEXT('Address 1')
A                CSADD2        30               TEXT('Address 2')
A                CSCITY        30               TEXT('City')
A                CSSTATE        2               TEXT('State')
A                CSZIP         11               TEXT('Zip Code')
A                CSPHONE       21               TEXT('Phone Number')
A                CSFAX         21               TEXT('Fax Number')
A                CSCRDLMT       9S 2             TEXT('Credit Limit')
A                CSAMTOPN       9S 2             TEXT('Amount Open')
```

Figure 6.8: DDS for the customer file CUSTPF.

The file will be populated with some fictitious data so that we can produce a report. Some customers will be over their credit limit, and others will be in the clear. Table 6.2 shows the customer number and name, credit limit, and amount open for six customers who we have set up in the CUSTPF file. We will use this as a reference for when we view the output from our e-RPG program.

Table 6.2: Customers and Their Credit.

Customer	Credit Limit	Amount Open
1 – Customer 1	$100.00	$57.00
2 – Customer 2	$5000.00	$5001.00
3 – Customer 3	$100.00	$340.00
4 – Customer 4	$100.00	$0.00
5 – Customer 5	$1500.00	$1700.00
6 – Customer 6	$50.00	$49.00

Now, let's work on the e-RPG program to produce output for this example. The first thing we should do is decide which field information from the CUSTPF file we are going to display on the browser. Because this list shows customers that are over their credit limit, a phone call might be made to the customers to alert them of their credit status. Therefore, we will display the customer name, phone number, and fax number. This should be plenty of information to get started. We can add more fields later as we become more comfortable with writing e-RPG programs.

Examine Figure 6.9. This is the e-RPG code that produces our HTML report. I will name the program OVRLMT. Don't let the tags scare you. All that is happening is some simple string concatenations of HTML tags and field data. Try to look past the HTML tags if they tend to be confusing. They will make more sense when you see the output.

```
FCUSTPF     IF   E              DISK
 *
D WPError          DS
D  EBytesP                   1     4B 0 INZ(%size(EData))
D  EBytesA                   5     8B 0
D  EMsgID                    9    15
D  EReserved                16    16
D  EData                    17    56
 *
D HTTPHeader       C              CONST('Content-type: text/html')
D NewLine          C              CONST(X'15')
 *
D WrtDta           S           1024
D WrtDtaLen        S              9B 0
 *
 * Write the HTTP Header Information
C                   eval      WrtDta = HTTPHeader + NewLine + NewLine +
C                             '<HTML><BODY>       '
C                   EXSR      $WrtStOut
 *
 * Write the report headings
C                   eval      WrtDta = '<TABLE border=1>' + NewLine +
C                             '<TR>' + NewLine +
C                             ' Customer Name</TD>' +
C                             ' Phone Number</TD>' +
C                             ' Fax Number</TD>' +
C                             NewLine + '</TR>' + NewLine
C                   EXSR      $WrtStOut
```

Figure 6.9: e-RPG program OVRLMT (part 1 of 2).

```
C                     READ      CUSTPF
C                     dow       (not %eof)
C                     if        (CSAMTOPN > CSCRDLMT)
C                     eval      WrtDta = '<TR>' + NewLine +
C                               '<TD>' + %trim(CSNAME) + '</TD>' +
C                               '<TD>' + %trim(CSPHONE) + '</TD>' +
C                               '<TD>' + %trim(CSFAX) + '</TD>' +
C                               NewLine + '</TR>' + NewLine
C                     EXSR      $WrtStOut

C                     endif
C                     READ      CUSTPF
C                     enddo
 *
C                     eval      WrtDta = '</TABLE>' + NewLine
C                     EXSR      $WrtStOut
 *
C                     eval      WrtDta = '</BODY></HTML>' + NewLine
C                     EXSR      $WrtStOut

C                     eval      *INLR = *ON
 *
C     $WrtStOut       BEGSR
C                     eval      WrtDtaLen = %len(%trim(WrtDta))
C                     CALLB     'QtmhWrStout'
C                     PARM                  WrtDta
C                     PARM                  WrtDtaLen
C                     PARM                  WPError
 *
C                     ENDSR
```

Figure 6.9: e-RPG program OVRLMT (part 2 of 2).

To create program OVRLMT after you have entered the source, use the following command:

```
CRTBNDRPG PGM(AS400CGI/OVRLMT) SRCFILE(AS400CGI/QRPGLESRC) +
  SRCMBR(OVRLMT) DFTACTGRP(*NO) ACTGRP(QILE) BNDDIR(CGIBNDDIR)
```

After the program is successfully created, enter the following URL into the location parameter of your browser:

```
http://youras400/cgi-bin/OVRLMT
```

---

e-Note: If you set up your HTTP configuration with *.PGM wildcard mapping, you will not need to specify .PGM in the URL. If you didn't use the *.PGM wildcard, and only specified a *, then you will need to attach the .PGM extension to the CGI program name in your URL.

Assuming everything works OK, your browser should resemble that shown in Figure 6.10. This lists customers 2, 3, and 5 as over their credit limit and displays their phone and fax number.

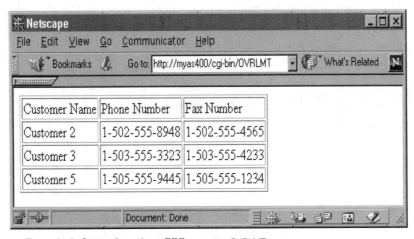

Figure 6.10: Output from the e-RPG program OVRLMT.

The example shown in Figure 6.10 is not meant to be pretty. It is simply meant to show you how easy it is to get output to a browser using an e-RPG program. You can add the flair later. Remember that the flair does nothing to make the information displayed any more accurate, and it should be your last priority in creating e-RPG applications.

What about Displaying Numeric Data?

You may have noticed in the examples given to this point that building HTML is nothing more than stringing different text values together. The example in Figure

6.10 only outputs fields from the CUSTPF file that contain text data. You are probably asking yourself now, "How do you output numeric data?"

The answer to this question is supplied by a great set of new Built In Functions (BIFs) that IBM supplied to RPG programmers in V3R7 and up of the AS/400 Operating System. You could perform this task yourself, but I would only recommend this if it's necessary, such as when you are on a version of the operating system that doesn't have the BIFs described available.

Using BIFs to Convert Numeric Data to Character Data

Outputting numeric data means that we need to somehow translate a numeric field into a text value. We can't concatenate a numeric value into a text string without converting that numeric value to a character value first. This is where some really neat BIFs come into play.

If you are on a version of the operating system in which these BIFs are not available, add this feature to your list of reasons to upgrade. If you are being asked to produce these types of programs, a subtle hint as to why upgrading will make the job easier never hurts.

The %EDITC BIF

The first and most frequently used BIF that we can use to convert numeric data to a text value is the Edit Code (%EDITC) BIF. The BIF takes the numeric value you pass into it, along with an edit code also supplied by you and returns a character value. An example of using the %EDITC BIF follows:

```
C                    eval      text = %editc(Number:'Z')
```

When this statement is executed, the value of Number is returned to the variable text using the edit code of Z. For example, if Number contained the numeric value 000121, after this statement is executed, text would contain the character value "121". The edit code Z will zero-suppress the numeric value. Refer to figure 6.11 for an explanation of each part of this statement.

The same rules that apply to using edit codes in other RPG reporting programs apply to using the Edit Code BIF. Familiarity with how the edit codes work for reporting will help in using the %EDITC BIF.

The %EDITW BIF

The %EDITW BIF is very similar in function to the %EDITC BIF; the only difference is that instead of using edit codes, you can supply and edit word.

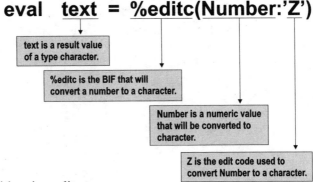

Figure 6.11: The %EDITC BIF.

Again, if you familiar with using edit words to format data in reports, this BIF is very similar. The rules for specifying an edit word on the %EDITW BIF are the same as using an edit word to edit a numeric value.

Applying the %EDITC and %EDITW BIFs to the Customer Report

Let's see how these two BIFs can help us make our Customer Report even more useful by displaying the Customer Number, Credit Limit, and the Amount Open on our report. If the user using the report calls the customer, they will have this information available to them.

Figure 6.12 contains the modified source for the program OVRLMT from earlier in this chapter. It uses the %EDITC BIF to display the Customer Number and the %EDITW BIF to display the Credit Limit and the Amount Open for the customers over their limit. Figure 6.13 shows the browser output for this updated program. For numeric data, notice how I specify the `align="right"` keyword in the table cell (<TD>) tag. This makes formatting numeric data easy and pleasing to the eye.

```
FCUSTPF    IF  E              DISK
 *
D WPError          DS
D  EBytesP                  1       4B 0 INZ(%size(EData))
D  EBytesA                  5       8B 0
D  EMsgID                   9      15
D  EReserved               16      16
D  EData                   17      56
 *
D HTTPHeader       C                    CONST('Content-type: text/html')
D NewLine          C                    CONST(X'15')
D EW               C                    CONST('$ ,   ,   . ')
 *
D WrtDta           S             1024
D WrtDtaLen        S                9B 0
 *
 * Write the HTTP Header Information
C                  eval      WrtDta = HTTPHeader + NewLine + NewLine +
C                            '<HTML><BODY>      '
C                  EXSR      $WrtStOut
 *
 * Write the report headings
C                  eval      WrtDta = '<TABLE border=1>' + NewLine +
C                            '<TR>' + NewLine +
C                            '<TD>Customer Name</TD>' +
C                            '<TD align="right">Customer Number</TD>' +
C                            '<TD align="right">Credit Limit</TD>' +
C                            '<TD align="right">Amount Open</TD>' +
C                            '<TD>Phone Number</TD>' +
C                            '<TD>Fax Number</TD>' +
C                            NewLine + '</TR>' + NewLine
C                  EXSR      $WrtStOut
 *
 * Read the customer file and output the detail records
C                  READ      CUSTPF
C                  dow       (not %eof)
C                  if        (CSAMTOPN > CSCRDLMT)
C                  eval      WrtDta = '<TR>' + NewLine +
C                            '<TD>' + %trim(CSNAME) + '</TD>' +
C                            '<TD alight="right">' +
C                            %trim(%editc(CSCST:'Z')) +
C                            '</TD>' +
C                            '<TD align="right">' +
C                            %trim(%editw(CSCRDLMT:EW)) +
C                            '</TD>' +
C                            '<TD align="right">' +
C                            %trim(%editw(CSAMTOPN:EW)) +
C                            '</TD> +
C                            '<TD>' + %trim(CSPHONE) + '</TD>' +
C                            '<TD>' + %trim(CSFAX) + '</TD>' +
C                            NewLine + '</TR>' + NewLine
```

Figure 6.12: Modifed e-RPG program OVRLMT to display numerical data (part 1 of 2).

```
C                        EXSR      $WrtStOut
C                        endif
C                        READ      CUSTPF
C                        enddo
 *
C                        eval      WrtDta = '</TABLE>' + NewLine
C                        EXSR      $WrtStOut
 *
C                        eval      WrtDta = '</BODY></HTML>' + NewLine
C                        EXSR      $WrtStOut

C                        eval      *INLR = *ON
 *
C        $WrtStOut       BEGSR
C                        eval      WrtDtaLen = %len(%trim(WrtDta))
C                        CALLB     'QtmhWrStout'
C                        PARM                    WrtDta
C                        PARM                    WrtDtaLen
C                        PARM                    WPError
 *
C                        ENDSR
```

Figure 6.12: Modifed e-RPG program OVRLMT to display numerical data (part 2 of 2).

The code in Figure 6.12 uses the %EDITC and %EDITW BIFS to translate numeric text to character data that can be displayed on a Web page. Figure 6.13 shows the output produced by this program.

Customer Name	Customer Number	Credit Limit	Amount Open	Phone Number	Fax Number
Customer 2	2	$ 5,000.00	$ 5,001.00	1-502-555-8948	1-502-555-4565
Customer 3	3	$ 100.00	$ 340.00	1-503-555-3323	1-503-555-4233
Customer 5	5	$ 1,500.00	$ 1,700.00	1-505-555-9445	1-505-555-1234

Figure 6.13: Browser output from modified OVRLMT program using BIFs to display numeric data.

In Figure 6.13, notice how both the headings and the data for the numerical data are aligned to the right. This is the same alignment that you would use when out-putting data to a screen or a report. To do this, all you need to use is the align="right" keyword on the HTML table cell (<TD>) tag.

You will also notice how the %EDITC and %EDITW BIFs affected the numerical data being displayed. Taking the time to format your data will make all the difference in how your result will turn out.

---

e-Tip: Using the `align="right"` keyword on the HTML table cell (‹TD›) tag will allow you to align the data to the right, making

---

MODULARIZING APIS FOR EASE OF USE

One trick I have found that makes e-RPG programs easier to develop, maintain, and follow is placing the APIs into subprocedures that can be called with a simple CALLP op-code. In the OVRLMT examples earlier in this chapter, I created a subroutine that only includes the code to call the `QtmhWrStout` API. While this is a good way to code this to show you how this API is used, you will soon find that you will be including this subprocedure in every e-RPG program that you write. There is a better way, and that is using subprocedures to place the code in an external location that can simply be called when needed.

Placing the `QtmhWrStout` API into a subprocedure might be easier than you think. If you are familiar with subprocedures, this will be no problem. If you are new to subprocedures, let's use this example to take your first step toward making your code modular.

The #WrStout Subprocedure

Thinking of a name for a subprocedure sometimes is hard if you aren't creative. Luckily for us, IBM already has a name for the API, which we can simply shorten for the name of our subprocedure. I named this subprocedure #WrStout simply by stripping the IBM Qtmh from the API name, and adding the pound sign (#) onto the beginning. I like to name my subprocedures starting with the pound sign simply because it tells me that this is a subprocedure when scanning through the code.

When using subprocedures, we must place them into a source member so that a module or service program can be created. Then we can access the subprocedure from a program. The source member name I will be placing my standard HTTP functions into is called F.HTTPSTD. Just for clarification, I preceded all my subprocedure source members with "F.", which tells me that this source is a set of functions for use by other programs.

The first step in creating a subprocedure to use the QtmhWrStout API is to define what information we will pass to the subprocedure. In all the examples given in this chapter, the only bit of information that really changes, or that we cannot determine on our own, is the text that we pass to the QtmhWrStout API. This is the HTML text that we are writing to the browser. The parameter that tells the API the length of the data can be found after we have the text, and the standard error parameter is an output parameter, so it doesn't need to be passed into the subprocedure.

After we know what we want to pass the subprocedure, the next step is determining if we want to return anything to the calling program. For this subprocedure, I have decided not to return anything. An error flag or information from the error parameter data structure could be returned, but this is such a simple subprocedure that this really isn't necessary. Figure 6.14 contains the code for the #WrStout subprocedure.

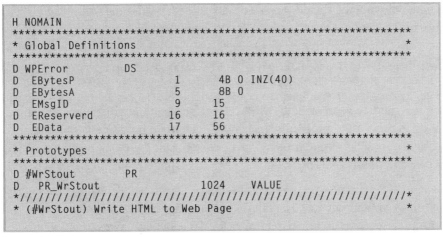

```
H NOMAIN
*****************************************************************
* Global Definitions                                           *
*****************************************************************
D WPError         DS
D  EBytesP               1      4B 0 INZ(40)
D  EBytesA               5      8B 0
D  EMsgID                9     15
D  EReserverd           16     16
D  EData                17     56
*****************************************************************
* Prototypes                                                   *
*****************************************************************
D #WrStout        PR
D  PR_WrStout                1024     VALUE
*///////////////////////////////////////////////////////////////*
* (#WrStout) Write HTML to Web Page                            *
```

Figure 6.14: Code for the #WrStout subprocedure in source member F.HTTPSTD (part 1 of 2).

```
*///////////////////////////////////////////////////////////////////*
P #WrStout         B                      EXPORT
*-                                                                 -*
D #WrStout         PI
D   WrtDta                      1024    VALUE
*
D WrtDtaLen        S             9B 0
*-                                                                 -*
C                  eval        WrtDtaLen = %len(%trim(WrtDta))
*
C                  CALLB       'QtmhWrStout'
C                  PARM                    WrtDta
C                  PARM                    WrtDtaLen
C                  PARM                    WPError
*-                                                                 -*
P #WrStout         E
```

Figure 6.14: Code for the #WrStout subprocedure in source member F.HTTPSTD (part 2 of 2).

The code for the #WrStout subprocedure looks similar to the code for the subroutine used in the OVRLMT examples in this chapter, and it should. The only difference is that all the special declarations are now self-contained within the subprocedure. Placing this information into the subprocedure cleans up our main processing program. And, once this subprocedure has been tested, it can literally be forgotten.

To create the module for the #WrStout subprocedure, use the following command:

```
CRTRPGMOD MODULE(AS400CGI/F.HTTPSTD) SRCFILE(AS400CGI/QMODSRC) MBR(F.HTTPSTD)
```

Once this module is created, the #WrStout subprocedure will be available to your main processing programs. Instead of each main program calling the QtmhWrStout API, all that needs to be done is to call the #WrStout subprocedure and pass it to the HTML text that you want to display on the browser.

You might wonder what is the point of placing this code in a subprocedure, because it is a rather small amount of code. To show you an example, Figure 6.15 contains the modified source for the HELLOW example used earlier in this chapter.

```
 * Prototype for #WrStout
D #WrStout          PR
D   PR_WrStout                  1024      VALUE
 *
D HTTPHeader         C                    CONST('Content-type: text/html')
D NewLine            C                    CONST(X'15')
 *
D HTML               S          1024
 *
C                    eval       HTML = HTTPHeader + NewLine + NewLine +
C                               '<HTML><BODY>' + NewLine +
C                               'Hello World' + NewLine +
C                               '</BODY></HTML>' + NewLine
 *
C                    CALLP      #WrStout(HTML)
 *
C                    eval       *INLR = *ON
```

Figure 6.15: e-RPG program HELLOW modified to use the #WrStout subprocedure.

What a difference, right? Not only did we move a bunch of declarations just for the QtmhWrStout API, but we made the process to write HTML data to a browser just one line!

To compile the new version of HELLOW to use the #WrStout subprocedure in the F.HTTPSTD module, use the following commands:

```
CRTRPGMOD MODULE(AS400CGI/HELLOW) SRCFILE(AS400CGI/QRPGLESRC)
CRTPGM PGM(AS400CGI/HELLOW) MODULE(AS400CGI/HELLOW AS400CGI/F.HTTPSTD)
```

The example uses a process called *bind by copy* in which the source for the subprocedure is physically placed into the finished program. First, the modules are created using the Create RPG Module (CRTRPGMOD) command. Then, a program is created binding all of the modules together using the Create Program (CRTPGM) command.

Another, and more accepted, method would be to create a service program from the F.HTTPSTD module and then use a process called *bind by reference*. In this case, the subprocedure is not physically added to the end program, but the reference to it is verified at compile time.

To create a service program from the F.HTTPSTD module, use the following command after the module has been created:

```
CRTSRVPGM SRVPGM(AS400GI/F.HTTPSTD) MODULE(AS400CGIL/F.HTTPSTD)
```

After the service program is created, you can create a program that uses the service program with the following commands:

```
CRTRPGMOD MODULE(AS400CGI/HELLOW) SRCFILE(AS400CGI/QRPGLESRC)
CRTPGM PGM(AS400CGI/HELLOW) MODULE(AS400CGI/HELLOW) +
BNDSRVPGM(AS400CGI/F.HTTPSTD)
```

If you are unfamiliar with these terms or how they work, it might be a good idea to brush up on the Integrated Language Environment (ILE). ILE is a powerful tool and is extremely useful when writing e-RPG programs. After all, these programs will be entirely new developments, so what better excuse to start using ILE? You will see more examples of the use of ILE as the other APIs used for e-RPG programming are discussed in this book. Whether you decide to use subprocedures or not is up to you, but I think in the long run you'll be glad you did.

Is e-RPG in Your Future?

Hopefully this chapter has convinced you just how easy and valuable e-RPG programs can be for your e-commerce solutions. In the chapters to come, there will be additional examples that are more functional, as well as more involved.

Before you go any further, I encourage you to get the examples in this chapter working. And more important, I encourage you to take the time to understand how these examples work. Once you have an understanding of the basics needed to produce Web output with e-RPG, you're on your way to creating usable Web applications in RPG!

7

READING INPUT FROM A BROWSER

What is output without input? Displaying pretty pictures on a Web page is entertaining for a while, but after the novelty wears off, we will soon find ourselves wanting more. The purpose of building robust Web-based applications is to interact with the user. We want to build real applications that do something, no matter how trivial, so that we can continue our learning experience.

Almost every application that we use today relies on some sort of user input. Whether this input consists of parameters needed to run a sales report, or information required for an order entry application, we need some way to allow the user to input data. We also need a way to read this information and process it.

It is a safe bet to say that in all e-business solutions available on the Web today, whether it is buying books or buying cars, some sort of input is needed so that the company can take an order. This chapter will discuss two different ways that you can read input from a browser, as well as describe the tools available that allow you to create input fields on your Web page.

HTML's Input Tools

HTML has all of the tools to provide input fields on your page. You've no doubt seen them before. From text fields to checkboxes, these input fields make your experience on the Web mean something.

When creating DDS screens on the AS/400, we are limited to input, output, or input/output fields. These are plain text fields. Although there is nothing fancy about these types of text-based input applications, they are functional. Think back to the last time you visited an airport reservation desk or talked to your insurance agent. If you caught a glimpse of the screen the person was using, chances are that it was a strictly text screen—something we are very familiar with in our AS/400 environment. Text screens most likely will not go away for some time, no matter how much hype you hear to the contrary.

But, there comes a time in every user's life (or every programmer's life) when an application requires a little jazzing up. For example, a project may come along that requires building a Web solution simply because using a browser is familiar to end-users of the application.

Although it is true that we could install a 5250 emulation package on every machine that wanted to use our new application, that would be silly, especially if the application was Web based. If you wanted to provide a solution so that users around the world could purchase items from your business, you certainly would not want a requirement such as Client Access/400. Home users have grown accustomed to their Web browser, and if you don't provide a Web solution, they will simply go to your competitor who does offer such a solution.

Creating interfaces with HTML gives you the chance to create something that is usable by anyone with a browser. Just think—all you have to do is write the application. The user most likely has a browser already installed on his or her machine, and from hours of surfing at home (or at work) the users are comfortable with this interface. Building a Web application in this day and age is almost a perfect solution.

Web applications do not apply only to those types of applications that sell your company's specific resources, either. Creating Web applications to provide reports to those on your intranet is a solution as well.

To get started with these ideas, let's see what types of HTML coded input fields can be used on a Web browser.

HTML allows you to create input fields by using a host of different input tools. These fields are included between the <FORM> tags, which define the entire form and set of fields. A form is an HTML object that defines a certain set of input on a Web display. If you relate a form to a DDS screen, a form could be thought of as a record format.

Each input field can be one of many types. Table 7.1 displays the most often used types of input available for an HTML form.

Table 7.1: Input Fields Available in HTML.

Type	HTML Code	Example
Text	Text:<input type="text" size="20">	Text:
Text Area	<Textarea rows="2" cols="20"></textarea>	
Select Box	<Select > <option value="Selection One">Selection One</option> <option value="Selection Two">Selection Two</option> </select>	Selection One ▼ Selection One Selection Two
Button	<Input type="button" value="Button" name="B1">	Button
Checkbox	<Input type="checkbox" name="C1" value="ON">Checkbox 1 <input type="checkbox" name="C2" value="ON">Checkbox 2	☑ Checkbox 1 ☐ Checkbox 2
Radio Button	<Input type="radio" value="V1" checked name="R1">Radio Button	⦿ Radio Button

With all the different types of input fields available in HTML, you'll never look at green-screen programming in the same way again. Finding uses for each type of input would be a challenge, but when used correctly, they will make the flow of your page very easy.

Passing the information from these fields to the processing CGI program is yet another task that must be performed. What good is a Web page with entry fields if we don't process the data that is entered? Not much. Reading this data from a Web page can be done in different ways.

QUERY STRING INPUT VS. STANDARD INPUT

Getting the data from these input fields to your CGI program is yet another story. There are two ways to accomplish this: by reading Query String environment variables and by reading the data directly from the page using standard input.

It is important when developing Internet applications to understand the difference between these two types of input. Not only is the data passed to a CGI program used differently in each case, but a different API is used to read from each type of input.

If we look at a basic RPG program, besides using a database file, there are two ways to get data into a program. The first would be passing parameters into the program using an entry parameter list. The second would be reading information from fields on a display screen. The two different methods of reading input from a browser can be thought of as the same two methods as used in RPG programs.

Query String Input

Reading input from the query string environment variables is similar to passing data into a program using an entry parameter list. In RPG, we specify the following code to tell the program to expect variables coming into the program:

```
C       *ENTRY      PLIST
C                   PARM                    INVOICE
C                   PARM                    CUSTOMER
```

The entry parameter list tells the program to expect a variable named INVOICE and another named CUSTOMER to be sent to the program as parameters. Once they are there, you are free to do with them what you wish.

In the same sense, query string environment variables are sent into your RPG program as parameters in a very similar fashion. Query string parameters are located after the URL following a question mark (?). Each parameter name is followed by an equal sign (=) and the data that is assigned to that variable. If more than one parameter is used, these sets of data are separated by an ampersand symbol (&). Examine the following URL:

```
http://www.mysite.com/cgibin/pgmname?INVOICE=109&CUSTOMER=225
```

Notice that following the question mark in this URL, we have two variables, one named INVOICE with a value of 109 (INVOICE=109), and one named CUSTOMER with a value of 225 (CUSTOMER=225). The similarity between the query string method and the use of an entry parameter list is that the data is passed into the program to be used. How query string variables are read and parsed for use in the program will be covered later in this chapter.

Standard Input

The second method we will use to make data from a Web page available to our CGI program is using what is called standard input. This method is very similar to using a display screen and the EXFMT or READ op-codes in an RPG program. First you design a screen with input fields, then you write a program to process this screen. When the user enters data into these fields, and you perform an EXFMT or READ on the record format of the display file, the data is magically available in your RPG program for you to manipulate.

The same holds true for standard input. You design a Web form with input fields on it specifying the POST method. You assign some sort of interface for users to activate when they are done, usually in the form of a submit button. When the user presses this button, your CGI program is called and you are able to read the data entered into these fields through standard input.

Both of the methods used for reading input described here have their time and place to be used. The following sections describe each method in detail as well as give examples of how and when to use them correctly.

USING QUERY STRING INPUT

As discussed in chapter 5, we learned that one way to read input is through the Query String environment variable. This is the data that follows the question mark (?) at the end of the URL. For example, the following URL contains Query String environment data:

```
http://www.mypage.com/cgi-bin/REPORT?month=jan
```

This URL specifies that the user is requesting to run a CGI program named RE-PORT in the cgi-bin directory. In addition, this URL will pass data in the form of a Query String environment variable that can be accessed by the program RE-PORT. More specifically, we are passing a value of "jan" as a value for the parameter month into this CGI program.

The previous example is a static method used to send data to a CGI program. Dynamic data also can be passed into a CGI program. A static method may be compared to a menu on the AS/400. Parameter data can be specified on the call that relates to a menu option. But, if the same program is called from an RPG program, the data passed into the program might be dynamic, such as data entered on a screen by a user, or read from a file.

The next sections covers static and dynamic input when using query string data in your Web application.

Static Query String Input

Static data is usually simple to produce. This data rarely changes, and when it does, user intervention is required. First, let's focus on what is needed in your HTML documents to use static query string variable data. You simply need a way to call a CGI program and include the query string variables and data following the URL.

The Web page in Figure 7.1 shows a menu that allows a user to run a sales report for months January through June. Each of the options passes a different Query String variable into the processing program. When a user clicks on one of the links, a CGI program is run with different Query String parameters. This is a very simple example of using static query string data.

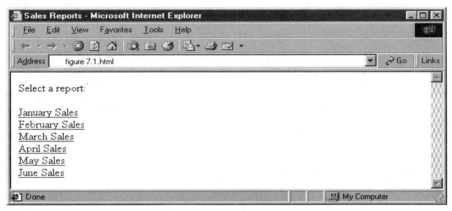

Figure 7.1: A Web page that uses static query string environment data for input.

If we were to view the HTML source for Figure 7.1, we would see that it really is simple. Each hyperlink points to the same URL, but includes different query string data being passed to the processing CGI program. This would be the equivalent of calling an RPG program with a different parameter value for each option. Figure 7.2 includes the HTML source for this example.

```
<HTML>
<HEAD>
<TITLE>Sales Reports</TITLE>
</HEAD>
<BODY>
Select a report: <BR><BR>
<A HREF="http://www.mypage.com/cgi-bin/REPORT?month=jan">
January Sales</A><BR>
<A HREF="http://www.mypage.com/cgi-bin/REPORT?month=feb">
February Sales</A><BR>
<A HREF="http://www.mypage.com/cgi-bin/REPORT?month=mar">
March Sales</A><BR>
```

Figure 7.2: HTML source for Figure 7.1 (part 1 of 2).

```
<A HREF="http://www.mypage.com/cgi-bin/REPORT?month=apr">
April Sales</A><BR>
<A HREF="http://www.mypage.com/cgi-bin/REPORT?month=may">
May Sales</A><BR>
<A HREF="http://www.mypage.com/cgi-bin/REPORT?month=jun">
June Sales</A><BR>
</BODY>
</HTML>
```

Figure 7.2: HTML source for Figure 7.1 (part 2 of 2).

As you can see, each hyperlink is identical except for the query string data following the URL. Each link specifies the value of the month for each report. When this data is read into the processing CGI program, it will know what month is to be run for the sales report.

Dynamic Query String Input

Building dynamic query string input is a more useful method of passing data to a CGI program. Dynamic data is usually retrieved from Web page fields that you are requesting the user to fill in. There are two ways to retrieve the values of these fields. The first is using JavaScript, and the second is using the GET method.

Dynamic Query String Input using JavaScript

For dynamic data, such as that entered into a text input field, you can use JavaScript embedded into your HTML to extract the values entered and pass them along to your CGI program. This method works great when you are simply passing nonsensitive data to your CGI program, such as search text. If you are having the user enter such information as user IDs, passwords, or any other sensitive information, this method is not advised, because the data will be visible in the URL using this method.

Figure 7.3 shows a simple example of a Web browser that displays a text entry field used for a text search. Because the data entered into this text field isn't sensitive data, passing the data as query string data shouldn't be a security problem. This example also uses JavaScript to extract the data from the field and pass it to the processing CGI program.

Figure 7.3: An example of using dynamic query string data.

Figure 7.4 shows the HTML source and JavaScript needed for the Web page shown in Figure 7.3. One important item to notice is the way control is passed to the processing CGI program. The JavaScript method `window.location` is used in this example to change the URL on the current window to the new one specified after the `window.location` method. This JavaScript method acts identically if the user were to enter the data into the location bar of the browser.

```
<html>
<head>
<title>Search Sample</title>
<script language="JavaScript">
function Redirect(form) {
    window.location="/cgi-bin/SEARCHPGM?query=" + form.query.value;
}
</script>
</head>
<body>
Enter your search string and press "Search!"<BR>
<form name="search">
<input type=text name=query size=30>
<input type=button value="Search!" onClick="Redirect(this.form);">
</form>
</body>
</html>
```

Figure 7.4: Dynamic query string input using JavaScript.

If we examine the code in Figure 7.4, we see the form, named search, consists of a text box where the user can enter a search string. The name of this field is query. There is also another input device on the form that is a button. When the user clicks on this button, the onClick event gets control and calls the JavaScript function Redirect(). The values of the input fields in the form are passed to the Redirect() function by specifying this.form as the parameter. (The value document.search could also be used in place of this.form.) Once inside the Redirect() function, the data value of the field query is parsed by specifying the form.query.value property. We use the value retrieved to pass along as a Query Sting environment variable to the CGI program named SEARCHPGM.

When the CGI program executes in this example, the query string data will be visible following the URL, which is why you should not use this method when sending sensitive data, such as user names or passwords, to your CGI programs. The preferred method is reading the data directly from the Web page using standard input described in the Standard Input section.

Dynamic Query String Input Using the GET Method

Another way to retrieve dynamic form information from your Web page, without the need for JavaScript, is to use the GET method within a form. The biggest difference between this method and the JavaScript method can be seen in the HTML source in Figure 7.5. The main areas to pay attention to are the FORM tags and the button. The button in this example is an input of type Submit. This keyword tells the browser to create a button that will submit the information from the form when pressed.

```
<html>
<head>
<title>Search Sample</title>
</head>
<body>
Enter your search string and press "Search!"<BR>
<form action="/cgi-bin/SEARCHPGM" method="GET">
<input type=text name=query size=30>
<input type=submit value="Search!">
</form>
</body>
</html>
```

Figure 7.5: Dynamic query string input using the GET method.

154

Figure 7.5 includes a couple of slight differences from the JavaScript example used in Figure 7.4. The first is obvious; there is no JavaScript. The next difference is the `action` and `method` tags used on the form. The `action` tag specifies the CGI program to run when the form is submitted by pressing the submit button. The `method` tag defines which method to use for the input. Lastly, the input button is no longer of type *button*, rather it's of type *submit*. This button is the Enter button for the form. When it is pressed, the action specified in the form tag is executed. In this case, it is the CGI program SEARCHPGM.

Both of the HTML examples shown in Figures 7.4 and 7.5 produce the same output to the browser. Whether JavaScript or the GET method is used to parse the data, the browser will still look the same to the user. The real advantage to using the JavaScript method, as discussed in chapter 2, is that the data can be validated before the form is submitted. JavaScript can be used to validate the data using the GET method as well, but it is a little more complicated.

All three of these methods are very handy in their own way. You might find that you need to use one of the dynamic methods rather than the static methods for most programs. Also, I find it easier to use the JavaScript method to verify and redirect the browser because I can perform both in one step.

The GET method example, which doesn't include any JavaScript, lacks any interactive error checking. If errors were encountered, you would have to display a new Web page in your CGI program to report errors. This is cumbersome and slow. Interactive verification can be done, but this requires the use of JavaScript. Figure 7.6 shows the GET example with a small piece of JavaScript to perform interactive field verification.

```
<html>
<head>
<title>Search Sample</title>
<script language="JavaScript">
function Validate(form) {
    if (form.query.value == "") {
        alert("Search String Cannot be Blank");
        return false;
```

Figure 7.6: Using JavaScript to verify form fields using the GET method (part 1 of 2).

```
    } else {
        return true;
    }
}
</script>
</head>
<body>
Enter your search string and press "Search!"<BR>
<form action="/cgi-bin/SEARCHPGM" method="GET"
 onsubmit="return Validate(this);">
<input type=text name=query size=30>
<input type=submit value="Search!">
</form>
</body>
</html>
```

Figure 7.6: Using JavaScript to verify form fields using the GET method (part 2 of 2).

You'll notice in Figure 7.6 that the onSubmit method has been added to the form tags. When the submit button is pressed, the JavaScript function Validate() is called. This function either returns a value of false if no text was entered, or a value of true if text was entered. When control is returned to the form, if the value returned was false, the action tag is not executed. If the value was true, the action is carried out and the CGI program is called.

As you can see, when you start doing more complicated things with your Web pages, JavaScript almost cannot be ignored. I encourage you to research all you can about using JavaScript for your Web pages. It will not only make your pages more interactive, but will also make them easier to maintain. If you were not interested in JavaScript and skipped chapter 2 of this book, I encourage you to give it another chance.

Reading Query String Input with e-RPG

No matter which method you use to place data into query string environment variables, in time you will want to read and process this data in your CGI program. Reading query string data from your Web is a two step process. First, you read the data into your page. Next, you parse the data into a usable format. The Get Environment Variable (QtmhGetEnv) API is used to read environment variables that are available. In this case, the environment variable is query string data.

To tell the `QtmhGetEnv` API to retrieve query string data, we must specify the particular environment variable we wish to retrieve. In the case of reading in query string data, we specify the value QUERY_STRING on the request variable parameter. This tells the API to retrieve the query string data and return it to us. Figure 7.7 shows a code snippet that is used to retrieve the query string environment variable.

```
D WPError          DS
D   EBytesP                  1      4B 0 INZ(40)
D   EBytesA                  5      8B 0
D   EMsgID                   9     15
D   EReserverd              16     16
D   EData                   17     56
 *
D EnvRec           S              1024
D EnvLen           S                9B 0
D EnvRecLen        S                9B 0 INZ(%size(EnvRec))
D EnvName          S               12    INZ('QUERY_STRING')
D EnvNameLen       S                9B 0 INZ(%size(EnvName))
 *
C                    CALLB     'QtmhGetEnv'
C                    PARM                    EnvRec
C                    PARM                    EnvRecLen
C                    PARM                    EnvLen
C                    PARM                    EnvName
C                    PARM                    EnvNameLen
C                    PARM                    WPError
C                    ENDSR
```

Figure 7.7: Using the QtmhGetEnv API to retrieve query string data.

After the `QtmhGetEnv` API is called, it returns the query string data into the receiver variable. In Figure 7.7, the receiver variable is named `EnvRec`. When the data is returned, the data resembles the following:

```
var1=value1&var2=value2
```

Once you have this data, parsing it into useable fields in your program is done with the second of the two APIs needed. This API is the Convert to Database API (`QtmhCvtDB`). If you feel adventurous, you could parse the data yourself, but I think you'll find that using the `QtmhCvtDB` API will be much easier.

Figure 7.8 shows the code that will parse the data retrieved from the code in Figure 7.7. Again, it's a simple call to an API. All of the data that you need to pass into the API has already been retrieved from a successful call to the QtmhGetEnv API.

```
D EnvDS           E DS                    EXTNAME(FILENAME)
D EnvFile           DS
D  File                     1      10     INZ('FILENAME  ')
D  Lib                     11      20     INZ('LIBRARY   ')
D CvtLen          S                 9B 0  INZ(%size(EnvDS))
D CvtLenAv        S                 9B 0
D CvtStat         S                 9B 0
C                   CALLB     'QtmhCvtDb'
C                   PARM                     EnvFile
C                   PARM                     EnvRec
C                   PARM                     EnvLen
C                   PARM                     EnvDS
C                   PARM                     CvtLen
C                   PARM                     CvtLenAv
C                   PARM                     CvtStat
C                   PARM                     WPError
```

Figure 7.8: Using the QtmhCvtDB API to parse query string data.

Notice that the second and third parameters used in Figure 7.8 are the same variables used to call the QtmhGetEnv API in Figure 7.7. These parameters contain the query string data retrieved and the length of that data.

The other variables used are fairly simple. The first contains the name of an AS/400 database file, which contains field names and definitions so that the QtmhCvtDB API knows where and how to parse the data. Similarly, the fourth parameter is the name of a data structure where the data will be placed. You'll notice that I used the same file name for both parameters. The data structure uses the file name as an external definition reference. This technique reduces the chances that the data definitions will differ between the file I tell this API to use to parse the data, and the actual structure that will hold the data.

This method of reading input was confusing to me until I used it a couple of times. To explain this method and make it a little easier to understand, let's look at a step-by-step process of how this method works.

1. You build an HTML file that includes a form. This form includes two variables, a text field named NAME that is 30 characters long and a numeric field (represented as text in the form) named AGE that is three characters long.

2. You enter the URL .../cgi-bin/CGIPGM?NAME=Brad&AGE=29 into the location bar. This calls a CGI program named cgipgm.

3. You call the QtmhGetEnv API in CGIPGM. This retrieves a string of data that looks like NAME=Brad&AGE=29 and places it in a field named envrec.

4. You call the QtmhCvtDB API specifying three things:

   ➣ A database name of agedata. This is a physical file that resides on your AS/400 and has two fields. The first is NAME and has 30 characters. The second is AGE and is a signed field with a size of three.

   ➣ A data structure built using an external reference of the physical file agedata.

   ➣ The envrec variable that contains the query string data retrieved from the QtmhGetEnv API.

5. If the call to the API is successful, the data structure will contain "Brad" for the variable NAME and the numeric value 29 for the variable AGE.

6. Like magic (well, almost magic), you now have the data available to your e-RPG program.

There are a couple of peculiar things about this process. First, in an HTML form, you really can't specify a numeric field. An example is the AGE variable used in the previous explanation. Because of this, you may have to do some error checking to verify that the field contains only numeric data. I usually do this with JavaScript, another reason to revisit chapter 2.

Second, even though the field AGE is character on the HTML page, we can still place it in a numeric field in our e-RPG program by specifying a numeric data type in the physical file used to parse the data. This is very convenient, because if you've ever tried to convert a character field into numeric, you know how difficult it can be if the fields are of different sizes, or if the data isn't left justified in the character field.

Using APIs to read input sounds a lot more complicated than it really is. Once you see it in action, and experienced how easily it works, you will gain confidence. I encourage you to try a few simple samples on your own; soon you'll see it's not that difficult.

USING STANDARD INPUT

Standard input is the second way that you can retrieve values entered from a Web page form. This method is much more convenient when you are reading sensitive data such as user ID, password, or credit card information. Because this data is not passed through environment variables, someone trying to capture the data from your page will have a harder time doing so.

Standard Input in HTML

Using standard input in your Web page is almost identical to using the GET method for query string data, described earlier in this chapter. The main difference is that you will use the POST method in your form. You will recall that in the query string example, we used JavaScript to process the form. Using the POST method requires no JavaScript unless you want to perform error checking before passing control to your CGI program. This is done in exactly the same way as using the GET method, shown earlier in this chapter.

Figure 7.9 shows a simple input screen that asks the user to enter his or her name and e-mail address. When the user presses the button labeled Done, the POST method is used to call the processing CGI program.

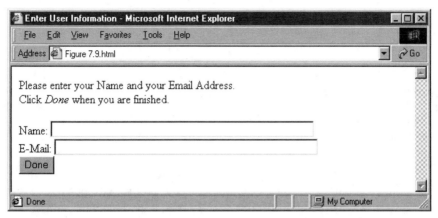

Figure 7.9: A sample screen that uses the POST method to send data through Standard Input.

Figure 7.10 contains the HTML code for Figure 7.9. The first difference you will notice when comparing this code to that used in the query string example is the form tags. The `action` tag specifies what to do when the form is posted. This is the same as using the GET method. The `method` tag tells the browser to use the POST method. The last difference is with the Submit button. This tells the browser that this button is used to pass control to the `action` form tag when pressed.

```
<HTML>
<HEAD>
<TITLE>Enter User Information</TITLE>
</HEAD>
Please enter your Name and your Email Address.<BR>
Click <i>Done</i> when you are finished. <BR>
<FORM action="/cgi-bin/CGIPGM" method="post">
Name: <input type="text" name="NAME" size=50><BR>
E-Mail: <input type="text" name="EMAIL" size=50><BR>
<input type="submit" value="Done">
</FORM>
</BODY>
</HTML>
```

Figure 7.10: HTML form that uses the POST method.

As you can see from the code in Figure 7.10, the only real difference between this method and the GET method is that POST is specified on the `method` tag. The rest of the HTML code remains the same. The same holds true if you wanted to use JavaScript for error checking. It is the same method as shown earlier using the GET method.

Reading Standard Input with e-RPG

Reading standard input data from your Web is, as with the query string input, a two-step process. The Read Standard Input (QtmhRdStin) API is used to read the standard input from your browser. Figure 7.11 shows a code snippet that is used to read standard input variables into a CGI program. After the QtmhRdStin API is executed, the standard input data is available to the program as a character string, exactly as it was when reading from the query string environment variable.

```
D WPError          DS
D  EBytesP                    1        4B 0 INZ(40)
D  EBytesA                    5        8B 0
D  EMsgID                     9       15
D  EReserverd                16       16
D  EData                     17       56
 *
D RcvRec           S                1024
D RcvLen           S                  9B 0
D RcvRecLen        S                  9B 0
C                  CALLB     'QtmhRdStin'
C                  PARM                      RcvRec
C                  PARM                      RcvLen
C                  PARM                      RcvRecLen
C                  PARM                      WPError
```

Figure 7.11: Using the QtmhRdStin API to read standard input data.

After the QtmhRdStin API is called, it returns the standard input data into the receiver variable. In Figure 7.11, the receiver variable is named RcvRec. When the data is returned, the data looks similar to the query string data in the previous section.

```
var1=value1&var2=value2
```

Once the data is available, the process is the same for parsing this data into fields usable in your CGI program. The QtmhCvtDB API is used to do this for standard input data as well.

Let's assume that the form in Figure 7.9 was used. I enter my name and e-mail address and click the Done button. CGI program CGIPGM is called. The first thing performed in CGIPGM is to read standard input variables using the QtmhRdStin API. After this is done, the receiver variable will contain the value below:

```
NAME=Brad Stone&EMAIL=bstone@midrangecomputing.com
```

Once we have this data available to us in our program, we would parse this data into a data structure using the same method described in the section on query string variables. The QtmhCvtDB API is used to parse the data into a data structure containing fields of the same name as on our HTML form.

READ ON

Reading information from a browser cannot be ignored. If you want to have a successful Web application, you need some way to read information from a browser.

The methods discussed here should get you started building Web applications. The APIs used to both read and parse data are described in further detail in chapter 5. Also, chapter 9 contains a set of service programs that will make the use of the APIs as simple as a CALL or EVAL statement.

8

PUTTING HTML, JAVASCRIPT, AND RPG TOGETHER

Prior to this point, we examined all of the single necessities for e-commerce programming in detail. This chapter brings together what you have learned in order to make a sample e-commerce solution.

The application that this chapter uses is a simple order-entry system for a fictional company that sells computers. A user signs in to the site using their account information, which consists of a user name and password. The user is then able to view computer hardware available for sale. When the user clicks on an item, it is added to the user's shopping basket. When a user is finished shopping, the user checks out and an invoice for the equipment purchased is generated.

Because this example contains many different source files and types, all of the complete source is available in appendix F. Important snippets of code are included for examples only.

BVS-COMPUTERS

Because I'm not the most creative person, I will make this simple. Our fictional company is named BVS-Computers. (I was going to name it Computers-n-Stuff, but on checking, that name is already taken). BVS-Computers sells complete computer systems and accessories. The Web page is www.BVS-Computers. com.

Signing in to BVS-Computers

The first thing users see when they log onto our site is an index page. This page allows the user to sign into our site and do some shopping. The name of this file is index.html. The page is automatically viewed when a user goes to our site because we have the following directive set up in our configuration file:

```
Welcome index.html
```

When the HTTP server gets a request and a specific document is not specified, it searches for the Welcome directive. If it finds it, the file specified is used. The front page to our imaginary site is shown in Figure 8.1. In this figure, I have started to enter my user information so that I can sign in and shop for computers. One thing you will notice is that the password field contains all asterisks (*) for each character I enter. This is done by specifying the input field as type password. This provides at least one layer of protection when entering sensitive data.

Let's assume for a moment that the information I entered into the fields on the page is invalid. If I were to leave the User ID field blank, a dialog box would be displayed that says I must enter a user ID. This is done by using interactive validation with JavaScript.

Now let's assume that either I entered an invalid user ID or the password entered was invalid. This will need to be verified using a CGI program. We could use JavaScript and hard-code all the user IDs and passwords into the script, but this would make it not only unsecured, but difficult to maintain. All a user would have to do to obtain a list of user IDs and passwords is click on the browser's View Source option.

We want to use our AS/400 as the database server for this model, so when we update a file, the page will automatically be updated. For example, if we updated a price on an item, the updated price would be displayed on the Web page the next time a user visited that page.

Figure 8.1: The front page for BVS-Computers.

The action tag for the form in this Web page says to execute the program SIGNIN in the /cgi-bin/ directory. The validation for user ID and password is performed in the SIGNIN e-RPG program. The values entered on the Web page are read from standard input and the values are checked in the same way we would verify information in almost any RPG program. We simply chain to the USER file. If we don't get a hit on the user name, or we do and the password is invalid, then we display an error. Figure 8.2 shows the display if invalid data is entered for the BVS-Computers sign-in page.

Figure 8.2: CGI Script signin output for invalid user ID or password.

Now let's assume that we entered a valid user ID and password on the first screen. In this case, a screen would be displayed that allows us to go shopping. Figure 8.3 shows what this screen looks like. The Go Shopping hyperlink will take us to a page that displays items available for purchase.

Figure 8.3: Web page displayed when a valid user ID and password are entered.

E-RPG program SIGNIN first reads standard input and then converts the data read into a data structure that is usable in our program. The values in this data structure are then used to CHAIN to the USER file to verify that a valid user ID and password were entered. To give you an idea of how this is done, let's look at a small code snippet in Figure 8.4 from e-RPG program SIGNIN.

```
C     USERID        CHAIN     USERPF
 *
C                   if        (not %found) or (PASSWORD   USPASSWORD)
C                   eval      WrtDta = '<CENTER>' +
C                                      'Error!' +
C                                      '<BR>' +
C                                      'Invalid User ID or Password!' +
C                                      '</CENTER>' +
C                                      NewLine
```

Figure 8.4: The main processing in e-RPG program SIGNIN (part 1 of 2).

```
C                else
C                eval       WrtDta = '<CENTER>' +
C                                   'Welcome ' +
C                                   %trim(USFNAME) + ' ' +
C                                   %trim(USLNAME) + '.' +
C                                   '<BR><BR>' +
C                                   '<a
href="/cgi-bin/items?userid=' +
C                                   %trim(USERID) + '">' +
C                                   'Go Shopping!' +
C                                   '</CENTER>' +
C                                   NewLine
C                endif
 *
C                EXSR       $WrStout
```

Figure 8.4: The main processing in e-RPG program SIGNIN (part 2 of 2).

The value that we use to chain to the user file is named USER. This is a field that exists in the data structure that we use in the QtmhCvtDB API. The data received from standard input is parsed with this API into the data structure we specify. The variable PASSWORD also exists in this data structure.

Depending on whether we get a hit when we chain to the USER file, and if the password is valid, we either display an error or a welcome message. The welcome message uses the first and last name fields from the USER file (USFNAME and USLNAME respectively) to display a welcome message. Finally, it displays a hyperlink to the shopping page and passes the user ID as a query string environment variable. The user ID will follow the shopper as an identifier throughout the rest of the shopping process so we know who is shopping and whose shopping basket items are placed into.

Go Shopping at BVS-Computers

The URL for the Go Shopping! page references the e-RPG program ITEMS. This e-RPG program reads through our item file (ITEMPF) and displays items for sale. Processing the Web page this way ensures that the page truly represents the items we have available. If we add an item, or change any information, this will be reflected immediately on our Web page. Figure 8.5 shows the Web page produced by the ITEMS e-RPG program.

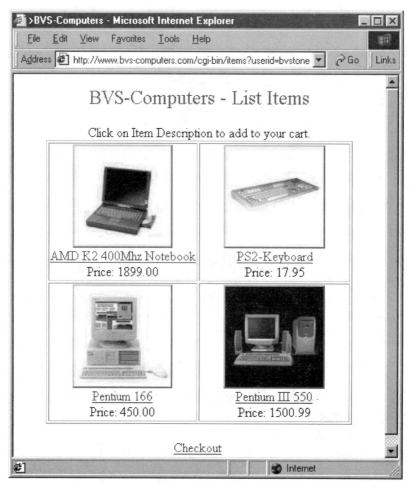

Figure 8.5: A listing of items produced by e-RPG program ITEMS.

After the users have viewed the items available, they may choose to add an item to their shopping basket. To do this, they simply click on the item description. The description is a hyperlink that calls e-RPG program BUYITEM. It also passes along as a query string environment variable the item number and the user ID. (Remember that we will pass the user ID along to every program as a customer identifier.) The image that is displayed for the item and hyperlink to the BUYITEM e-RPG program is built dynamically. If we take a look at a portion of the code from e-RPG program ITEMS in Figure 8.6, we see how this is done.

```
… begin loop to read ITEMPF file
 *
 * Display image of item.  ITITG is the path to the image in the IFS
 *
C                      eval      WrtDta = '<td width="50%" align="center">' +
C                                '<img src="' +
C                                %trim(ITIMG) + '"><br>' +
C                                NewLine
C            EXSR      $WrStout
 *
 * Build a hyperlink to e-RPG program BUYITEM using the item number
 * (ITITEM) and the user id as query string environment variables.
 * The item description (ITDESC) becomes the hyperlink text.
 *
C                      eval      WrtDta = '<a href=' +
C                                '"/cgi-bin/buyitem?USERID=' +
C                                %trim(USERID) +
C                                '&ITEM=' +
C                                %trim(ITITEM) + '">' +
C                                %trim(ITDESC) + '</a><br>' +
C                                NewLine
C            EXSR      $WrStout
 *
 * Display the item price (ITPRC) below the hyperlink.
 *
C                      eval      WrtDta = 'Price: ' +
C                                %trim(%editc(ITPRC:'3')) +
C                                '</td>' +
C                                NewLine
C            EXSR      $WrStout
… end loop
```

Figure 8.6: Code that produces a dynamic image and hyperlink from e-RPG program ITEMS.

If we were to add an item or change any item information, the Web page would be automatically updated with the information read from the ITEMPF file. This is the same for item number, image, and price. This is one of the main factors that makes e-RPG programming so powerful.

We now wish to add the Pentium III 550 machine to our shopping cart. When we click on the description for this item, e-RPG program BUYITEM is called. BUYITEM produces a Web page telling the user that an item has been added to the shopping cart. Figure 8.7 shows this page.

Figure 8.7: Output from e-RPG program BUYITEM.

The output from e-RPG program BUYITEM is rather simple. After adding the information to the invoice files (shopping cart), the item information is displayed on the page. You will also notice that the user now has two options. The user can either click the Return to Shopping hyperlink, which returns to the item display, or the user can click on the Checkout hyperlink. The Checkout hyperlink takes the user to a page to view the contents of the shopping cart and finalize the purchase.

Just to make this more interesting, let's assume that I return to the item display page and select to purchase a keyboard and a notebook computer. After this, I will select the Checkout hyperlink. When I click on this hyperlink, e-RPG program CHECKOUT is called, again passing along the user ID. Figure 8.8 shows the output produced when I check out.

E-RPG program CHECKOUT produces a display that looks similar to an invoice. It displays items, quantities, descriptions, and prices of items. Also, a grand total for all purchases is displayed. On this page, we have three options. Return to Shopping will take us back to the items page where we can continue shopping. Ship Order will confirm that these items are what we want, and will signal BVS-Computers to ship the order. The last option is to remove a line item from an invoice. This is a hyperlink that calls e-RPG program RMVITEM. The invoice number and line item sequence number are passed to this program. This program deletes the specified line item from the invoice. Let's assume I remove the Pentium III 550 computer from the invoice. I would do this by clicking on the hyperlink on this line (the *). Figure 8.9 shows the output produced when this hyperlink is selected.

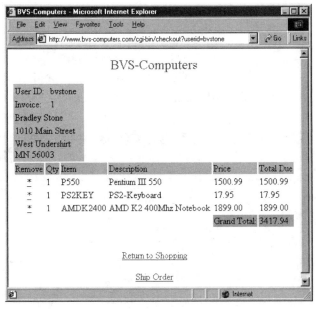

Figure 8.8: Output from e-RPG program CHECKOUT.

Figure 8.9: Output from e-RPG program RMVITEM.

When a user selects to remove an item from the shopping cart, we display a page that tells the user the item was removed, and gives the user the option to continue shopping or to check out.

Now, let's assume we returned to the checkout so that we can ship our order. When Ship Order is selected, a screen thanking the customer for the order is displayed. This is performed by e-RPG program INVSHIP. The invoice number and user ID are passed along to this program, and the invoice is marked as processed. This process empties our shopping cart and tells BVS-Computers to send the items to the customer. Figure 8.10 shows the final display after confirming the order and selecting the Ship Order link.

Figure 8.10: Output from program INVSHIP after the user selects to ship the order.

You'll notice that this page has one more link that lets the user return to shopping. If the user clicks here, the user returns to the page that displays items, and may fill the shopping basket again. This would create a new invoice in the process.

One final note about the BVS-Computers page. You'll notice that there aren't any flashy graphics or anything else appealing. But it is functional. I purposely designed the site this way so that you understand that functionality should come before glamor, something that is overlooked not only by Web developers but project managers as well.

Now that the page is functional, we can fine-tune everything, adding fancy graphics to please the customers and make them feel like they want to return to the site.

SET-UP FOR BVS-COMPUTERS

With the fun comes the work. Setting up your AS/400 for an e-business page requires a little time and understanding of how things work. One thing we do not want to do is compromise the security of our system. This section will take you through the basic steps that are needed to set up BVS-Computers.

HTTP Configuration

Setting up the HTTP configuration for a page such as BVS-Computers isn't that difficult. It only requires a couple Exec and Pass directives as well as a couple more.

I mentioned earlier in this chapter that using the Welcome directive will specify the first page a user will see when they come to your site. If this were not specified, the user could not punch in the URL into the browser and expect a page to appear. Instead, the user would have to specify a document, such as index.html to start. This isn't fun for the user, which is why using the Welcome directive is so powerful, yet easy to use.

Figure 8.11 shows all of the directives that I set up to make BVS-Computers work. As you can see, there really isn't much to it. If you are unsure what each of the directives is doing, please refer back to chapter 4, which discusses each of these directives in detail.

```
Enable GET
Enable HEAD
Enable POST
Exec /cgi-bin/* /QSYS.LIB/AS400CGI.LIB/*.PGM %%EBCDIC%%
Pass /* /bvscomputers/* www.bvs-computers.com
Welcome index.html
```

Figure 8.11: HTTP configurations needed for BVS-Computers.

The Enable directives do exactly what they sound like they would do. They enable certain operations, such as GET and POST, to be performed on our server. Without these, we would not be able to allow users to enter information into forms and process them with our e-RPG programs.

The next directive, Exec, tells the server which directory CGI programs exist in. When a request is made for the /cgi-bin/ directory, the system looks for programs in the AS400CGI library on the AS/400.

The Pass directive tells the server where the user is permitted access. We want them to have access to our files. One thing to make a note of is the www.bvs-computers.com following the Pass information. This specifies to only use this Pass directive when a request is made to this URL. This is handy when setting up an AS/400 with multiple domains.

When a request is made and no path is given, the server looks in the directory BVSCOMPUTERS located in the root file system of the IFS. We locate things such as HTML documents and images in the IFS simply because we will have the best access time locating them here compared to storing them in a folder or QSYS.LIB structure of the AS/400. Another reason for using the root system of the IFS is that it is easier to work with and more like other file systems that are used on other machines.

Finally, the Welcome directive tells the server which document to serve up if no document is requested. When a user enters http://www.bvs-computers.com into their browser, no specific document is requested. The Welcome directive tells the server to display the index.html document in this case. Most servers have this ability. The most common welcome pages used are named index.html or welcome.html.

After you have made these entries in your HTTP configuration, you will have to restart the server instance that is associated with this configuration to let the changes take effect.

Physical Files

The BVS-Computers Web site uses four physical files to process and store data. These files are:

- USERPF – This file stores user information such as user ID, password, and address information.

- ITEMPF – This file stores item information such as item number, description, location of image, and price.

- INVHDRPF – This is the invoice header file. It contains a status code field, a user name and an invoice number. When a user places an item into the shopping basket, this file is checked for an invoice with a status of "O", or open. If one is not found, a new invoice is created.

- INVDETPF – This is the invoice detail file, or shopping basket. When an item is added to the shopping basket, a record is added to this file containing the item information. If the item already exists, the quantity is increased and the file is updated.

All of these files are basic in structure, and similar to what most of us use every day (minus a few details). These files store data the same as any other physical file we use, and they are created with the Create Physical File (CRTPF) command. These files, for convenience sake, should be placed in the library that will contain the CGI programs as specified on the Exec directive in the HTTP configuration. If they are stored in a library other than the CGI, you will need to manipulate the library list before opening the files in your CGI programs.

External Data Structure

BVS-Computers uses one external data structure. The name of the physical file used to reference this data structure is named BVSCOMP. This physical file is also used when calling the QtmhCvtDB API. It is referenced as the physical file descriptions to use when parsing data. This file contains fields that are used for standard input or query string environment variables. This file contains the following fields:

- USERID – The User ID
- PASSWORD – The User Password
- ITEM – Item Number
- INV – Invoice Number
- SEQ – Sequence Number

If you review the URLs in the illustrations throughout this chapter for the BVS-Computers Web page, you would see these field names used. These names also are used when building the HTML forms. The names must be the same; otherwise the QtmhCvtDB API will not know what to do with them.

Be careful to use the correct case when using these field names. This really only applies to building HTML files, since e-RPG programs will automatically convert letters to upper case. But, if you name a field EMAIL (all caps) in your HTML form, you must reference it in the rest of the HTML page, including any JavaScript, in all capital letters.

To make this easier, I tend to always use lowercase when building HTML forms and naming fields. This also tends to not draw so much attention to them when they are passed as query string environment variables. For example, examine the following URLs:

```
www.bvstools.com/cgi-bin/CGIPGM?NAME=Brad&AGE=29
www.bvstools.com/cgi-bin/cgipgm?name=Brad&age=29
```

You'll notice that the first URL draws more attention to it because of the capital letters. The second URL is not noticed as easily. In the end, though, it's entirely up to you how you want to specify your field names.

E-RPG Programs

The e-RPG programs in this example each perform a specific function and output unique information to the Web page. When building Web pages using CGI programming, you will find that it almost forces you to create a modular application.

This is good in that creation and maintenance will be easier, because you can work on each part while not affecting others. This also helps split up the work among more than one programmer. The programs used are as follows:

- SIGNIN – This program processes the information passed from the first page. It displays an error if the user ID or password is invalid, or a page that allows the user to go shopping if the information is correct.

- ITEMS – This program displays available items by reading through the ITEMPF file. It uses the information from this file to display the item image and create the hyperlink, which allows the user to add this item to the shopping cart.

- BUYITEM – This program adds the selected item to the user's shopping cart.

- CHECKOUT – This program displays the items currently in the user's shopping cart. It allows the user to ship the items or to remove certain line items from the shopping cart.

- RMVITEM – This program removes the selected line item from the invoice. This option is available from the screen created by program CHECKOUT.

- INVSHIP – This program runs when the user selects the ship option from the checkout page. This program marks the invoice as processed and displays a thank you message for the user.

Because the HTTP APIs are used in each of these programs, when creating them you must bind the QTMHCGI service program to them. You can do this in one of two ways. The first is by specifying the QTMHCGI service program in a binding directory. The second is by creating modules from these programs first, and then specifying the QTMHCGI service program with the Create Program (CRTPGM) command.

I prefer to use a binding directory rather than create modules first and then use CRTPGM to bind them together. When you specify a binding directory on the

CRTBNDRPG command, it automatically searches the binding directory for any modules or service programs used in the program.

If you are using a version of OS/400 that allows you to specify H-Specs for this type of information, it makes the process even easier. If you specify the following in your H-Specs, you can still use option 14 in PDM to create your programs without having to worry about specifying other parameters on the CRTBNDRPG program.

```
H DFTACTGRP(*NO) BNDDIR('CGIBNDDIR')
```

This H-Spec will take care of it for you. As you can see in the example, I call my binding directory CGIBNDDIR. If you name yours something different, be sure to specify it in place CGIBNDDIR.

The HTML File

This example only includes an HTML file. This file is named index.html and is stored in the root structure of the IFS. I placed my index.html file in a directory named /bvscomputers because the Pass directive I use tells the server to look in this directory for documents.

All other Web pages in this example are created dynamically using e-RPG programs. If I had any other pages that could remain static, I would place them in this directory as well. An example of another static page could be a page named aboutus.html. When the user views this page, the user would see information about BVS-Computers. Because this information would not depend on data stored on the AS/400, it could be created as a static HTML file and uploaded to the IFS.

THE FUTURE OF BVS-COMPUTERS

While BVS-Computers is a purely fictional Web page and company, it is a good example of how you can use the AS/400 for e-commerce in your business. Creating a successful site not only depends on making the site aesthetically pleasing, but it also must be functional, fast, and consistent.

The AS/400 has the potential to provide all of these features. Because it is already a leading database server, it is already ahead of the pack. With new AS/400 models being delivered and marketed as server machines, the speed will also be there.

We've all depended on the AS/400 for years as one of the most stable machines in the industry. This translates to more up-time, the ability to handle more requests, and the use of RPG to handle database serving needs, something most of us already know how to do.

With the prices of the newer, faster AS/400 models dropping from day to day, you can't afford not to invest in an AS/400 as your e-commerce solution. It's time to build your own BVS-Computers site!

9

HTTP SERVICE PROGRAMS

Throughout this book, I have given examples of how to write e-RPG programs using the APIs supplied by IBM. Although these examples are functional, they lack the luster and maintainability that we have become accustomed to using every day RPG op-codes such as EXFMT, WRITE, UPDATE, and EVAL.

When I first started writing e-RPG programs, I ran into this very situation. I was having a ball writing Web applications with RPG, but I found that when I needed to make changes, it wasn't always as easy as I had hoped. This is mainly because of two things. First, the use of APIs usually results in cumbersome code that is hard to decipher. Second, writing HTML to a browser requires the use of a lot of string manipulation.

I quickly found that applying my ILE skills to these Web applications made writing e-RPG programs much easier. It helped with maintainability and with the ability to read what the code was doing. I ended up reusing a large portion of the code I had already written by creating service programs for the APIs used and also for formatting HTML text.

If you haven't looked into what ILE can do for you, I strongly suggest that you do. ILE will help in your everyday applications, and will especially come in handy when writing CGI programs. The biggest help I have found with ILE is the ability to encapsulate system APIs into easy-to-use subprocedures.

This chapter will give a few examples of the service programs that I have created as well as describe the subprocedures contained within, and how they are used. I will also show you how you can use them in your Web programming to make your life easier, as well as allowing you to produce applications much more quickly.

STANDARD HTTP SUBPROCEDURES

The first service program I created contained a collection of subprocedures that made the interfaces to the APIs used for CGI programming much easier. Because this service program takes advantage of the Integrated Language Environment (ILE), it could also be used by programmers who don't program in RPG. COBOL, for instance, can use the same service program and the subprocedures defined within.

In taking the step from using APIs to subprocedures, I first looked at all of the API calls that I had made up to this point. One thing that was constant in almost all of the cases was that even though the API required from three to five parameters, only one or two of them contained data that I had to produce before the call. Most of them required input parameters, and returned data. I really only needed to change one or two parameters because the other parameters could be derived before the call to the API from the data that I was sending to the API.

For example, a lot of these APIs require the use of a string that is used to send or receive data from the API. Along with this parameter is another that specifies the size of the data. The size of the data can, in most cases, be figured directly before the call, so this is a parameter that I could omit from my subprocedures.

This may seem confusing, but you will see how this all falls into place after studying the subprocedures that follow. The naming schemes I used for the suprocedures are rather simple. I removed the standard Qtmh prefix from the API names and substituted the pound sign (#).

Using the pound sign as the first character in subprocedures is a standard that I use simply so that I know that what I am using is a user-created subprocedure. You could choose to do the same, or you can use your own standard.

The #WrStout Subprocedure

The first and easiest subprocedure to write was #WrStout. This subprocedure uses the Write to Standard Output (QtmhWrStout) API and makes the interface as simple as passing a string of text. This means I was able to reduce the number of parameters needed to write standard output to a browser from three to one.

Figure 9.1 contains the source for the #WrStout subprocedure. As you can see, all it does is call the QtmhWrStout API. The data passed into the subprocedure is the text you wish to write to the browser. The length of the data is determined using the %LEN Built In Function (BIF) immediately before the call to the API.

```
*//////////////////////////////////////////////////////////////*
* (#WrStout) Write HTML to Web Page using the QtmhWrStout API  *
*                                                              *
* Use: #WrStout(HTML_string)                                   *
*//////////////////////////////////////////////////////////////*
P #WrStout        B                    EXPORT
 *                                                          -*
D #WrStout        PI
D  WrtDta                      1024    VALUE
 *
D WrtDtaLen       S              9B 0
 *                                                          -*
C                 eval      WrtDtaLen = %len(%trim(WrtDta))
 *
C                 CALLB     'QtmhWrStout'
C                 PARM                    WrtDta
C                 PARM                    WrtDtaLen
C                 PARM                    WPError
 *                                                          -*
P #WrStout        E
```

Figure 9.1: The #WrStout subprocedure.

The #WrStout subprocedure accepts one parameter as input. The parameter is the string of HTML text that you wish to output to the browser. What a time saver! So, instead of a piece of code that calls the QtmhWrtStout API (shown in Figure 9.2).

```
C                    eval       WrtDta = '     Table Data</TD>'
C                    eval       WrtDtaLen = %len(%trim(WrtDta))
 *
C                    CALLB      'QtmhWrStout'
C                    PARM                      WrtDta
C                    PARM                      WrtDtaLen
C                    PARM                      WPError
```

Figure 9.2: The QtmhWrtStout API.

You end up with a simple call as shown in Figure 9.3.

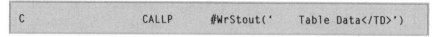

```
C                    CALLP      #WrStout('     Table Data</TD>')
```

Figure 9.3: The time-saving #WrStrout subprocedure.

The data that is used in the input parameter of the #WrStout subprocedure can be a text literal or a variable name containing the HTML text that you wish to write to standard output. I usually build the HTML that I want to write to the browser and place it in a variable. Then I call the #WrStout subprocedure using the variable as a parameter. It is much easier to use this method, rather than have all literal text values if I needed to debug the value.

I use the #WrStout subprocedure in virtually every e-RPG program that I write. I am sure that you will find it very useful as well. If you want to test it out, I encourage you to go back to the examples given earlier in this book, and convert the calls to the QtmhWrStout API to statements using the #WrStout subprocedure.

The #GetEnv Subprocedure

The #GetEnv subprocedure is used to retrieve environment variables. The QtmhGetEnv API is the core of this subprocedure. If you recall from previous chapters, this API is used to retrieve environment variable information such as query string data or content length data.

The source for the #GetEnv subprocedure is shown in Figure 9.4.

```
 *//////////////////////////////////////////////////////////////*
 * (#GetEnv)  Get Environment Variables                          *
 *                                                               *
 * Use: #GetEnv(environment record :                             *
 *              environment record length :                      *
 *              environment variable name)                       *
 *                                                               *
 *//////////////////////////////////////////////////////////////*
 P #GetEnv          B                        EXPORT
 *                                                              -*
 D #GetEnv          PI
 D  EnvRec                        1024
 D  EnvLen                           9B 0
 D  EnvName                         64    VALUE
 *
 D  EnvRecLen      S                 9B 0 INZ(%size(EnvRec))
 D  EnvNameLen     S                 9B 0
 *                                                              -*
 C                  eval           EnvNameLen = %len(%trim(EnvName))
 *
 C                  CALLB          'QtmhGetEnv'
 C                  PARM                         EnvRec
 C                  PARM                         EnvRecLen
 C                  PARM                         EnvLen
 C                  PARM                         EnvName
 C                  PARM                         EnvNameLen
 C                  PARM                         WPError
 *                                                              -*
 P #GetEnv          E
```

Figure 9.4: The #GetEnv subprocedure.

The #GetEnv subprocedure uses three variables. The first is an output parameter that will contain the value of the environment variable after a call to the subprocedure is made. The second parameter is also an output parameter and returns the length of the data in the first parameter. The third parameter is an input parameter and must contain the name of the environment variable you wish to retrieve. For example, if you wanted to retrieve the query string data, you would specify QUERY_STRING in this parameter. If you wanted to retrieve the content length value, you would specify CONTENT_LENGTH.

The #GetEnv subprocedure is called using the CALLP op-code. For example, in an e-RPG program, the call to this subprocedure would look like the example in Figure 9.5, if we were receiving the query string environment variables.

```
C                          eval      EnvName = 'QUERY_STRING'
C                          CALLP     #GetEnv(EnvRec:EnvLen:EnvName)
```

Figure 9.5: The CALLP op-code for the #GetEnv subprocedure.

First, we fill the variable EnvName with the name of the environment variable we wish to retrieve. In this case, we wish to retrieve the query string data, so we use the value QUERY_STRING. Next, we call the #GetEnv subprocedure using the CALLP op-code. When the call is complete, the variable EnvRec will contain the value of the query string data, and EnvLen will contain the length of that data.

If you refer back to an example using the QtmhGetEnv API in a previous chapter, it should be obvious, especially in this case, why using a subprocedure in your e-RPG program makes this process much easier.

The #RdStin Subprocedure

Reading input from a browser is another great example of an API that can be transformed into a subprocedure for a reduction in code. Once this subprocedure is available in a service program, you'll never look at reading from standard input as a chore again. Figure 9.6 contains the source for the #RdStin Subprocedure.

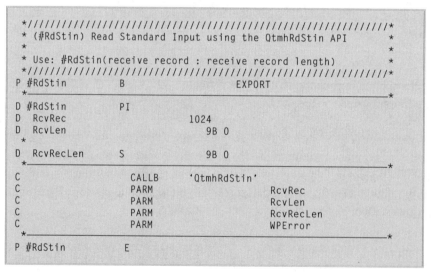

```
 *///////////////////////////////////////////////////////////*
 * (#RdStin) Read Standard Input using the QtmhRdStin API     *
 *                                                            *
 * Use: #RdStin(receive record : receive record length)       *
 *///////////////////////////////////////////////////////////*
P #RdStin         B                   EXPORT
 *-----------------------------------------------------------*
D #RdStin         PI
D  RcvRec                        1024
D  RcvLen                          9B 0
 *
D  RcvRecLen      S                9B 0
 *-----------------------------------------------------------*
C                     CALLB     'QtmhRdStin'
C                     PARM                    RcvRec
C                     PARM                    RcvLen
C                     PARM                    RcvRecLen
C                     PARM                    WPError
 *-----------------------------------------------------------*
P #RdStin         E
```

Figure 9.6: The #RdStin subprocedure.

188

The #RdStin subprocedure requires two variables. The first variable is an output variable that will contain the standard input data upon completion of the call to the QtmhRdStin API. The second is an input variable that contains the length of the data to read from standard input.

If you remember from the chapter that discussed the HTTP APIs, you will recall that reading from standard input is a two step process. First, we must retrieve the content length environment variable, convert this value into a numeric value, and then pass it to the Read from Standard Input (QtmhRdStin) API. If we do not use this process, most likely the last parameter from standard input will be dropped.

Lucky for us we already have a subprocedure that will read environment variables in the form of #GetEnv! The only thing that is required now is for you to write your own subprocedure that converts character data into numeric data. I have one written that is named #CtoN (CharactertoNumeric) and is included in appendix G, along with the full source for all of these subprocedures.

Now, how does the call to retrieve standard input look? Well, it involves three steps as shown in Figure 9.7.

```
C                eval      EnvName = 'CONTENT_LENGTH'
C                CALLP     #GetEnv(EnvRec:EnvLen:EnvName)
C                eval      RcvLen = #CtoN(EnvRec)
C                CALLP     #RdStin(RcvRec:RcvLen)
```

Figure 9.7: The call to retrieve standard input.

First, we set the environment variable to be read to CONTENT_LENGTH. Next, we call the #GetEnv subprocedure to retrieve the content length environment variable. Next, we convert the value returned from the #GetEnv subprocedure from character into numeric using the #CtoN subprocedure. Lastly, we call the #RdStin subprocedure, which will return the standard input variable into the field RcvRec.

The #CvtDb Subprocedure

The #CvtDb subprocedure is used to convert standard input or query string environment variable data into a format that is usable in your programs. This data is done using the QtmhCvtDB API. This process requires that you supply two items:

- A data structure containing field names that are the same as those on the HTML input form.

- A file name containing field names that are the same as those on the input form.

The file name that you supply is used to convert the data retrieved into the correct data type. After the data is converted, the values are placed into the data structure that you provide.

Figure 9.8 contains the source for the #CvtDB subprocedure.

```
*////////////////////////////////////////////////////////////////////*
 * (#CvtDB) Convert to DB                                             *
 *                                                                    *
 * Use: #CvtDb(receive record : receive record length :              *
 *             convert status : data structure pointer)              *
 *                                                                    *
 *////////////////////////////////////////////////////////////////////*
P #CvtDB          B                   EXPORT
  *-----------------------------------------------------------------*
D #CvtDB          PI
D   RcvRec                      31000     VALUE
D   RcvLen                         9B 0
D   CvtStat                        9B 0
D   RcvDS@                          *
 *
D File_DS         E DS                   EXTNAME(FILENAME)
 *
D RcvFile         DS
D   File                     1    10     INZ('FILENAME  ')
D   Lib                     11    20     INZ('FILELIB   ')
 *
D RcvRecLen       S               9B 0 INZ(%size(RcvRec))
D CvtLen          S               9B 0 INZ(%size(File_DS))
  *-----------------------------------------------------------------*
C                   CALLB     'QtmhCvtDb'
C                   PARM                    RcvFile
C                   PARM                    RcvRec
C                   PARM                    RcvRecLen
```

Figure 9.8: The #CvtDB subprocedure (part 1 of 2).

190

```
C                      PARM                      File_DS
C                      PARM                      CvtLen
C                      PARM                      RcvLen
C                      PARM                      CvtStat
C                      PARM                      WPError
 *
C                      eval       RcvDS@ = %addr(File_DS)
 *------------------------------------------------------------*
P #CvtDB           E
```

Figure 9.8: The #CvtDB subprocedure (part 2 of 2).

You might wonder why the file name and library values are not passed as input parameters, because these could change from application to application. The main reason that I chose to code them in the subprocedure is because it is important that the file used and the data structure used contain the same field names and data types for each of the fields.

There is another part of this subprocedure that might seem unclear to you. This is the use of a pointer to return the data structure information to the calling program.

This subprocedure uses a data structure named FILE_DS as the receiver of the data. Because we cannot return a data structure as a parameter, I have chosen to return a pointer that contains a reference to the location of this data structure to any calling program. The calling program will then use this pointer to point a duplicate data structure to the location of the FILE_DS data structure, thus filling it with the data retrieved by the QtmhCvtDB API.

Figure 9.9 contains an example of how the #CvtDB subprocedure is used.

```
D EnvDS           E DS                      EXTNAME(BADDLRDS)
D                                           BASED(EnvDS@)
D EnvDS@          S                    *
D EnvRec          S               1024
D EnvLen          S               9B 0
D EnvName         S               64
 *
C                      eval       EnvName = 'QUERY_STRING'
C                      CALLP      #GetEnv(EnvRec:EnvLen:EnvName)
C                      CALLP      #CvtDB(EnvRec:EnvLen:EnvDS@)
```

Figure 9.9: Using the #CvtDB subprocedure.

First, the variable EnvName is set to retrieve the query string variable. Next, a call to the #GetEnv subprocedure is performed. After this call, the variable EnvRec will contain the query string variable. Let's assume for this example that the following data is retrieved into the EnvRec variable:

```
FNAME=Brad&LNAME=STONE&GENDER=M&AGE=30
```

The information retrieved was entered on a form using the GET method. The form contained four fields: First Name (FNAME), Last Name (LNAME), Gender (GENDER), and Age (AGE).

The value of EnvLen will contain the value 38, because this is the length of the data retrieved.

Now we have all the information for the query string variables. We now want to use the #CvtDB subprocedure to parse the data so that we can use it. The first two parameters used in the #CvtDB subprocedure are exactly the same as those retrieved from the #GetEnv subprocedure. The variables EnvRec and EnvLen contain the data and length of data, respectively, that the #CvtDB subprocedure requires.

The last parameter is named EnvDS@. This is a pointer data type. If you remember from the source code for the #CvtDB subprocedure, this third parameter is an output parameter and contains the pointer location for the data structure that contains the parsed data. After this call, the variable EnvDS@ will contain this value. Because the data structure EnvDS is based on this pointer, it will contain a mirror image of the data that was retrieved into the File_DS data structure after the call to the QtmhCvtDB API used in the #CvtDB subprocedure.

Now you can see why applications will require their own #CvtDB subprocedure. The File_DS data structure in the #CvtDB subprocedure and the EnvDS data structure in your CGI program must be exactly the same. Because they are external data structures, the EXTNAME keyword should contain the same filename in both instances. The file used to externally describe these data structures is usually the same file used as the filename parameter in the QtmhCvtDB API call.

HTML SUBPROCEDURES

Along with creating subprocedures that make HTTP programming easier, I also have created a few subprocedures that make coding HTML a little easier. The subprocedures do one thing. They accept a string of text, and return a formatted HTML statement that can be pasted directly into your Web page.

The subprocedures listed here may or may not be of use to you. I found most of them useful because it was easier to read a call to a function than a long concatenation of strings and HTML tags. If you find that these subprocedures make CGI and HTML programming easier, you may want to try creating a few of your own or modifying those given here. Now, let's take a look at what they do.

Create Hyperlink (#Link)

The #Link subprocedure was the first HTML function that I created. I was simply getting tired of coding a long concatenation for each hyperlink that I was placing on my Web page with an e-RPG program. The #Link subprocedure may not seem very useful at first, but after coding hyperlinks a few times, I think you'll see why I found it useful.

The #Link subprocedure accepts a total of three parameters: the last parameter is optional. The first parameter is the URL of the page you want the hyperlink to link to. The second parameter is the text that you want to appear on the screen as a hyperlink.

For example, if you want to display the text "My Homepage!" as a hyperlink that, when clicked, redirects the user to the URL http://www.myhomepage.com, you would specify the following statement in your e-RPG program to return the formatted HTML statement:

```
C                eval      Link = #Link("http://www.myhompage.com" :
C                                        "My Homepage!")
```

After the call to the #Link subprocedure, the variable Link will contain the formatted HTML text that you can write to the browser to produce a link with the
text specified.

The last parameter is optional. If this parameter is used, you should specify the
name of a JavaScript function to call when the hyperlink is clicked on. This can
be useful when you would rather execute JavaScript instead of redirecting the
browser. The code for the #Link subprocedure is shown in Figure 9.10.

```
 *//////////////////////////////////////////////////////////////*
 * (#Link) Return HTML code for an href link                    *
 *                                                              *
 * Use: #Link(URL : Text {:onClick function})                   *
 *                                                              *
 *//////////////////////////////////////////////////////////////*
P #Link           B                   EXPORT
 *------------------------------------------------------------------*
D #Link           PI           1024
D  Link                         512    VALUE
D  Text                         512    VALUE
D  onClick                      256    VALUE OPTIONS(*NOPASS)
 *
D RtnText         S            1024
 *------------------------------------------------------------------*
C                 eval      RtnText = '<a href="' +
C                                     %trim(Link) + '"'
 *
C                 if        (%parms > 2) and (onClick <> ' ')
C                 eval      RtnText = %trim(RtnText) + ' ' +
C                                     'onClick="' +
C                                     %trim(onClick) + '"'
C                 endif
 *
C                 eval      RtnText = %trim(RtnText) +
C                                     '>' +
C                                     %trim(Text) +
C                                     '</a>'
 *
C                 RETURN    RtnText
 *------------------------------------------------------------------*
P #Link           E
```

Figure 9.10: The #Link subprocedure.

As with any of the subprocedures in this chapter, feel free to modify them to suit
your needs. These subprocedures work well for me, but everyone likes to use
their own style.

Create MailTo: Hyperlink (#MailTo)

The #MailTo subprocedure is similar to the #Link subprocedure. It is used to return the formatted HTML text for a mailto hyperlink. If you remember from
chapter 1, a mailto hyperlink is used to open an e-mail document instead of redirecting the browser. A mailto hyperlink is useful when you want to list names on
a page and allow the user to click on any of the names and automatically open a
mail document with an e-mail address already entered in the To: location.

The #MailTo subprocedure accepts two parameters. The first parameter is the
e-mail address you wish to send mail to when the link is clicked. The second is the
name of the person you wish to be assigned to the e-mail address. The name used
in the second parameter will be the name shown on the browser as the mailto
hyperlink. The source for the #MailTo subprocedure is shown in Figure 9.11.

```
*//////////////////////////////////////////////////////////////*
* (#MailTo) Return HTML code for mailto tag                     *
*                                                               *
* Use: #MailTo(E-Mail Address : Name)                           *
*                                                               *
*//////////////////////////////////////////////////////////////*
P #MailTo          B                      EXPORT
*                                                                *
D #MailTo          PI           1024
D EMail                           50      VALUE
D User                            30      VALUE
*                                                                *
C                  RETURN       '<a href=mailto:' +
C                               %trim(EMail) +
C                               '>' +
C                               %trim(User) +
C                               '</a>'
*                                                                *
P #MailTo          E
```

Figure 9.11: The #MailTo subprocedure.

As you can see, the #MailTo subprocedure simply takes the e-mail address and
name passed as parameters, and formats a mailto hyperlink, which is then returned to the calling program as formatted HTML text.

A good use for the #MailTo subprocedure is to produce a database of names of
people in your department that includes a field for e-mail addresses. Creating a

dynamic list on your Web page would be a simple program that would read through this file and call the #MailTo subprocedure for each entry in the file. When the file is changed, so would the list displayed on the Web page.

Return Bold Text (#Bold)

The #Bold subprocedure is one of the more simple subprocedures in this section. This subprocedure accepts only one parameter: the text that you wish to display in a bold font on the browser.

I find this subprocedure useful because I grow tired of concatenating the <B> and </B> HTML tags around text that I want to display as bold. Call me lazy, but at least this way I will be sure that the tags I use are correct. (After coding boldface a few times, you might have the tendency to accidentally leave the slash out of the ending tag.) The source for the #Bold subprocedure is shown in Figure 9.12.

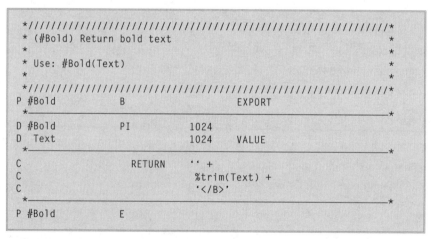

```
*///////////////////////////////////////////////////////////////*
* (#Bold) Return bold text                                       *
*                                                                *
* Use: #Bold(Text)                                               *
*                                                                *
*///////////////////////////////////////////////////////////////*
P #Bold           B                        EXPORT
 *------------------------------------------------------------------*
D #Bold           PI           1024
D  Text                        1024     VALUE
 *------------------------------------------------------------------*
C                 RETURN       '' +
C                              %trim(Text) +
C                              '</B>'
 *------------------------------------------------------------------*
P #Bold           E
```

Figure 9.12: Source for the #Bold subprocedure.

The #Bold subprocedure is rather simple. It takes the text parameter passed into it and returns the text surrounded by the HTML tags needed to display the text in bold on the browser.

Return Italic Text (#Italics)

The #Italics subprocedure is used to return text that you wish to display in italics on the browser. This subprocedure is similar to the #Bold subprocedure, in that it simply takes the single text parameter value passed into it and returns formatted HTML text that you can use on your Web page to display text in italics.

Again, the main purpose of making such a simple subprocedure is that the formatting for the italics HTML text will reside only in one place, this subprocedure. I don't have to worry about typos, such as leaving the slash out of the ending tag, which I might make if I were not using the subprocedure. The source for the #Italics subprocedure is shown in Figure 9.13.

```
*////////////////////////////////////////////////////////////*
 * (#Italics) Return italics text                             *
 *                                                            *
 * Use: #Italics(Text)                                        *
 *                                                            *
 *////////////////////////////////////////////////////////////*
P #Italics        B                    EXPORT
 *----------------------------------------------------------*
D #Italics        PI           1024
D Text                         1024    VALUE
 *----------------------------------------------------------*
C                 RETURN       '' +
C                              %trim(Text) +
C                              '</I>'
 *----------------------------------------------------------*
P #Italics        E
```

Figure 9.13: The source for the #Italics subprocedure.

Return Centered Text (#Center)

The #Center subprocedure is used to return a value that will display centered text on your browser. As with the #Bold and #Italics subprocedures, #Center simply places the beginning and ending HTML tags around the single text parameter passed into it. The source for the #Center subprocedure is shown in Figure 9.14.

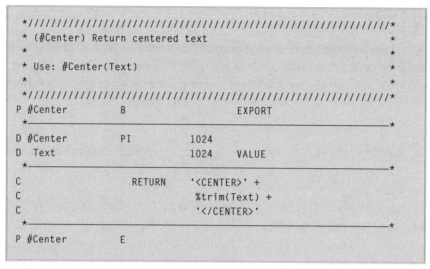

```
*////////////////////////////////////////////////////////////*
* (#Center) Return centered text                               *
*                                                              *
* Use: #Center(Text)                                           *
*                                                              *
*////////////////////////////////////////////////////////////*
P #Center          B                        EXPORT
*------------------------------------------------------------*
D #Center          PI            1024
D  Text                          1024    VALUE
*------------------------------------------------------------*
C                  RETURN        '<CENTER>' +
C                                %trim(Text) +
C                                '</CENTER>'
*------------------------------------------------------------*
P #Center          E
```

Figure 9.14: The source for the #Center subprocedure.

One interesting note about the previous three subprocedures is that they can all be used together in one EVAL statement to produce text that is bold, italic, and centered. Let's assume the text we are formatting is "Welcome" and we want this text to contain all three attributes. We could use the following RPG statement:

```
C                    eval      Out = #Center(#Italics(#Bold('Welcome')))
```

When executed, the variable Out will contain the value:

```
<CENTER>Welcome</B></I></CENTER>
```

This is what makes writing your own subprocedures powerful, whether they are to be used for CGI programming or not. This is one feature that I definitely was happy to be able to use in RPG, as well as in languages that I have used in the past.

Return Input Field (#Input)

The #Input subprocedure is a little more involved than the previous three subprocedures. The #Input subprocedure returns the text for an input object.

This subprocedure can accept up to five parameters, the first of which is the only required parameter.

The first parameter is used to tell the compiler what type of input object you wish to create. In our examples, we have seen types such as Text, Button, and Submit; each one performs a different function. The value used in this parameter should be the same as the HTML type you would specify if you were coding the input object in HTML.

The rest of the parameters are optional, but you should remember that if you want to use one, you must use all the parameters that come before it. For example, if you want to use the fourth parameter, you must specify a value for the second and third parameters as well. Specifying a blank is valid for any of the following parameters, and they will be treated as if you did not specify a value.

The second parameter should specify the name of the input object you wish to create. For example, if you were creating an input field that is to contain an e-mail address and want to name it EMAIL, you should specify this name in the second parameter. Remember that HTML is case sensitive, and so is this parameter.

The third parameter should specify the size of the input object you wish to create. Using the example above, you may want to specify that the field is 35 characters long. Specifying '35' in this parameter sets the size attribute of this input field to 35.

The fourth parameter can be used to specify an initial value of the object. For example, if you have a form that contains a field that holds a quantity, you may want to initialize it to a beginning value.

The fifth and last parameter is used to specify a JavaScript function to call when the object is clicked. This parameter will mainly be used when the type of the input object is specified as Button. When the button is clicked, the JavaScript function specified in this parameter will be called. The source for the #Input function is shown in Figure 9.15.

```
 *///////////////////////////////////////////////////////////////*
 * (#Input) Return Input                                          *
 *                                                                *
 * Use: #Input(Input Type : {Name : Size : Value :               *
 *             onClick function})                                 *
 *                                                                *
 *///////////////////////////////////////////////////////////////*
 P #Input           B                    EXPORT
 *---------------------------------------------------------------*
 D #Input           PI         1024
 D  Type                        256      VALUE
 D  Name                        256      VALUE OPTIONS(*NOPASS)
 D  Size                        256      VALUE OPTIONS(*NOPASS)
 D  VALUE                       256      VALUE OPTIONS(*NOPASS)
 D  onClick                     256      VALUE OPTIONS(*NOPASS)
 *
 D RtnText           S         1024
 *---------------------------------------------------------------*
 C                   eval      RtnText = '<INPUT TYPE=' +
 C                                       %trim(Type)
 *
 C                   if        (%parms > 1) and (Name  '< >')
 C                   eval      RtnText = %trim(RtnText) + ' ' +
 C                                       'NAME=' +
 C                                       %trim(Name)
 C                   endif
 *
 C                   if        (%parms > 2) and (Size  '< >')
 C                   eval      RtnText = %trim(RtnText) + ' ' +
 C                                       'SIZE=' +
 C                                       %trim(Size)
 C                   endif
 *
 C                   if        (%parms > 3) and (VALUE  '< >')
 C                   eval      RtnText = %trim(RtnText) + ' ' +
 C                                       'VALUE=' +
 C                                       %trim(VALUE)
 C                   endif
 *
 C                   if        (%parms > 4) and (onClick  '< >')
 C                   eval      RtnText = %trim(RtnText) + ' ' +
 C                                       'onClick="' +
 C                                       %trim(onClick) + '"'
 C                   endif
 *
 C                   eval      RtnText = %trim(RtnText) + '>'
 *
 C                   RETURN    RtnText
 *---------------------------------------------------------------*
 P #Input           E
```

Figure 9.15: Source for the #Input subprocedure.

The #Input subprocedure takes the values passed into it and builds a formatted HTML statement that will create the desired input field. This is one subprocedure that you might wish to modify for your specific needs.

Write Source Member (#WrtSrcMbr)

The #WrtSrcMbr subprocedure is used to write a section of HTML or JavaScript code to your Web page. The source that is written is stored in the source physical file member of your choice.

You will find this useful when you have a collection of JavaScript functions that you use over and over, such as the basic functions used in creating and retrieving values from cookies. Also, if you have standard headings or sections of HTML that are static, storing this code in a source member and using the #WrtSrcMbr subprocedure will take hours off your development time.

The #WrtSrcMbr subprocedure accepts three parameters. The first is the library that contains the file in which the source member containing the JavaScript is located. The second is the file name. I tend to store all my JavaScript in a source physical file named QHTMLSRC. The third parameter is the name of the member that contains the JavaScript source. Figure 9.16 contains the source for the #WrtSrcMbr subprocedure.

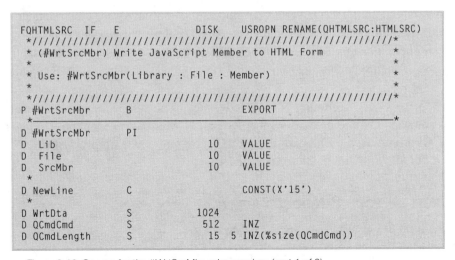

```
FQHTMLSRC  IF   E           DISK    USROPN RENAME(QHTMLSRC:HTMLSRC)
 *//////////////////////////////////////////////////////////////////*
 * (#WrtSrcMbr) Write JavaScript Member to HTML Form               *
 *                                                                  *
 * Use: #WrtSrcMbr(Library : File : Member)                        *
 *                                                                  *
 *//////////////////////////////////////////////////////////////////*
P #WrtSrcMbr      B                   EXPORT
 *-----------------------------------------------------------------*
D #WrtSrcMbr      PI
D  Lib                          10    VALUE
D  File                         10    VALUE
D  SrcMbr                       10    VALUE
 *
D NewLine         C                   CONST(X'15')
 *
D WrtDta          S           1024
D QCmdCmd         S            512    INZ
D QCmdLength      S             15  5 INZ(%size(QCmdCmd))
```

Figure 9.16: Source for the #WrtSrcMbr subprocedure (part 1 of 2).

```
 *──────────────────────────────────────────────────────────────*
 C          if          (Lib = ' ')
 C          eval        Lib = '*LIBL'
 C          endif
 *
 C          eval        QCmdCmd = 'OVRDBF FILE' +
 C                                '(QHTMLSRC) ' +
 C                                'TOFILE(' +
 C                                %trim(Lib) + '/' +
 C                                %trim(File) +
 C                                ') MBR(' +
 C                                %trim(SrcMbr) + ')'
 *
 C          CALL        'QCMDEXC'                               99
 C          PARM                    QCmdCmd
 C          PARM                    QCmdLength
 *
 C          OPEN        QHTMLSRC
 C          READ        QHTMLSRC                                69
 *
 C          dow         (not *IN69)
 C          eval        WrtDta = SRCDTA + NewLine
 C          CALLP       #WrStout(WrtDta)
 C          READ        QHTMLSRC                                69
 C          enddo
 *
 C          CLOSE       QHTMLSRC
 *────────────────────────────────────────────────────────────*
 P #WrtSrcMbr      E
```

Figure 9.16: Source for the #WrtSrcMbr subprocedure (part 2 of 2).

You will see that the #WrtSrcMbr subprocedure simply overrides the member with the values passed into it via the Override Database File (OVRDBF) command. Then, it simply reads and writes the source, adding a new-line character to the end of each statement.

If you have a large section of HTML code, such as headings that rarely change, and you want them to be consistent among all of your pages, even those created by CGI programs, the first part of your CGI program could simply write the static HTML from the member specified.

MISCELLANEOUS SUBROCEDURES

In addition to the subprocedures described above, I have also written a few subprocedures that I find very useful not only in e-RPG programming, but also in everyday programming.

Convert Character to Numeric (#CtoN)

The Convert Character to Numeric (#CtoN) subprocedure returns the numeric representation of the character value passed into it. This is useful when converting the values returned from the CONTENT_LENGTH environment variable for use with the Read Standard Input API.

The only parameter that you need to pass to the #CtoN suprocedure is the value that you wish to convert to numeric. After the call, #CtoN returns the numeric representation of that value. Figure 9.17 contains the source for the #CtoN subprocedure.

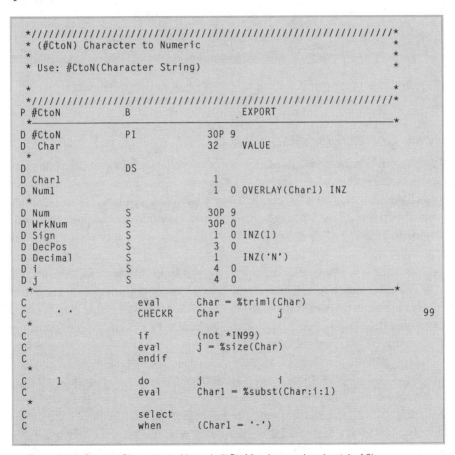

```
*//////////////////////////////////////////////////////////////*
* (#CtoN) Character to Numeric                                  *
*                                                               *
* Use: #CtoN(Character String)                                  *
*                                                               *
*                                                               *
*//////////////////////////////////////////////////////////////*
P #CtoN           B                     . EXPORT
 *                                                              *
D #CtoN           PI            30P 9
D  Char                         32     VALUE
 *
D                 DS
D Char1                          1
D Num1                           1  0 OVERLAY(Char1) INZ
 *
D Num             S             30P 9
D WrkNum          S             30P 0
D Sign            S              1  0 INZ(1)
D DecPos          S              3  0
D Decimal         S              1    INZ('N')
D i               S              4  0
D j               S              4  0
 *
C                   eval      Char = %triml(Char)
C         ' '       CHECKR    Char          j                   99
 *
C                   if        (not *IN99)
C                   eval      j = %size(Char)
C                   endif
 *
C         1         do        j             i
C                   eval      Char1 = %subst(Char:i:1)
 *
C                   select
C                   when      (Char1 = '-')
```

Figure 9.17: Convert Character to Numeric (#CtoN) subprocedure (part 1 of 2).

```
C                   eval      Sign = -1
C                   when      (Char1 = '.')
C                   eval      Decimal = 'Y'
C                   when      (Char1 >= '0') and (Char1 <= '9')
C                   eval      WrkNum = (WrkNum * 10 + Num1)
C *
C                   if        (Decimal = 'Y')
C                   eval      DecPos = (DecPos + 1)
C                   endif
C *
C                   endsl
C *
C                   enddo
C *
C                   eval(h)   Num = (WrkNum * Sign / (10 ** DecPos))
C                   RETURN    Num
C *-----------------------------------------------------------------*
C      *PSSR        BEGSR
C                   RETURN    0
C                   ENDSR
C *-----------------------------------------------------------------*
P #CtoN             E
```

Figure 9.17: Convert Character to Numeric (#CtoN) subprocedure (part 2 of 2).

Replace Characters (#Replace)

The Replace Characters (#Replace) subprocedure is useful to replace one character string with another when writing HTML code. Sometimes you might want to output characters such as a Greater Than or Less Than symbol. These symbols are usually used in HTML as tag delimiters and may corrupt the page that you are trying to create.

Another scenario is a page that includes an input field. In the field, the user can type in characters such as Greater Than, Less Than, quotation marks, etc. After the entry is processed, you want to fill the field with the last value they typed. If this is a quotation mark, you may find this difficult. For example, you can't use the following HTML statement:

```
<input type="text" name="string" value="""">
```

The three quotation marks following the value keyword will confuse the browser. Instead, you need to use a special keyword that tells the browser to display a quotation mark. In this case, the value is ". To correctly display a quotation mark in the value of a text field, the following HTML code is used:

```
<input type="text" name="string" value="&quot;">
```

I stumbled upon this in a CGI program where I had created an input field. After I loaded the page with the criteria entered by the user, I wanted to fill the text field with what the user had entered to produce the output. If this text contained quotation marks, it confused the browser. So, I created the #Replace subprocedure to handle this. When my e-RPG program wrote HTML to display the input field, I used the statement shown in Figure 9.18.

```
C                eval      WrtDta = 'Customer Name: ' +
C                                  %trim(#Input('TEXT':'"customer"':
C                                  '30':'"' +
C                                  %trim(#Replace(CustNam:
C                                  '"':'&quot;')) +
C                                  '"')) +
C                                  NewLine
C                CALLP     #WrStout(WrtDta)
```

Figure 9.18: Using the #Replace subprocedure to replace a quotation mark with the HTML keyword ".

The #Replace subprocedure accepts three parameters. The first is the string you wish to convert. The second is the character(s) that you want to search through the string to replace. The third parameter contains the character(s) that you wish to replace the character(s) supplied in the second parameter.

The only thing this subprocedure won't do is replace spaces. It could be modified to do so, but I use this subprocedure exclusively for replacing characters with special HTML keywords as shown in the example in Figure 9.18. The code for the #Replace subprocedure is shown in Figure 9.19.

```
*//////////////////////////////////////////////////////////////////*
* (#Replace) Replace Characters to Numeric                         *
*                                                                  *
* Use: #Replace(String : Replace_This : With_This)                 *
*                                                                  *
*//////////////////////////////////////////////////////////////////*
D #Replace       PR             1024
```

Figure 9.19: The #Replace subprocedure (part 1 of 3).

```
D  InString                        1024    VALUE
D  From                              56    VALUE
D  To                                56    VALUE
*/////////////////////////////////////////////////////////////////*
*  (#Replace) Replace character(s) with new character(s)          *
*                                                                 *
*  Use: #Replace(String : Replace_This : With_This)              *
*                                                                 *
*/////////////////////////////////////////////////////////////////*
P  #Replace         B                         EXPORT
*-----------------------------------------------------------------*
D  #Replace         PI               1024
D  InString                         1024    VALUE
D  From                              56    VALUE
D  To                                56    VALUE
*
D  String           S               1024
D  Temp             S               1024
D  i                S                  4 0
D  j                S                  4 0
D  len              S                  4 0
D  lenTo            S                  4 0
*-----------------------------------------------------------------*
C                       eval      String = InString
C                       eval      i = 1
C          ' '          CHECKR    From          len                   99
*
C                       if        (not *IN99)
C                       eval      len = %size(From)
C                       endif
*
C          ' '          CHECKR    To            lenTo                 99
*
C                       if        (not *IN99)
C                       eval      lenTo = %size(To)
C                       endif
*
C      From:len         SCAN      String:i      j
*
C                       dow       (j< >0)
C                       eval      Temp = %trim(To) + %subst(String:j+len)
*
C                       if        (j = 1)
C                       eval      String = Temp
C                       else
C                       eval      String = %subst(String:1:j-1) + Temp
C                       endif
*
C                       eval      i = (j + lenTo)
C      From:len         SCAN      String:i      j
C                       enddo
*
C                       RETURN    String
```

Figure 9.19: The #Replace subprocedure (part 2 of 3).

206

Figure 9.19: The #Replace subprocedure (part 3 of 3).

SERVICE PROGRAMS

The subprocedures listed in this chapter are easily placed into modules or service programs to make using them in your CGI programs a snap.

If you haven't had the chance to use service programs or modules before, now is a good time to start understanding and applying these basic ILE principals.

There are three major service programs used in most CGI programs.

- Standard HTTP subprocedures - #WrStout, #ReadStin, #GetEnv.

- HTML subprocedures - #Link, #Img, #Bold, #WrtSrcMbr, etc.

- Application specific subprocedures - #CvtDB and other subprocedures specific to the application.

The first service program is one that can be created and left alone. The subprocedures that write to standard output, read from standard input, and get environment variables can be used in all of your applications. These procedures will not change.

The second service program also contains subprocedures that can be used in every CGI. Again, these are simply created once and used everywhere functions.

The third set of service programs is more application specific. The main subprocedure included in this service program is #CvtDB, which is application specific is because the data retrieved might differ from application to application.

The other subprocedures contained in this service program are contain any application-specific function that you deem useful to be coded as a subprocedure.

SERVICE PROGRAMS:
YOUR SECRET WEAPON FOR E-RPG PROGRAMMING

Using subprocedures to encapsulate standard functions, whether APIs or often-used routines, will make your job easier. Instead of coding the same routines over and over again in each application, you simply call your procedures. The code for the function is stored in one location, meaning that any changes needed will only need to be made in one location.

The APIs used for CGI programming on the AS/400 are a bit cumbersome, but the use of subprocedures will make using them a lot easier. Use the secret weapons provided in the functionality of the Integrated Language Environment and you'll see your production soar, not only with CGI programming, but all programming.

10

E-RPG TIPS AND TECHNIQUES

This chapter is a potluck of tips and techniques that I have used since I first started CGI programming. Because I originally started CGI programming on the AS/400 as a proof-of-concept project, I was able to tinker and test most any method that came to mind. I have found the tips explained here to be the most useful, and I hope you do as well. They range from debugging your CGI programs, to using Server Side Includes (SSI), to using the Open Query File (OPNQRYF) command to select and sort data to be displayed on your Web page.

DEBUGGING E-RPG PROGRAMS

We've covered the basics of e-RPG programming, but up until now we have left out a very important piece of the puzzle: debugging. When you build applications, there will be times when you're not sure why something is happening, or why you have a certain error. You most likely know how to debug normal RPG programs and feel that debugging an e-RPG program should be quite similar. Well, it is, in fact. The only real difference is finding where the program is and how to debug it.

The first step in any debugging scenario is to decide if the problem is actually with the program. This is usually a simple step, but you'd be surprised how many times I've debugged an e-RPG program only to find that a PTF was needed to fix the problem. Of course, this is only after hours of checking and double-checking the code. After I have ruled out any operating system problems, debugging is the next step. Sometimes you will find the problem in your CGI program, and other times you will find that it is an internal software problem that requires a call to IBM for help. The latter I can't help you with, but I can help you with debugging.

To start debugging an e-RPG program, end the HTTP server instance in which your CGI program is running. If you are not sure which instance your programs are running in, or you are not the Web administrator of your company, by all means, contact someone who can help you. You wouldn't want to put a halt to any production programs using the instance that you are ending. (This is why it is a good rule to use a separate instance, configuration, and CGI library for the purpose of debugging and testing.)

To end the HTTP server instance that runs the e-RPG programs that you will be debugging, issue the following command:

```
ENDTCPSVR *HTTP HTTPSVR(instance_name)
```

Before going on to the next step, make sure that the instance has indeed ended. To view the status of your instance, use the Work With Active Jobs (WRKACTJOB) command, qualifying the command with the job name you want to view. In this case, the job name will be the same as the HTTP server instance. Use the following command to view your instance jobs:

```
WRKACTJOB JOB(instance_name)
```

Each instance of the HTTP server has one or more (usually five) utility jobs associated with it. These utility jobs are known as Batch Immediate (BCI) jobs. If you look at Figure 10.1, you'll see that there are six jobs with the same instance name of Stone. The first job is of the job type Batch (BCH). That job is the actual HTTP server; it handles all Web requests. The server job in turn asks one of the utility BCI jobs to process the request, otherwise the HTTP Server would lock out requests from other users until the response was sent back to the browser.

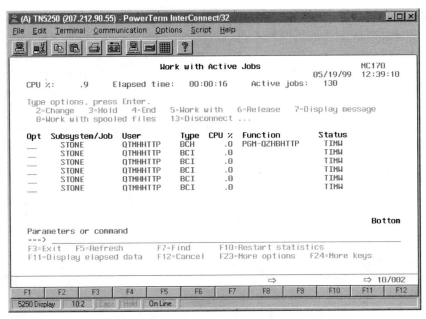

Figure 10.1: Viewing the active jobs for a particular HTTP server instance.

When you are debugging an e-RPG application, it is difficult to know which of these five jobs are invoking the program you want to debug. You need to restart the server so you can make sure that only one of the BCI utility jobs is started. Wait until all the jobs shown on the Work with Active Jobs (WRKACTJOB) display have completed. Refresh the screen until there are no jobs listed on the display. Once there are no jobs listed, you can proceed to restart the instance. When you restart the instance, you will specify a couple of extra parameters that tell the server to limit the number of BCI utility jobs. To do this, use the following command:

```
STRTCPSVR *HTTP HTTPSVR(instance_name '-minat 1 -maxat 1')
```

The minat and maxat parameters tell the server to start a minimum and a maximum of one of the BCI utility jobs. You want to limit the number of BCI jobs during debugging so that you will not have a hard time finding which BCI job to debug.

Return to the screen where you are viewing the instance jobs. Refresh the screen until there are at least three jobs displayed as running. The first job is always the job that runs the server instance. The next two jobs are BCI jobs. You'd expect only one BCI job because that's what you specified in the `minat` and `maxat` parameters, but the HTTP server starts two. One is for running single-threaded CGI programs and the other is for running multithreaded CGI programs. Single-threaded CGI programs are RPG or COBOL programs. Multithreaded CGI programs are Java programs.

View the job log of each of the last two jobs running. Find the one that states that this is a single-threaded job by using the display job (option 5) and then selecting the view job log (option 10) from the menu. The single-threaded job will have a job log that resembles the one shown in Figure 10.2.

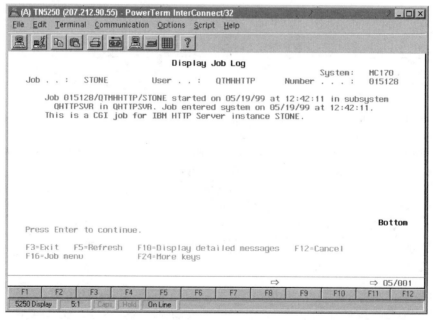

Figure 10.2: The job log of the BCI job that we want to use to debug our e-RPG program.

Once the correct job is found, write down the number, and user and job parameters for this job. In Figure 10.2, these parameters are found at the top of the display. Return to the command line and enter the following command:

```
STRSRVJOB <Number/User/Job>
```

This command starts a service job for the job that will be running our e-RPG application. Remember, there is only one application running now, so we can count on the fact that this is the correct job. Next, issue the Start Debug (STRDBG) command and enter the name of the e-RPG program you wish to debug in the program parameter. Be sure to specify UPDPROD(*YES) if your e-RPG program updates any database files. Enter your breakpoints and then press F12 to return to the command line.

Lastly, invoke the e-RPG program by opening your browser and entering the URL to run your e-RPG program in your browser's location bar. Once the first breakpoint is reached in your program, you will see the debug screen displayed on the display that you issued the STRSRVJOB command on. From here, debugging the program is exactly the same as debugging a normal RPG application.

One thing to keep in mind when debugging e-RPG (or any CGI applications), you must stop and restart your server instance after each compile, especially if you are debugging service programs. If you do not, you will find that in some cases you are not only running the old version of the program or service program, but debugging the old version while viewing the newer source because there is no way to reclaim eligible activation groups that the server jobs are using. Only stopping and restarting your server instance will allow you to do this.

SERVER SIDE INCLUDES (SSIs)

Server Side Includes (SSIs) are features that will make your applications sizzle, and ease your design. SSIs allow you to embed any HTML document on your server, or execute a CGI application from inside an HTML document, whether it is static or built dynamically using an e-RPG or any CGI program.

There are also some standard SSI variables that you can include in your document such as current date and time, last change date of the document, and file size of the document. These are used by specifying reserved directives in your SSI statements. Let me show you a quick example of an SSI that shows the current time and last change date of the document to further explain this concept.

Figure 10.3 contains the source code that includes some simple SSI code. This code will display "The current date and time is:" followed by the current system time and date. On the next line, the document information is presented.

```
<HTML>
<HEAD>
<TITLE></TITLE>
</HEAD>
The current date and time is:
<!-#echo var=DATE_GMT  -> <BR>
The document name is:
<!-#echo var=DOCUMENT_NAME -> <BR>
</BODY>
</HTML>
```

Figure 10.3: Sample code using Server Side Includes (SSIs).

The source from Figure 10.3 is short and sweet, as is the output. Figure 10.4 contains the output for Figure 10.3.

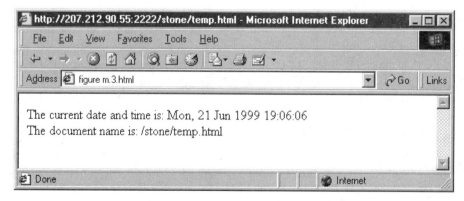

Figure 10.4: The output from the SSI example in Figure 10.3.

As you can see, the document time and the document name are placed into the document using the SSI directive #echo. This directive is similar to other echo commands you might have seen. It simply echos the data onto the screen. One other curious aspect of SSIs is that if you were to use your browser's view source option on this display, you would not see the SSI directives. Instead, you would see the source, as if the information were manually typed into an HTML document.

The only thing that I had to add to my HTTP configuration was one directive. The directive is named Embeds and tells the server that embedded commands such as SSI directives are allowed. The entire directive looks like the example below:

```
embeds on html
```

What this is saying is first to allow embedding (Embeds on), and second to treat normal HTML files as SSI files. Usually HTML files that have a type of shtml or htmls are specifically reserved for SSI-type HTML files, but for this explanation, I wanted to make it as simple as possible.

Inserting CGI execution calls with SSI is also simple. This is done using the following format:

```
<!-#exec cgi="/cgipath/cgiprogram" ->
```

If you have a CGI program that produces dynamic output, you might be able to use this method to embed the output of the CGI program in an HTML file.

Let's assume that all of the pages on your Web site have the same look and feel. The only problem is that this look and feel was designed with a WYSIWYG editor, and the HTML code is rather complex. Now you have created a CGI program that will output a list of messages, such as a discussion forum topic list display. It would be difficult to place all of the HTML into your CGI program. Instead, you can simply build the page with your editor and include the #Exec SSI directive in the page. When the browser reaches this statement, it will execute your CGI program and the output produced will appear to be embedded on your page.

Figure 10.5 shows an example of using an SSI to include output from a CGI program.

```
<html>
<head>
<meta http-equiv="Content-Type" content="text/html; charset=iso-8859-1">
<title>Forums</title>
</head>
Here is a list of discussion forums available.

<p><!-#exec cgi="/cgi-forum/forumlist"-> <br>
<br>
</body>
</html>
```

Figure 10.5: Using SSI to include dynamic output from a CGI program.

As you can see in Figure 10.5, the code for this Web page is rather small. The SSI statement is really doing all the work. The SSI statement will execute a CGI program named forumlist. This program lists the currently available forums, the number of postings in each, as well as when the last posting was. Figure 10.6 shows an example of what this might look like.

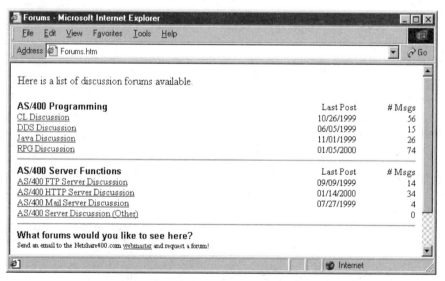

Figure 10.6: Output from the SSI example in Figure 10.5.

As you can see from Figure 10.6, you can create pages rather easily with SSI. Almost the entire Web page is created by a CGI program. This means that if you have pages that require dynamic creation, you can make them look like the rest of the static pages on your site by simply using a SSI statement in the HTML code.

PAGING

Paging is a method of CGI programming that allows the user to view a certain number of records on a display at one time. This method can be tricky at times because one user could use one HTTP server job for the first request, and another for the second request. Remember, there are multiple jobs running and the user only uses the job until the request—whether a document or CGI request—has completed.

You may be familiar with paging when using subfiles in RPG programming. Controlling the page that the user is displaying is rather simple with subfiles because the user uses his own job. This job retains its own access paths for the files being used. Other jobs running the same program do not affect the file pointer except for that job. When a user displays records 1 through 10 of a subfile, it is almost guaranteed that the next record read with that job will be record 11.

This scenario is not true with a CGI program. Let's assume that you have written a CGI program that will display items currently in your inventory. Because you have thousands of items, you don't want to display all of the items on one screen. Not only would this waste processing time, forcing the user to wait until all the records are loaded, it also would make the display very cumbersome for the user to search through. So, you write your CGI application to display 25 items at a time with a link at the bottom of the list that reads "Next Page". When the user clicks on this link, the next 25 items are displayed.

If we will always have one user using this display, little programming is needed to control the file pointer for this CGI program. After the first request, the file will be positioned to read the next 25 lines. The only problem is, you will no doubt have multiple users running a particular application at one time. The jobs accessing the data do not remain in a persistent state, as they do with interactive jobs used on AS/400 green screens.

Paging with a Sequential File

The method I use to control paging when reading from a sequential file involves sending a query string environment variable with the last relative record number (RRN) read from the file to the processing program. This method allows me to keep a persistent state for the job without getting into the complex and sometimes unneeded processes involved with persistent CGI programming.

When building an HTML page from within a CGI program, after writing the last record for that page, I save the RRN of the last record read and build my Next Page hyperlink using this value. The hyperlink looks like the following example:

```
<a href="/cgi-bin/cgipgm?LastRRN=25">Next Page</a>
```

Assuming that the CGI program that I am running is named CGIPGM, this hyperlink will pass a query string environment variable into the same program when it is called from this hyperlink. The first process in CGIPGM will be to retrieve this environment variable and process it. Then the value is used to perform a Set Greater Than (SETGT) operation on the file that I am reading from. This places the file pointer in a position so that the next record that I read will be the record directly following the last record read for the particular job.

What about the first time this program is called, you ask? That is a good question since there will most likely be no value passed in for the LastRRN query string environment variable. You can either leave the query string data off of the URL, or you can specify an RRN of zero. Either way, the LastRRN value will contain zero, and when the SETGT operation is performed, you will be positioned at the first record that you wish to read.

This method assumes that you are reading records from a file sequentially. This would be the case on a nonkeyed file or if the access path of the file you are reading was built with an Open Query File (OPNQRYF) command. (More on using OPNQRYF will be discussed later in this chapter). The pseudocode for this method would look like the example in Figure 10.7.

```
Get Query String Environment Variables using the QtmhGetEnv API
Extract the value of LastRRN with the QtmhCvtDB API
SETGT using the value of LastRRN
READ file
Do While (not EOF) and (Count < Number_on_Page)
    Increment Number_On_Page
    Write data to Standard Output using the QtmhWrStout API
    Save value of last RRN read
    READ file
EndDo

If (not EOF)
    Write hyperlink using the RRN of the last record read
Else
    Write message stating "End of File"
EndIf
```

Figure 10.7: Using SETGT to position the file pointer for paging on a sequential file.

Using the last RRN as a query string variable will help in this case because the file will be positioned differently for each user requesting the page. If Bob is on the 100th record, the Next Page link will contain the value 100 as the last RRN read. Mary, who just started using the page, will have no value for LastRRN (or zero), and will be positioned at the front of the file.

This is a simple technique that I have found very useful when you want to keep data in a persistent state for one user, or for 100 users. In a sense, each visitor to the page has a custom-built page just for them.

Paging with Keyed Files

Fortunately, the AS/400's database system is not composed of strictly sequential files. We are allowed to create access paths in the form of logical files to make selecting and sorting data much easier. This is the norm in today's world. The previous example using sequential files is not, although it is still used in those cases where it is deemed necessary.

Paging using keyed files is very similar to the last method described. We will still create a Next Page link, but instead of specifying the last RRN read from the file, we will specify the last unique field value or values read from the file as the query string environment variable parameters. We will then use these values to perform the same SETGT operation to position the file pointer to the next set of records for the current user. The values used on the SETGT operation will be those that are read in from the environment variables.

In this example, let's assume that we have an item file that is uniquely keyed by item type and item number. We have created a CGI program to display items on the user's browser so that they can see certain information, such as quantity on hand, for the items in the system. We again assume that there will be 25 items displayed per page.

The first time this CGI program is called, no query string values will be passed into it. This means that the values used to perform the SETGT operation will be blanks or zeros, depending on the data type of the key fields in the file. After displaying the first 25 items, we create our next page link, using the last values of item type and item number, which were read from the file. The next page link resembles the following:

```
<a href="/cgi-bin/CGIPGM?LastType=100&LastItem=CARROT">Next Page</a>
```

When this next page link is clicked, the same CGI program that created the first display is called. The only difference is that we specify query string variables, which tell the program the last uniquely keyed values that were displayed. In this case, the last item type read is 100, and the last item number read is CARROT. If we perform a SETGT on the item file with these values, the file pointer is positioned directly after the last item read. This process is repeated until the last item number is read. Figure 10.8 shows an example of how paging using keyed files is accomplished.

```
H DFTACTGRP(*NO) BNDDIR('CGIBNDDIR')
FITEMS1LF   IF   E          K DISK
 /COPY QSRVSRC,P.ITEMLIST
D EnvDS          E DS                    EXTNAME(ITEMSPF) BASED(EnvDS@)
D HTTPHeader       C                     CONST('Content-type: text/html')
D NewLine          C                     CONST(X'15')
 *
D WrtDta           S            1024
 *
```

Figure 10.8: Code for program ITEMLIST that uses keyed paging (part 1 of 3).

```
D EnvDS@          S                  *
D EnvRec          S              1024
D EnvLen          S                 9B 0
D EnvVar          S                64
D CvtLen          S                 9B 0 INZ(%size(EnvDS))
D LastType        S                      LIKE(ITTYPE)
D LastItem        S                      LIKE(ITITEM)
D Count           S                 4S 0
 *
C       ItemKey       KLIST
C                     KFLD                      ITTYPE
C                     KFLD                      ITITEM
C                     eval      EnvVar = 'QUERY_STRING'
C                     CALLP     #GetEnvQS(EnvRec:EnvLen:EnvVar)
C                     CALLP     #CvtDB(EnvRec:EnvLen:CvtLen:EnvDS@)
C                     EXSR      $Header
C                     EXSR      $Main
C                     EXSR      $Footer
C                     SETON                                            LR
C       $Header       BEGSR
 *
C                     eval      WrtDta = %trim(HTTPHeader) +
C                                        NewLine + NewLine
C                     CALLP     #WrStout(WrtDta)
 *
C                     eval      WrtDta = '<html><head>' +
C                                        '<title>' +
C                                        'Item List' +
C                                        '</title>' +
C                                        '</head><body>' +
C                                        '<p align="center">' +
C                                        '<big><big>' +
C                                        'Item List' +
C                                        '</big></big></p>' +
C                                        NewLine
C                     CALLP     #WrStout(WrtDta)
 *
C                     ENDSR
C       $Main         BEGSR
 *
C                     eval      WrtDta = '<table border="1"><tr>' +
C                                        NewLine +
C                                        '<td>Item Type</td>' +
C                                        '<td>Item Number</td>' +
C                                        '<td>Description</td>' +
C                                        '<td>On-Hand</td>' +
C                                        NewLine
C                     CALLP     #WrStout(WrtDta)
C                     eval      Count = 0
C       ItemKey       SETGT     ITEMS1LF
C                     READ      ITEMS1LF
 *
C                     dow       (not %eof) and (Count < 2)
C                     eval      WrtDta = '<tr><td>' +
```

Figure 10.8: Code for program ITEMLIST that uses keyed paging (part 2 of 3).

```
C                                       %trim(ITTYPE) +
C                                       '</td><td>' +
C                                       %trim(ITITEM) +
C                                       '</td><td>' +
C                                       %trim(ITDESC) +
C                                       '</td><td>' +
C                                       %trim(%editc(ITONH:'3')) +
C                                       '</td></tr>' +
C                                       NewLine
C                   CALLP     #WrStout(WrtDta)
C                   eval      Count = (Count + 1)
C                   eval      LastType = ITTYPE
C                   eval      LastItem = ITITEM
C                   READ      ITEMS1LF
C                   enddo
C     *
C                   eval      WrtDta = '</tr></table>' +
C                                       '</center>' +
C                                       NewLine
C                   CALLP     #WrStout(WrtDta)
C     *
C                   ENDSR
C     $Footer       BEGSR
C     *
C                   if        (not %eof)
C                   eval      WrtDta = '<a href="/cgi-bin/ITEMLIST?' +
C                                       'ITTYPE=' +
C                                       %trim(LastType) +
C                                       '&ITITEM=' +
C                                       %trim(LastItem) +
C                                       '">Next Page</a>' +
C                                       NewLine
C                   CALLP     #WrStout(WrtDta)
C                   endif
C     *
C                   eval      WrtDta = '</body></html>' +
C                                       NewLine
C                   CALLP     #WrStout(WrtDta)
C     *
C                   ENDSR
```

Figure 10.8: Code for program ITEMLIST that uses keyed paging (part 3 of 3).

First, the query string environment variables are read using the #GetEnv subprocedure. Next, the values read are placed into the data structure named EnvDS, using the #CvtDB subprocedure. If no values are retrieved, then these values will be blanks.

Then, the header information of the Web page is written in the $Header subroutine. This is the standard information included on every page, such as the headers and title of the page.

After the header information is written, the main body of the page is written by executing the $Main subroutine. This routine first writes the report headers. It then uses the data passed into the program via the query string environment variables to position the item file immediately after the last item read. Again, if no data is passed into the program, the file will be positioned at the top of the file. The item file is then read, and the next 25 items are written to the browser.

Lastly, the footer portion of the page is written by executing the $Footer subroutine. This subroutine first checks to see if the file pointer of the item file is at the end of the file. If not, it writes the Next Page hyperlink using the last item type and last item number as query string variables. If the end of the file was reached, the hyperlink is not written to the browser.

Figure 10.9 shows what this display might look like. I have changed the number of items to display per page from 25 to two for simplicity.

Figure 10.9: The itemlist program.

If you look at the status bar in Figure 10.9, you will see the hyperlink that is created for the Next Page link. The last item type is 100, and the last item number is BANANA. When we click on the Next Page link, we will get the next two items, as shown in Figure 10.10.

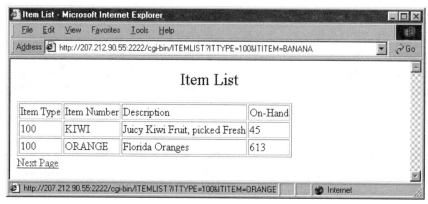

Figure 10.10: The itemlist Web page after clicking on the Next Page Link.

The URL displayed in Figure 10.10 shows the values passed into the ITEMLIST program. Again, the status bar shows the location that the Next Page hyperlink is pointing to. This time the last item type read is 100, and the last item number is ORANGE.

If the user clicks on the Next Page hyperlink, the cycle is repeated the next 25 items. This continues until the end of the file is reached and the Next Page hyperlink is not displayed. If you choose, you could display text that reads "End of List" instead of nothing, as I do in my example. This is entirely up to you.

SELECTING AND SEQUENCING WITH DYNAMIC OPNQRYF

The examples given have been rather simple, and rely on the fact that no selection or abnormal sorting criteria is used on the display. This is not always the case, and you will find times when a user wants to not only select the sorting method used, but also select items that they wish to view.

A good example of this might be a used car Web site that allows the user to select criteria to display a list of used cars that are available. The selection could be made on make, model, year, or even price. When the information is viewed, the user might also want to sort the data viewed differently than displayed.

Let's think back to how we would accomplish this if we were simply producing a report for a user. The first thing we would do is display a screen that would allow the user to enter in selection and sorting criteria. After the screen is processed, we would use the information entered by the user to select and sort the data, finally printing the list out on a report. The method used for this in most cases is the Open Query File (OPNQRYF) command.

OPNQRYF is a great tool used for selecting and sorting data. It takes a lot of the work out of the process so that when the report program is called, we only have to read through the new temporary file created by OPNQRYF. The same process can be used for creating dynamic Web pages.

Let's assume that we have a company called BVS-Cars that sells used cars on the Internet. We will allow users to browse our selection as described previously. The following examples guide you through a step-by-step process to accomplish this using OPNQRYF as the main selection and sorting engine to produce the Web pages.

The Web Page

The front-end Web page to BVS-Cars will allow the user to select cars by make, year, or price range. After the user has selected the criteria, we will read the form and process the data to show the user only the cars that meet the criteria they selected. Figure 10.11 shows an example of what the page looks like.

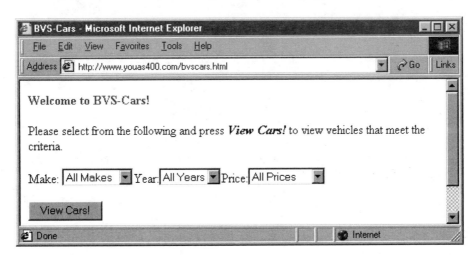

Figure 10.11: The front page to BVS-Cars.

The first thing the user sees when coming to BVS-Cars is a display with three select boxes. The first box allows users to select a make of car, the second lets them select a year, and the last lets them select a price range.

The special value "ALL" is used for each selection box when the user selects all. When the user clicks on the View Cars! button, e-RPG program LISTCARS is called. The GET method is used so the data will be passed as query string environment variables. Figure 10.12 shows the source for this HTML page.

```html
<html>
<head>
<title>BVS-Cars</title>
</head>
<body>
<p><font color="#FF0000"><strong>Welcome to BVS-Cars!</strong></font></p>
<p>Please select from the following and press <em><strong>View
Cars!</strong></em> to view
vehicles that meet the criteria.</p>
<form method="GET" action="/cgi-bin/ListCars" method="GET">
  <p>Make: <select name="MAKE" size="1">
    <option value="ALL">All Makes</option>
    <option value="Ford">Ford</option>
    <option value="Cheverolet">Cheverolet</option>
    <option value="Honda">Honda</option>
    <option value="Toyota">Toyota</option>
  </select>Year:<select name="YEAR" size="1">
    <option value="ALL">All Years</option>
    <option value="1999">1999</option>
    <option value="1998">1998</option>
    <option value="1997">1997</option>
    <option value="1996">1996</option>
    <option value="Pre1996">Pre 1996</option>
  </select>Price:<select name="PRICE" size="1">
    <option value="ALL">All Prices</option>
    <option value="0002000">Up to 2000</option>
    <option value="0005000">Up to 5000</option>
    <option value="0010000">Up to 10,000</option>
    <option value="0020000">Up to 20,000</option>
  </select></p>
  <p><input type="submit" value="View Cars!"> </p>
</form>
</body>
</html>
```

Figure 10.12: The HTML source for the BVS-Cars page.

The source in Figure 10.12 is not complicated at all. And because we chose to use select boxes, the data passed to the processing program has little chance to be corrupt. As you can see, the select box uses the option tag to specify selection values. Also, the value in the box is not necessarily the value that has to be passed to the processing program.

Because the action property of the form tag specifies to execute program LISTCARS in the /cgi-bin/ directory, the e-RPG program LISTCARS will be used to process the data when the user presses the View Cars! button.

Let's assume that the user selected Ford for the model, selected all years for the year, and selected less than $20,000 for the price. The list would look similar to Figure 10.13.

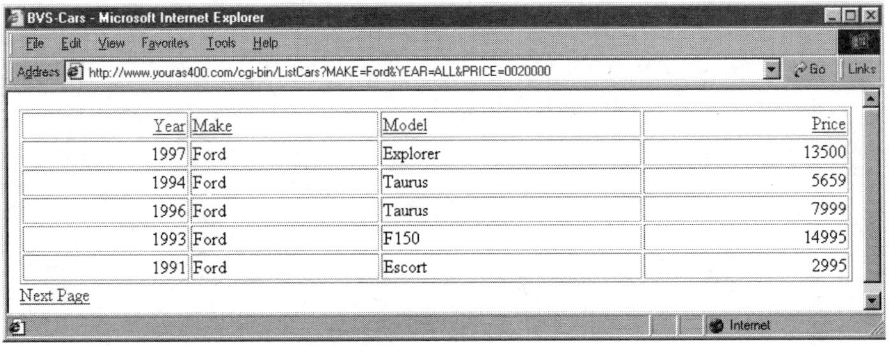

Year	Make	Model	Price
1997	Ford	Explorer	13500
1994	Ford	Taurus	5659
1996	Ford	Taurus	7999
1993	Ford	F150	14995
1991	Ford	Escort	2995

Next Page

Figure 10.13: Output from e-RPG program listcars.

After the user has a list of cars to view, there are a couple of options. The first option, if there are more cars than can fit on one page, is to click on the Next Page link. This will display the next cars that meet the search criteria. There can be multiple pages depending on how the user selects to view the cars.

The next option the user has on this display is to sort the results by any of the headings. If you looked closely, you will notices that the headings in Figure 10.13 are hyperlinks. If the user clicks on one of the headings, it will sort the information by that heading.

The e-RPG Program

We noticed in the Web page that the processing program for the BVS-Cars page is named LISTCARS. This program handles everything that can be done on this page. From displaying the list of cars, to sorting the way the information is displayed. The entire program is listed in appendix H.

e-RPG program LISTCARS uses OPNQRYF to both select and sort the data that it is to display. It reads in the values from the form using the #GetEnv and #CvtDB subprocedures, and then builds an OPNQRYF statement from these values. Figure 10.14 shows the code that is used to build the select statement for the OPNQRYF.

```
C       $QRYSLT        BEGSR
*
C                      if          (MAKE < > 'ALL')
C                      EXSR        $AND
C                      eval        QrySlt = %trim(QrySlt) +
C                                  ' (CMAKE *EQ "' +
C                                  %trim(MAKE) + '")'
C                      endif
*
C                      if          (YEAR < > 'ALL')
C                      EXSR        $AND
*
C                      if          (YEAR = 'Pre1996')
C                      eval        QrySlt = %trim(QrySlt) +
C                                  ' (%digits(CYEAR) *LT ("1996")'
C                      else
C                      eval        QrySlt = %trim(QrySlt) +
C                                  ' (%digits(CYEAR) *EQ "' +
C                                  %trim(YEAR) + '")'
C                      endif
*
C                      endif
*
C                      if          (PRICE < > 'ALL')
C                      EXSR        $AND
C                      eval        QrySlt = %trim(QrySlt) +
C                                  ' (%digits(CPRICE) *LE "' +
C                                  %trim(PRICE) + '")'
C                      endif
*
C                      ENDSR
*********************************************************************
C       $AND           BEGSR
*
C                      if          (QrySlt < > ' ')
C                      eval        QrySlt = %trim(QrySlt) +
C                                  ' *AND'
C                      endif
*
C                      ENDSR
```

Figure 10.14: The code used to build the select portion of the opnqryf statement.

The field QrySlt is used to store the selection parameter of the query. Most of us should be familiar with the process as we no doubt have many programs that do this that are written in either CL or RPG.

After we have the query select parameter built, we must next build the key value parameter. This will be used to sort the data the way the user has specified. In this initialization subprocedure of e-RPG program LISTCARS, if the sort field is blank, I default the value to sort by make. If the user clicks on one of the four headings, the data will be sorted by that heading.

The code that builds the key field parameter of the OPNQRYF statement is shown in Figure 10.15.

```
C        $KEYFLD        BEGSR
 *
C                       eval      KeyFld = ' '
 *
C                       select
C                       when      (SORTBY = 'YEAR')
C                       eval      KeyFld = %trim(KeyFld) +
C                                           ' (CYEAR)'
C                       when      (SORTBY = 'MAKE')
C                       eval      KeyFld = %trim(KeyFld) +
C                                           ' (CMAKE)'
C                       when      (SORTBY = 'MODEL')
C                       eval      KeyFld = %trim(KeyFld) +
C                                           ' (CMODEL)'
C                       when      (SORTBY = 'PRICE')
C                       eval      KeyFld = %trim(KeyFld) +
C                                           ' (CPRICE)'
C                       other
C                       eval      KeyFld = %trim(KeyFld) +
C                                           ' (CYEAR)'
C                       endsl
 *
C                       eval      KeyFld = 'KEYFLD(' +
C                                           %trim(KeyFld) + ')'
 *
C                       ENDSR
```

Figure 10.15: The code that builds the key value of the opnqryf statement.

As the program reaches the select statement in Figure 10.15, the value of the field KeyFld is filled with a value if the sort parameter is equal to its corresponding keyword. If no values are met, the sort defaults to Year. Finally, the entire KeyFld parameter is built.

Now that the select and key field parameters have been built, we can perform the OPNQRYF on the file that contains the cars that BVS-Cars has for sale.

First, as with any OPNQRYF statement, we override the file that we are performing the query on by specifing the SHARE(*YES) option. Next, the values of the fields QRYSLT and KEYFLD are used to build the OPNQRYF command, which is then executed with the QCMDEXC API. Figure 10.16 contains this source.

```
C                    if        (QrySlt < > ' ')
C                    eval      QCmdCmd = 'OPNQRYF FILE(CARSPF) ' +
C                                        'OPTION(*INP)' + ' QRYSLT(' +
C                                        '''' + %trim(QrySlt) + ''') ' +
C                                        %trim(KeyFld)
C                    else
C                    eval      QCmdCmd = 'OPNQRYF FILE(CARSPF) ' +
C                                        'OPTION(*INP)' + ' ' +
C                                        %trim(KeyFld)
C                    endif
    *
C                    CALL      'QCMDEXC'                               99
C                    PARM                    QCmdCmd
C                    PARM                    QCmdLength
```

Figure 10.16: The source code that executes the OPNQRYF command.

You will notice in Figure 10.16 that I am checking for a value in the QrySlt parameter. Only if I find a value, do I specify the QRYSLT keyword on the OPNQRYF command. This is a simple way to make sure the command executes.

Now that we know how the sorting and selecting are done, let's focus on how the hyperlinks are built on the page.

The hyperlinks for the headings that allow the user to sort the selected data are built while the page is being created. First, all the values of the other query string parameters are placed into a string so that we do not lose the values the user previously selected. Next, the sort by query string variable is tacked onto the end of the URL. Figure 10.17 shows the code that builds these headings.

```
      * Note:   The InLink variable is built in the *INZSR
      C                 eval       InLink = %trim(W$PGM) +
      C                            '?MAKE=' + %trim(MAKE) +
      C                            '&YEAR=' + %trim(YEAR) +
      C                            '&PRICE=' + %trim(PRICE)
      *
      C                 eval       WrtDta = '<table border="1" width="100%">' +
      C                            NewLine
      C                 CALLP      #WrStout(WrtDta)
      *
      C                 eval       WrtDta = '<tr>' +
      C                            '<td align="right">' +
      C                            '<a href="' + %trim(InLink) +
      C                            '&sortby=YEAR">' +
      C                            'Year</a>' +
      C                            '</td>' +
      C                            '<td>' +
      C                            '<a href="' + %trim(InLink) +
      C                            '&sortby=MAKE">' +
      C                            'Make</a>' +
      C                            '</td>' +
      C                            '<td>' +
      C                            '<a href="' + %trim(InLink) +
      C                            '&sortby=MODEL">' +
      C                            'Model</a>' +
      C                            '</td>' +
      C                            '<td align="right">' +
      C                            '<a href="' + %trim(InLink) +
      C                            '&sortby=PRICE">' +
      C                            'Price</a>' +
      C                            '</td>' +
      C                            NewLine
      C                 CALLP      #WrStout(WrtDta)
      *
      C                 EXSR       $Detail
      *
      C                 eval       WrtDta = '</table>' +
      C                            NewLine
      C                 CALLP      #WrStout(WrtDta)
```

Figure 10.17: The source code to build the headings that allow the user to sort the results.

Before I explain Figure 10.17, I must say that the code that appears first to build the InLink variable is actually performed in the initialization subroutine (*INZSR) after the query string variables are read in and parsed. Also, the portion of code near the end that executes the $Detail subroutine is used to display the list of cars. These two portions of code were included in Figure 10.17 simply to make the code more clear.

As shown in Figure 10.17, for each heading, we are building a hyperlink to the same CGI program that created the page, LISTCARS. We are also including the data read in from the variables as part of the link. This way we do not lose the values that the user entered. Last, depending on the heading, we are adding another query string variable to the URL that will determine how the data will be sorted should the user click on one of the headings.

The last link that takes some special processing is the Next Page link. While we are reading through the file that contains the car information, we are counting records to make sure we only display a certain amount per page. In this case that number is five. Figure 10.18 shows the source for the portion of the program that displays the information requested by the user.

```
C                    OPEN      CARSPF
C                    eval      Count = 0
C                    eval      *IN69 = *OFF
 *
C                    if        (LRRN > 0)
C         LRRN       CHAIN     CARSPF                                    99
C                    endif
 *
C                    dow       (not *IN69) and (Count < 5)
C                    READ      CARSPF                                    69
 *
C                    if        (*IN69)
C                    ITER
C                    endif
 *
C                    eval      WrtDta = '<tr>' +
C                                       '<td align="right">' +
C                                       %trim(%editc(CYEAR:'Z')) +
C                                       '</td>' +
C                                       '<td>' +
C                                       %trim(CMAKE) +
C                                       '</td>' +
C                                       '<td>' +
C                                       %trim(CMODEL) +
C                                       '</td>' +
C                                       '<td align="right">' +
C                                       %trim(%editc(CPRICE:'3')) +
C                                       '</td>' +
C                                       '</tr>' +
C                                       NewLine
C                    CALLP     #WrStout(WrtDta)
 *
```

Figure 10.18: Code that displays the car information to the Web page (part 1 of 2).

```
C                    eval      Count = (Count + 1)
C                    enddo
 * LRRN is filled here for the Next Page Link.
C                    if        (not *IN69)
C                    eval      LRRN = F$RRN
C                    READ      CARSPF                              69
C                    endif
```

Figure 10.18: Code that displays the car information to the Web page (part 1 of 2).

The first thing we check when processing the file is the field LRRN. This field will contain a value if, and only if, the page was accessed from a Next Page link on a previous page. You'll see why later.

If the variable LRRN contains a value, we will use the CHAIN op-code to position the file so that the first record read will be the one following the last record read. If there is no value in the LRRN field, we do nothing.

When we enter the loop, we will start reading the file that contains the information on the cars. No checking has to be done on the values since the OPNQRYF already did the selecting and sorting. We will read the file until we have read five records, or until we reach the end of the file.

After one of the conditions is met, we have one final step. If we didn't reach the end of the file, we will save the relative record number of the last record read. This value is retrieved from the program status data structure and stored in the LRRN field. Also, we perform one last read to make sure that the last record we read wasn't the last record in the file. If it was, we wouldn't know unless we performed this last read.

The reason for reading one last record from the file is simple. If we don't and the loop terminated because we had already read five records, there is a chance that the fifth record read was the last in the file. If it was, this last read will set on the end of file indicator. If it wasn't, the end of file indicator will remain off. It is important to note that we store the last relative record number before we perform this final read.

Now that all our records are displayed, we display the footer. This is where we will determine if we will display the Next Page link or not. You will see why we did that last read after exiting the loop. We wouldn't want to display a next page link for the user that will display a blank page. The code for the footer is shown in Figure 10.19.

```
C                   if        (*IN69)
C                   CALLP     #WrStout('End of Listing' +
C                                      NewLine)
C                   else
C                   eval      OutLink = %trim(InLink) +
C                                      '&lrrn=' +
C                                      %trim(%editc(LRRN:'L'))
   *
C                   eval      WrtDta = '<a href="' + %trim(OutLink) +
C                                      '&SORTBY=' + %trim(SORTBY) +
C                                      '">Next Page</a>' +
C                                      NewLine
C                   CALLP     #WrStout(WrtDta)
C                   endif
   *
C                   eval      WrtDta = '</BODY></HTML>' +
C                                      NewLine
C                   CALLP     #WrStout(WrtDta)
```

Figure 10.19: The code that produces the footer of the BVS-Cars Web page.

The first thing we do before writing the footer information to the Web page is to check the end of file indicator. If it is off, we will display the Next Page link. This link is built using the parameters read into the page and adding one more parameter for the last relative record number read. If this link is clicked, then all the same values the user entered on the first selection screen will be used, as well as any sorting parameters, and finally the value of the last record read. When the code displayed in Figure 10.18 is reached again, the file will be positioned by using the value in a CHAIN.

All of the code for the HTML page, RPG program, and the DDS for the files used in this example are given in appendix H. I strongly encourage you to try this out. Paging is important, and I believe that this is one of the best methods available to you to perform paging as well as record selection and sorting.

WHY OPNQRYF?

You may be wondering why I choose to use OPNQRYF for record selection and sorting in my CGI programs. The answer is actually quite simple. First, it's something that I am familiar with, as are most AS/400 programmers. Second, I know it works.

Using OPNQRYF in your CGI programs will be very handy and will speed the development if you are not familiar with other forms of sorting and record selection, such as embedded dynamic SQL statements. You also have the added benefit of the Query Optimizer doing most of the work, such as searching for access paths that already exist for your queries.

OPNQRYF will also have very good performance since no records are read until you perform a read on the file. This is similar to an SQL fetch. No real record processing is done until the first record is fetched. This is what makes it easy to page with OPNQRYF. By performing the OPNQRYF statement, chaining to the relative record number (RRN) of the last record read, you will be positioned exactly where you need to be.

Remember, the more tools you use with your CGI programs, the quicker development will be and the easier maintenance will be.

OLD DOG, NEW TRICKS

This chapter shows you a few of the tricks and techniques I have found very useful in my CGI programming applications. As you become more comfortable writing CGI programs, you will no doubt come up with some tricks of your own.

AFTERWORD

With the tremendous growth of the Internet and e-commerce in today's world, you can either keep up or be left in the dust. Establishing a Web presence for your company today will help ensure your company's e-commerce strategy will be a worthwhile business venture instead of just a page with pretty pictures.

The AS/400 is the machine on which we all rely for our day-to-day business operations, from production to payroll. Now the same AS/400 can be used as an all-in-one e-commerce solution.

This book has touched on the main areas that I believe will get your company up and running on the Web. From HTML to JavaScript to Common Gateway Interface programming with RPG—all of these ingredients play an important role in whether your site succeeds or not.

Let's take a very quick look at how each part works to help you develop your Web strategy.

HTML

Hypertext Markup Language (HTML) is the foundation of the Web. Without it, you cannot create a Web page. The first step in training your staff to be able to provide a successful Web presence begins and ends with HTML.

It is important to learn what tricks and techniques are involved in making a Web site both functional and appealing. I strongly suggest, though, that you focus mainly on functional features. As you have seen or experienced, many Web developers have the skills to make a Web page look good, but lack the business fundamentals to understand how to make the functionality of a page a reality.

Functionality first. Appeal later.

JavaScript

JavaScript (not Java) plays another very important role in your Web page design. A site can be made to function without JavaScript, but you will find that with it, your site will become more interactive and user friendly.

JavaScript not only shifts some of the processing to the client machine (freeing up your server), but it also provides solutions to interactive error checking, page manipulation, and the ability to implement a shopping basket.

JavaScript is a very easy language to learn. Also, with the many resources available today in the form of online manuals and discussion forums, there is no reason that any problem with JavaScript should leave you stumped.

Common Gateway Interface (CGI) Programming

Once you have your Web page designed, adding interactivity and dynamic content can be done with CGI programming. CGI programs are used mainly to keep information on your site up to date, and to cut down on maintenance performed on the site.

By building functional and useful CGI programs, your pages can run for months, or even years, with little or no intervention. CGI programs can do for e-business applications what green-screen applications have traditionally done for back office applications.

THE AS/400 HTTP SERVER

The heart and soul of any Web page is the server that it runs on. We are lucky enough to have the AS/400 as our Web server. Since the release of OS/400 V3R2M0, the AS/400's capabilities have moved from green-screen to fully interactive Web applications.

The AS/400 now serves Web pages, as well as adds the capability of using RPG or COBOL to provide CGI application programming with little or no learning curve.

Learning the basics of creating server instances, HTTP configurations, and security setup for your HTTP server is a must in your company. The AS/400 provides a very easy-to-use setup interface, and also provides some of the setup utilities as green-screen as well—the best of both worlds.

HTTP APIs

To make your CGI programs function, you will need to learn how to use a small set of APIs. APIs allow your CGI programs to write to standard output (the Web page) and read from standard input (Web page forms).

With any application, input and output are the basic necessities. The APIs provided to you as part of the operating system of the AS/400 allow you to create interactive Web pages for your company.

USING RPG FOR CGI APPLICATIONS

RPG has served most AS/400 programmers well for quite some time. There really isn't anything you cannot do with RPG. Now RPG does even more—it allows you to use it as a CGI programming language to provide interactive content to your Web applications.

Sure, there are a few other solutions out there today, but if RPG is your company's forté, why mess with a good thing? Why mess with a learning curve that isn't needed? If the Web application you are trying to provide is a priority, it is best to start with something that you are familiar with and will provide predictable results.

I have found that RPG has met or exceeded my expectations as a CGI programming solution. It's not the only solution, but if it is all you have, by all means use it. And if you use another solution, I'm sure that you will find situations where RPG can complement your existing solution. RPG was built solely for the AS/400 database, so I don't see how any other solution, on its own, could do more or be easier to use than RPG.

GET STARTED!

Now is the time that you have all been waiting for. Go out there and prove that the AS/400 is still the machine to use in the 21st century. IBM has done an excellent job in keeping up with the needs of today's business, and I feel they have outdone themselves when it comes to providing an e-commerce solution with the AS/400.

We are still able to use the same database, tools, programming languages, and programming techniques that we have all grown accustomed to. While others are scrambling to learn new technologies, we only need to learn a few new things as the bulk of the processing can be performed on a machine we already know.

Now, go out there and make some noise with e-RPG. It's the secret weapon we've all been waiting for!

APPENDIX A

The following sections include information to help you get started with HTML, as well as todetermine what some of the common error messages that you receive are trying to tell you. The error messages listed here are those you will find most commonly while working with HTML and CGI programming on the AS/400. For a more complete list, please see the Web Programming Guide (under the subheading HTML References) or the *Web Programming Guide* IBM manuals.

HTML ERROR MESSAGES

Error: Error 403 – Forbidden

> Cause: The path is not accessible. If you get this error while trying to retrieve a document or execute a CGI program, you may have specified the Pass directive incorrectly.

> Solution: Examine the Map, Exec, and Pass directives closely. Be sure that you have not specified a Pass directive before an Exec or Map directive.

> For example:

```
Pass /QSYS.LIB/AS400CGI.LIB/*
Exec /QSYS.LIB/AS400CGI.LIB/*
```

> This directive is specified incorrectly. When the server reads the Pass directive, and it matches the request, all other checking is aborted.

> Be sure to place your documents and CGI programs in separate locations. This way you won't cause conflicts in the configuration.

Error: Error 403 – Can't Browse Selected File

> Cause: User profile QTMHHTTP does not have the proper authorities to the file.

> Solution: Change the authority of the object so that user profile QTMHHTTP has the proper authority to the object requested.

Error: Error 500 – Bad Script Request

Cause: A request for a invalid CGI program

Solution: Double check the reference to the CGI program. If in your HTTP configuration you specified:

```
Exec /cgi-bin/* /QSYS.LIB/AS400CGI.LIB/*.PGM
```

make sure that the reference to your CGI program does not contain the .PGM extension. If in your HTTP configuration you specified:

```
Exec /cgi-bin/* /QSYS.LIB/AS400CGI.LIB/*
```

make sure that the reference to your CGI program contains the correct extension, usually .PGM.

HTML REFERENCES

HTTP Server for AS/400 Webmaster's Guide V4R4:

```
http://publib.boulder.ibm.com/cgi-bin/bookmgr/BOOKS/QB3AE004/CCONTENTS
```

Web Programming Guide V4R4:

```
http://publib.boulder.ibm.com/cgi-bin/bookmgr/BOOKS/QB3AEQ03/CCONTENTS
```

The Compendium of HTML Elements:

```
http://www.htmlcompendium.org/index.htm
```

HTML Tag List:

```
http://utopia.knoware.nl/users/schluter/doc/tags/index.html
```

W3C HTML Home Page:

```
http://www.w3.org/MarkUp/
```

APPENDIX B

This appendix has the complete source for the two programs referenced in chapter 2.

SOURCE FOR COOKIE BASKET

The following is the source for the Cookie Basket example in chapter 2.

```
<HTML>
<HEAD>
<TITLE>Cookie Basket</TITLE>
</HEAD>
<BODY>
<script language="javascript">
<!- begin script

//Cookie Basket

var itemCookie = "itemCookie";
var qtyCookie = "qtyCookie";
var basketwinopen = "n";
```

Source for Cookie Basket (part 1 of 5).

```
// FindElement() will return the index of the array    //
// that contains the value passed in.  If the element //
// is not found, -1 is returned.                       //

function FindElement(value) {
   var i = 0;
   while(i < itemArray.length) {
      if (itemArray[i] == value)
         return i;
      i++;
   }
   return -1;
}


// WriteCookie() will write a cookie with the data     //
// passed in as well as the expiration date.           //

function WriteCookie(name,value,expireDays) {
   var expire = new Date();
   expire.setTime (expire.getTime() + (expireDays * 24 * 3500000));
   document.cookie = name + "=" + escape(value) +
                     "; expires=" + expire.toGMTString() ;
}


// GetCookie() will return the data that is contained //
// in the cookie specified by the name pass in.       //

function GetCookie(name) {
   var value = name + "=";
   var i = 0;
   while (i < document.cookie.length) {
      var j = (i + value.length);
      if (document.cookie.substring(i,j) == value) {
         var len = document.cookie.indexOf(";",j);
            if (len == -1)
            len = document.cookie.length;
            return unescape(document.cookie.substring(j, len));
      }
      i = document.cookie.indexOf(" ", i) + 1;
      if (i == 0) break;
   }
   return null;
}


// DeleteCookie() deletes the cookie by setting       //
// the expiration date to 2 days ago.                 //

function DeleteCookie(name) {
   var expire = new Date();
   expire.setTime(expire.getTime() - 2 * 86400001);
   document.cookie = name + "=*; expires=" + expire.toGMTString();
```

Source for Cookie Basket (part 2 of 5).

```
}
// LoadItemArray() loads the array itmArray with the   //
// values stored in the itemCookie.                    //

function LoadItemArray() {
   var i = 0,index = 0, len = 0;
   var cookieValue = GetCookie(itemCookie);
   itemArray = new Array();
   if (cookieValue == null )
      return;
   len=cookieValue.indexOf("`", index);
   while (len != -1) {
 itemArray[i]= cookieValue.substring(index, len);
      i++;
      index = len + 1;
      len=(cookieValue.indexOf("`", index));
   }
}


// LoadQtyArray() loads the array qtyArray with the    //
// values stored in qtyCookie.                         //

function LoadQtyArray() {
   var i = 0,index = 0, len = 0;
   var cookieValue = GetCookie(qtyCookie);
   qtyArray = new Array();
   if (cookieValue == null )
      return;
   len=cookieValue.indexOf("`", index);
   while (len != -1) {
      qtyArray[i]= cookieValue.substring(index, len);
      i++;
      index = len + 1;
      len=(cookieValue.indexOf("`", index));
   }
}


// BigCookie() writes two cookies.  The first stores   //
// the items select and the second stores the related  //
// quantity of that item.                              //

function BigCookie(cookieValue) {
   LoadItemArray();
   LoadQtyArray();
   var i = FindElement(cookieValue);
   if (i != -1) {
      qtyArray[i] = eval(qtyArray[i]) + 1;
   } else {
      itemArray[itemArray.length] = cookieValue;
      qtyArray[qtyArray.length] = 1;
   }
```

Source for Cookie Basket (part 3 of 5).

```
      var itemValue = itemArray.join("`") + "`";
      var qtyValue = qtyArray.join("`") + "`";
      WriteCookie(itemCookie,itemValue,1);
      WriteCookie(qtyCookie,qtyValue,1);
   }


   // AddItem() adds the selected item to the shopping   //
   // basket and notifies that the item has been added.  //

   function AddItem(item) {
      BigCookie(item);
      alert("A " + item + " has been added to your shopping basket.\n");
   }


   // DisplayBasket() displays the contents of the       //
   // shopping basket.                                   //

   function DisplayBasket() {
      LoadItemArray();
      LoadQtyArray();
      if ((basketwinopen == "y") && (! basketwin.closed)) {
         basketwin.close();
      }
      basketwin=window.open('','basketwin','width=300,height=300');
      basketwinopen="y";
      basketwin.document.write("<HTML><TITLE>Basket Contents</TITLE>");
      basketwin.document.write("Your shopping basket contains the
   following: <BR>");
      basketwin.document.write("<BODY onBlur=self.close>\n" +
                               "<TABLE border=1>\n" +
                               "<TR><TD>Item Number</TD>\n" +
                               "<TD align=right>Quantity</TD></TR>\n");
      var i = 0;
      while(i < itemArray.length) {
         basketwin.document.write("<TR><TD>" + itemArray[i] + "</TD>" +
                               "<TD align=right>" + qtyArray[i] + "</TD>");
         i++;
      }
      basketwin.document.write("</TABLE></BODY>");
   }


   // DeleteAllCookies() deletes the three cookies.      //
   // This clears the shopping basket.        .          //

   function DeleteAllCookies() {
      DeleteCookie(itemCookie);
      DeleteCookie(qtyCookie);
   }

   // end script ->
</script>
Click on the item you wish to add to your shopping basket.<BR>
```

Source for Cookie Basket (part 4 of 5).

```
<TABLE border="1"><TR>
<TD><a href="#" onClick="AddItem('Jackhammer');">Jackhammer</a></TD>
<TD><a href="#" onClick="AddItem('PickAxe');">PickAxe</a></TD></TR>
<TR><TD><a href="#" onClick="AddItem('Shovel');">Shovel</a></TD>
<TD><a href="#" onClick="AddItem('Auger');">Auger</a></TD></TR>
<TR><TD><a href="#" onClick="AddItem('Wheelbarrow');"> +
Wheelbarrow</a></TD>
<TD><a href="#" onClick="AddItem('Crowbar');">Crowbar</a></TD></TR>
</TABLE>
<form>
<input type="button" value="Clear Basket"
OnClick="DeleteAllCookies();"><BR>
<input type="button" value="View Basket" onClick="DisplayBasket();"><BR>
</form>
</BODY>
</HTML>
```

Source for Cookie Basket (part 5 of 5).

SOURCE FOR BVS-REPRINTS

The following is the source for the BVS-Reprints example in chapter 2.

```
<html>

<head>
<title>BVS-Reprints</title>
<script LANGUAGE="javascript">
<!-
pageArr = new Array(1,6,12);
qtyArr = new Array(25,50,75,100,250,500);
priceArr = new Array(pageArr.length);

for (i=0; i < priceArr.length; i++) {
    priceArr[i] = new Array(qtyArr.length)
}

priceArr[0][0] = 2.0232
priceArr[1][0] = 4.3424
priceArr[2][0] = 6.2376

priceArr[0][1] = 1.2646
priceArr[1][1] = 3.4642
priceArr[2][1] = 4.6012

priceArr[0][2] = 0.9980
priceArr[1][2] = 3.2164
```

Source for BVS-Reprints (part 1 of 6).

```
priceArr[2][2] = 4.2551

priceArr[0][3] = 0.8647
priceArr[1][3] = 3.0926
priceArr[2][3] = 4.0822

priceArr[0][4] = 0.4526
priceArr[1][4] = 2.7902
priceArr[2][4] = 3.1841

priceArr[0][5] = 0.3339
priceArr[1][5] = 2.5831
priceArr[2][5] = 2.7899

shipArr = new Array("1","2","3");
shipPgArr = new Array(2,4,8,16);
shipQtyArr = new Array(1000,5000,10000);
shipPriceArr = new Array(shipArr.length);

for (i=0; i < shipPriceArr.length; i++) {
    shipPriceArr[i] = new Array(shipPgArr.length)
    for (j=0; j < shipPriceArr[i].length; j++) {
        shipPriceArr[i][j] = new Array(shipQtyArr.length)
    }
}
//UPS Ground
shipPriceArr[0][0][0] = 0.00797
shipPriceArr[0][1][0] = 0.01397
shipPriceArr[0][2][0] = 0.02492
shipPriceArr[0][3][0] = 0.04875

shipPriceArr[0][0][1] = 0.005404
shipPriceArr[0][1][1] = 0.011934
shipPriceArr[0][2][1] = 0.023268
shipPriceArr[0][3][1] = 0.04424

shipPriceArr[0][0][2] = 0.005967
shipPriceArr[0][1][2] = 0.011634
shipPriceArr[0][2][2] = 0.02212
shipPriceArr[0][3][2] = 0.04424

//UPS 2nd Day
shipPriceArr[1][0][0] = 0.03275
shipPriceArr[1][1][0] = 0.057
shipPriceArr[1][2][0] = 0.1015
shipPriceArr[1][3][0] = 0.1975

shipPriceArr[1][0][1] = 0.0254
shipPriceArr[1][1][1] = 0.0494
shipPriceArr[1][2][1] = 0.126
shipPriceArr[1][3][1] = 0.2408
```

Source for BVS-Reprints (part 2 of 6).

```
shipPriceArr[1][0][2] = 0.0247
shipPriceArr[1][1][2] = 0.063
shipPriceArr[1][2][2] = 0.1204
shipPriceArr[1][3][2] = 0.2408

//UPS Overnight
shipPriceArr[2][0][0] = 0.051
shipPriceArr[2][1][0] = 0.0725
shipPriceArr[2][2][0] = 0.1235
shipPriceArr[2][3][0] = 0.25275

shipPriceArr[2][0][1] = 0.0311
shipPriceArr[2][1][1] = 0.06335
shipPriceArr[2][2][1] = 0.1484
shipPriceArr[2][3][1] = 0.2856

shipPriceArr[2][0][2] = 0.031675
shipPriceArr[2][1][2] = 0.0742
shipPriceArr[2][2][2] = 0.1428
shipPriceArr[2][3][2] = 0.2856

function stripSpaces(x) {
   while (x.substring(0,1) == ' ') x = x.substring(1);
   while (x.substring(x.length-1,x.length) == ' ') x =
x.substring(0,x.length-1);
   return x;
}


function isNumber(value) {
   var i, len = value.length;
   for (i = 0; i < len; i++) {
      if ((value.charAt(i) < '0') || (value.charAt(i) > '9'))
         return false;
   }
   return true;
}

function round (n) {
   n = Math.round(n * 100) / 100;
   n = (n + .001) + "";
   return n.substring(0, n.indexOf('.') + 3);
}

function pageElm(page) {
var i = 0;
   while (i < pageArr.length) {
      if (pageArr[i] >= page)
         return i;
      i++;
   }
   return pageArr.length-1;
```

Source for BVS-Reprints (part 3 of 6).

```
}

function qtyElm(qty) {
    var i = 0;
    for (i = 0; i < qtyArr.length; i++) {
        if (qtyArr[i] >= qty)
            return i;
    }
    return qtyArr.length-1;
}

function shipElm(carrierLevel) {
    var i = 0;
    for (i = 0; i < shipArr.length; i++) {
        if (shipArr[i] == carrierLevel)
            return i;
    }
    return 0;
}

function shipPgElm(page) {
    var i = 0;
    for (i = 0; i < shipPgArr.length; i++) {
        if (shipPgArr[i] >= page)
            return i;
    }
    return shipPgArr.length-1;
}

function shipQtyElm(qty) {
    var i = 0;
    for (i = 0; i < shipQtyArr.length; i++) {
        if (shipQtyArr[i] >= qty)
            return i;
    }
    return shipQtyArr.length-1;
}

function validForm(form,show) {
    form.copies.value = stripSpaces(form.copies.value);
    if (! isNumber(form.copies.value)) {
        if (show)
            alert("Copies must contain numbers only.");
        return false;
    } else {
        return true;
    }
}

function figurePrice(form) {
    var selectedPage = form.numpages[form.numpages.selectedIndex].value;
```

Source for BVS-Reprints (part 4 of 6).

```
    var selectedShip = form.shipopt[form.shipopt.selectedIndex].value;
    var unitPrice, shippingCost, totalPrice, weightPerc = 1,
        i = pageElm(selectedPage),
        j = qtyElm(form.copies.value),
        x = shipElm(selectedShip),
        y = shipPgElm(selectedPage),
        z = shipQtyElm(form.copies.value);

    if (validForm(form,1)) {
        if (form.paperstock[1].checked)
            weightPerc = 1.15;
        if (form.paperstock[2].checked)
            weightPerc = 1.30;
        unitPrice = round(priceArr[i][j] * weightPerc);
        shippingCost = round((shipPriceArr[x][y][z] * form.copies.value));
        totalPrice = round((unitPrice * form.copies.value +
eval(shippingCost)));
        form.unitPrice.value = ("$" + unitPrice);
        form.shippingCost.value = ("$" + shippingCost);
        form.totalPrice.value = ("$" + totalPrice);
    }

}

//-->
</script>
</head>

<body>

<p align="center"><big><big><strong><font color="#FF0000">BVS-Reprints
</font></strong></big></big></p>

<p align="left"><u>Please select from the following:</u></p>

<form name="form1">
  <table width="100%">
    <tr>
      <td><table>
        <tr>
          <td valign="top"><font size="2" face="Arial, Helvetica,
sans-serif">Paper Stock: </font></td>
          <td><font size="1" face="Arial, Helvetica, sans-serif"><input
type="radio"
          name="paperstock" value="70" checked
onClick="figurePrice(document.form1)">70 lb<br>
          <input type="radio" name="paperstock" value="80"
onClick="figurePrice(document.form1)">80
          lb<br>
          <input type="radio" name="paperstock" value="100"
onClick="figurePrice(document.form1)">100
          lb<br>
```

Source for BVS-Reprints (part 5 of 6).

```
           </font></td>
        </tr>
       </table>
      </td>
      <td><font size="2" face="Arial, Helvetica, sans-serif">Number of
Pages: <select
       name="numpages" onChange="figurePrice(document.form1);" size="1">
         <option value="1">1</option>
         <option value="6">6</option>
         <option value="12">12</option>
      </select> </font></td>
    </tr>
    <tr>
      <td colspan="2"><hr>
        <p><font size="2" face="Arial, Helvetica, sans-serif">Shipping
Options: <select
       name="shipopt" onChange="figurePrice(document.form1);" size="1">
         <option value="1">UPS Ground</option>
         <option value="2">UPS 2nd Day Air</option>
         <option value="3">UPS Overnight</option>
      </select> </font></td>
    </tr>
  </table>
  <hr>
  <table width="100%">
    <tr>
      <td><font size="1" face="Arial, Helvetica, sans-serif">Copies:<input
type="text"
       name="copies" maxlength="8" size="10" value="100"
onChange="figurePrice(document.form1);">
      </font></td>
      <td><font size="1" face="Arial, Helvetica, sans-serif">Unit
Price:<input type="text"
       maxlength="5" size="10" name="unitPrice"> </font></td>
      <td><font size="1" face="Arial, Helvetica, sans-
serif">Shipping:<input type="text"
       maxlength="5" size="10" name="shippingCost"> </font></td>
      <td><font size="1" face="Arial, Helvetica, sans-serif">Total
Price:<input type="text"
       maxlength="8" size="12" name="totalPrice"> </font></td>
    </tr>
  </table>
  <script>
figurePrice(document.form1);
</script>

</form>
</body>
</html>
```

Source for BVS-Reprints (part 6 of 6).

JavaScript References

Netscape DevEdge JavaScript Reference:

```
http://developer.netscape.com/docs/manuals/communicator/jsguide4/index.htm
```

The JavaScript Source:

```
http://javascript.internet.com/
```

JavaScript World:

```
http://www.jsworld.com/
```

APPENDIX C

The following is the source for a set of subprocedures that will let you easily manipulate the current job's library list. I find them useful when I need to access data that is not in a library that is in the HTTP job's library list.

```
H NOMAIN
*****************************************************************
 * Prototypes                                                   *
*****************************************************************
D #PushLib        PR
D   PR_Lib                       10    VALUE
D #PopLib         PR
D   PR_text                      10    VALUE OPTIONS(*NOPASS)
*****************************************************************
 * Global Definitions                                           *
*****************************************************************
D WPError         DS
D  EBytesP                1      4B 0 INZ(%size(EData))
D  EBytesA                5      8B 0
D  EMsgID                 9     15
D  EReserverd            16     16
D  EData                 17     56
```

Source for #PushLib and #PopLib (part 1 of 3).

```
 *
D QCmdCmd         S            512     INZ
D QCmdLength      S             15   5 INZ(%size(QCmdCmd))
 *//////////////////////////////////////////////////////////////*
 * (#PushLib) Push a library onto the top of the libary list.   *
 *//////////////////////////////////////////////////////////////*
P #PushLib        B                    EXPORT
 *                                                               *
D #PushLib        PI
D  Lib                          10     VALUE
 *                                                               *
C                 eval      QCmdCmd = 'ADDLIBLE LIB(' +
C                               %trim(Lib) +
C                               ') ' +
C                               'POSITION(*FIRST)'
 *
C                 CALL      'QCMDEXC'                         99
C                 PARM                  QCmdCmd
C                 PARM                  QCmdLength
 *
 *                                                               *
C      *PSSR      BEGSR
C                 ENDSR
 *                                                               *
P #PushLib        E
 *//////////////////////////////////////////////////////////////*
 * (#PopLib) Pop a library from the library list.  If no value  *
 *  is passed to this procedure, the first library is popped    *
 *  from the library list.                                      *
 *//////////////////////////////////////////////////////////////*
P #PopLib         B                    EXPORT
 *                                                               *
D #PopLib         PI
D  Lib                          10     VALUE OPTIONS(*NOPASS)
 *
D LibPtr          S              *
 *
D MaxLibs         C                    CONST(25)
 *
D LibData         DS                   BASED(LibPtr)
D  #Libs                        9B 0
D  LibArr                       10     DIM(MaxLibs)
 *                                                               *
 *
C                 if        (%Parms < 1) or (Lib = '*FIRST')
C                 eval      LibPtr = #RtvLibL('*USER')
 *
C                 if        (LibPtr *NULL) and (#Libs > 0)
C                 eval      Lib = (LibArr(1))
C                 endif
 *
C                 endif
```

Source for #PushLib and #PopLib (part 2 of 3).

```
 *
 C                    eval      QCmdCmd = 'RMVLIBLE LIB(' +
 C                                        %trim(Lib) +
 C                                        ') '
 *
 C                    CALL      'QCMDEXC'                           99
 C                    PARM                   QCmdCmd
 C                    PARM                   QCmdLength
 *
 *──────────────────────────────────────────────────────────────*
 C     *PSSR          BEGSR
 C                    ENDSR
 *──────────────────────────────────────────────────────────────*
 P #PopLib            E
```

Source for #PushLib and #PopLib (part 3 of 3).

COMMON GATEWAY INTERFACE (CGI) REFERENCES

The World Wide Web Consortium (W3C) CGI Reference Page:

```
http://www.w3.org/CGI/
```

The CGI Resource Index:

```
http://www.cgi-resources.com/
```

CGI Made Really Easy:

```
http://www.jmarshall.com/easy/cgi/
```

The Common Gateway Interface:

```
http://hoohoo.ncsa.uiuc.edu/cgi/overview.html
```

APPENDIX D

The following sections include a summary of the technical information covered in chapter 4. The default configuration file that comes with your AS/400 is also included. You can use these sections as a reference when setting up your HTTP server.

ACCESSING THE AS/400 TASKS PAGE

Start the *ADMIN HTTP server instance with the following command:

```
STRTCPSVR SERVER(*HTTP) HTTPSVR(*ADMIN)
```

Enter the following URL into your web browser replacing your.as400. ipaddress with the IP address of your AS/400.

```
http://your.as400.ipaddress:2001
```

IMPORTANT HTTP CONIFIGURATION DIRECTIVES

Directive	Action	Example
Map	Maps a directory or file to another location	Map /cgi-bin/* /QSYS.LIB/AS400CGI.LIB/*
Exec	Allows acess to executable programs in a particular library	Exec /QSYS.LIB/AS400CGI.LIB/*
Pass	Allows the client to access a particular directory or library on your HTTP Server	Pass /HTML/*orPass /QSYS.LIB/AS400CGI.LIB/*
Fail	Refuse access to a particular directory or library on your HTTP Server	Fail /Private/*orFail /QSYS.LIB/APDATA.LIB/*
Redirect	Redirects the client to a new location	Redirect /oldpages/* http://www.newpage.com
Welcome	Specifies the file to access when no file is specified in the URL	Welcome index.html

HTTP CONFIGURATION EXAMPLES

Default HTTP Configuration (V4R4M0)

The following is the default HTTP configuration (named CONFIG) that comes with a V4R4M0 machine.

```
# * * * * * * * * * * * * * * * * * * * * * * * * * * * * *
#                    IBM HTTP Server for AS/400
# * * * * * * * * * * * * * * * * * * * * * * * * * * * * *
#
#─────────────────────────────────────────────────────────────
# NOTE:    Lines starting with a "#" are comments.
#          Inline comments are not allowed.  For example,
#          do not have a "#" on the same line as MAP
#          statement.
#─────────────────────────────────────────────────────────────
#               *** HOSTNAME DIRECTIVES ***
#
# HostName your AS/400 uses when generating references
# to itself. This value will be set to the value set in
# CFGTCP, Option 12, when not specified here.
#
# Syntax:
#   HostName                    <your.full.host.name>
#
#─────────────────────────────────────────────────────────────
#               *** PORT DIRECTIVES ***
#
# The default port for HTTP is 80.  If you change this
# use a port number greater than 1024.
#
#
# Syntax:
#   Port                        <port number>
#─────────────────────────────────────────────────────────────
#   Port                        80
#
#─────────────────────────────────────────────────────────────
#               *** METHOD DIRECTIVES ***
#
# GET and HEAD are enabled by default.  POST will need to
# be enabled for CGI and Net.Data.
#
# Syntax:
#   Disable                     <GET ! HEAD ! POST>
#   Enable                      <GET ! HEAD ! POST>
#─────────────────────────────────────────────────────────────
#   Enable                      GET
#   Enable                      HEAD
#   Enable                      POST
#
#─────────────────────────────────────────────────────────────
#               *** MAPPING DIRECTIVES ***
#
# Mapping to AS/400 IFS library objects requires the
# object to have PUBLIC(*RX) authority.
#
# Mapping to AS/400 QSYS.LIB library objects requires
```

Default HTTP Configuration (part 1 of 5).

```
# the QTMHHTTP user profile to have read access to the
# object or the object to have PUBLIC(*USE) authority.
#
# The <template> is the string used to match the
# incoming request or HTML link (URL).  The template is
# mapped to replacement location on the server.  Once a
# matching Pass, Exec, Redirect, or Fail template is
# found, all subsequent rules are ignored.
# A match on Map rule changes the request to the
# value in replacement and continues searching for a
# Pass, Exec, Redirect or Fail.
#
#    - To serve documents or images, use Pass directives.
#    - To run CGI or Net.Data, use Exec
#      directives.
#    - To send the request to another server, use Redirect
#      directives.
#    - To prevent access to a particular location that
#      a subsequent rule would allow access to, use the
#      Fail directive.
#    - All requests that do not match a template on the
#      Pass, Exec or Redirect will Fail by default and
#      generate a "403 - Forbidden by rule" error.
#
# Syntax:
#    Map       <template> <replacement>
#    Pass      <template> <replacement>
#    Exec      <template> <replacement>
#    Redirect  <template> <replacement>
#    Fail      <template>
#
#    Map      /test/*     /as400/*
#    Pass     /as400/*    /QDLS/400HOME/*
#    Pass     /httpfile/* /QSYS.LIB/AS400LIB.LIB/HTML.FILE/*
#    Pass     /doc/*      /QDLS/graphics/*
#    Pass     /file/*     /www/webdata/*
#    Fail     /QIBM/UserData/private/*
#    Pass     /QIBM/UserData/*
#    Redirect /wsg        http://hostname:5061/WSG
#
# HTTP server CGI programs must find an Exec directive.
# This Exec directive refers to a path where the CGI
# program is stored.
#
# Exec  /cgi-bin/*  /QSYS.LIB/MYCGI.LIB/*
#
# The next two Pass directives are shipped in the IBM HTTP
# Server for AS/400 server configuration in
# V4R3.  The first Pass directive serves a sample file
# called Welcome.html for a request of the form
# http://hostname/. The second Pass directive allows
# image files referenced in the Welcome.html file to
```

Default HTTP Configuration (part 2 of 5).

```
#  be served.
#  To serve your own server home page change the first pass
#  directive to point to your welcome page location.
#
Pass /edi432pgm/*
   Pass /  /QIBM/ProdData/HTTP/Public/HTTPSVR/HTML/Welcome.html
   Pass /sample/*  /QIBM/ProdData/HTTP/Public/HTTPSVR/HTML/*
Pass /EDI432PGM/*
#
#─────────────────────────────────────────────────────────────
#                   *** WELCOME FILE ***
#
# Syntax:
#   Welcome                      <file.ext> <ip address>
#
# To serve a welcome file from QDLS, add:
#   Welcome                      Welcome.htm
#
# To serve hello.html to clients with IP addresses
# that map to 100.99.* and serve Welcome.html to
# all others, add:
#   Welcome                      hello.html 100.99.*
#   Welcome                      Welcome.html
#
# When the HTML is an AS/400 source physical file,
# the source type of the member must be set to HTML.
# The Welcome directive refers to the member name
# and the value specified for source type.
#─────────────────────────────────────────────────────────────
#   Welcome                      Welcome.html
#─────────────────────────────────────────────────────────────
#                 *** DIRECTORY LISTINGS ***
#
# Syntax:
#   DirAccess                    <Off ! On ! Selective>
#   DirShowMaxLen                <Maximum name length>
#   DirShowMinLen                <Minimum name length>
#   DirReadme                    <Off ! Top ! Bot>
#   DirShowData                  <Off ! On>
#   DirShowSize                  <Off ! On>
#   DirShowByte                  <On  ! Off>
#   DirShowOwner                 <Off ! On>
#   DirShowDescription           <Off ! On>
#   DirShowMaxDescrLength        <number>
#─────────────────────────────────────────────────────────────
#   DirAccess                    On
#   DirShowMaxLen                15
#   DirShowMinLen                15
#   DirReadme                    Top
#   DirShowDate                  On
#   DirShowSize                  On
#   DirShowBytes                 On
```

Default HTTP Configuration (part 3 of 5).

```
#   DirShowOwner                     On
#   DirShowDescription               On
#   DirShowMaxDescrLength            25
#------------------------------------------------------------
#                      *** AddIcon ***
#
#  To represent files with a specific MIME content-type
#  or encoding type with icons on directory listings,
#  use AddIcon.  To actually use these, you will need to
#  enable directory listings using DirAccess and
#  add a Pass directive that maps the IconPath to
#  /QIBM/ProdData/HTTP/Protect/HTTPSVR/HTML/ICONS/
IconPath /QIBM/HTTPSVR/Icons/
AddIcon text.gif        text    text/*
AddIcon html.gif        html    text/html
AddIcon binary.gif      bin     application/*
AddIcon compress.gif Z          application/x-compress
AddIcon compress.gif gzip       application/x-gzip
AddIcon image.gif       img     image/*
AddIcon movie.gif       vid     video/*
AddIcon sound.gif       au      audio/*
#------------------------------------------------------------
#                      *** AddType ***
#
#  To bind files with a particular suffix to a MIME
#  type/subtype, use AddType.  Multiple occurrences
#  are allowed.
AddType .java text/plain binary 1.0
AddType .html text/html   8bit   1.0
AddType .htm  text/html   8bit   1.0
AddType .gif  image/gif   binary
#------------------------------------------------------------
#                      *** LOGGING ***
#
#  To enable access logs to the AS/400 server, use
#  AccessLog.  To enable logs for HTTP server
#  errors, use ErrorLog.  AccessLog and ErrorLog
#  Filenames can be specified in these forms:
#
#  Access Log file, ACCESSLOG, created in QUSRSYS.
#  1 - AccessLog ACCESSLOG
#  Access Log file, ACCESSLOG, created in
#    Integrated File System directory, httplog.
#  2 - AccessLog /httplog/accesslog
#
#  Syntax:
#    AccessLog                      <Access_Log_FileName>
#    ErrorLog                       <Error_Log_FileName>
#    LogFormat                      <DDS ! COMMON>
#    LogTime                        <LocalTime ! GMT>
#    NoLog                          <ip address>
#------------------------------------------------------------
```

Default HTTP Configuration (part 4 of 5).

```
#   AccessLog                   ACCESSLOG
#   ErrorLog                    ERRORLOG
#   LogFormat                   COMMON
#   LogTime                     LocalTime
#
#                   *** TIMEOUT ***
#
#   InputTimeout - Client to send MIME header request.
#   OutputTimeout - Server to serve a document.
#   ScriptTimeout - Server to finish a CGI program.
#
#   Syntax:
#       InputTimeOut            <number> mins
#       OutputTimeOut           <number> mins
#       ScriptTimeOut           <number> mins
#
#   InputTimeOut                2 mins
#   OutputTimeOut               20 mins
#   ScriptTimeOut               5 mins
#
#               *** END OF DIRECTIVES ***
#
```

Default HTTP Configuration (part 5 of 5).

Sample of Basic HTTP Configuration

The following is a sample HTTP configuration. It assumes that your HTML files, style sheets, and graphics are stored in the root file system of the Integrated File System (IFS) in the /Webpages directory and that your CGI programs are stored in a library named AS400CGI.

Accessing the Web page will require the URL http://www.myas400.com and accessing CGI programs will require the cgi-bin directory in the URL without the use of the .PGM extension.

```
Exec /cgi-bin/* /QSYS.LIB/AS400CGI.LIB/*.PGM %%EBCDIC%%
Pass /* /Webpages/*
Welcome index.html
```

Granting Authority to Files in the IFS

First, grant authority to the root directory:

```
CHGAUT OBJ('/dir') USER(QTMHHTTP) DTAAUT(*R)
```

Next, grant authority to all objects within the root directory:

```
CHGAUT OBJ('/dir/*') USER(QTMHHTTP) DTAAUT(*R)
```

AS/400 HTTP Configuration References

HTTP Server for AS/400 Webmaster's Guide V4R4:

```
http://publib.boulder.ibm.com/cgi-bin/bookmgr/BOOKS/QB3AE004/CCONTENTS
```

Web Programming Guide V4R4:

```
http://publib.boulder.ibm.com/cgi-bin/bookmgr/BOOKS/QB3AEQ03/CCONTENTS
```

APPENDIX E

The following sections include the definitions for the APIs discussed in chapter 5. References to online documentation where you can get more information on these APIs are also included. You can use this information as a reference when you write CGI programs.

HTTP API PARAMETER DEFINITIONS

The following is a list of HTTP APIs that are available for use in your CGI programs.

QtmhWrStout (Write to Standard Output) Required Parameters		
Parameter	Type(Size) – Use	Description
Data	Char(*) – Input	A varying character field that contains the data, such as HTML code, that is to be written to the browser.
Length of Data	Bindary(4) – Input	A binary field that tells the API the length of the data in the Data parameter.
Error Parameter	Char(*) – Input/Output	The standard API Error structure.

QtmhRdStin (Read from Standard Input) Required Parameters

Parameter	Type(Size) – Use	Description
Receiver Variable	Char(*) – Output	The variable name that will hold the data received from the Read Standard Input API.
Length of Receiver Variable	Binary(4) – Input	A binary field that holds the length of the Receiver Variable.
Length of Response Available	Bindary(4) – Output	The length of the data read in by the Read Standard Input API.
Error Parameter	Char(*) – Input/Output	The standard API Error structure.

QtmhGetEnv (Get Environment Variables) Required Parameters

Parameter	Type(Size) – Use	Description
Receiver Variable	Char(*) – Output	The variable name that will hold the data received from the Read Standard Input API.
Length of Receiver Variable	Binary(4) – Input	A binary field that holds the length of the Receiver Variable.
Length of Response	Bindary(4) – Output	The length of the data read in by the Read Standard Input API.
Request Variable	Char(*) – Input	The name of the environment variable that the request is made for.
Length of Request Variable	Binary(4) – Input	The length of the request variable.
Error Parameter	Char(*) – Input/Output	The standard API Error structure.

QtmhCvtDB (Convert to Database) Required Parameters		
Parameter	**Type(Size) – Use**	**Description**
Database Name	Char(20) – Input	A variable that contains the qualified database name that contains the field descriptions for conversion. The first 10 characters are the file name and the last 10 characters are the library name.
Input String	Char(*) – Input	The variable name that contains the string received from the Read Standard Input API or the Query String environment variable.
Length of Input String	Binary(4) – Input	A binary field that holds the length of the input string to be parsed.
Response Variable	Char(*) – Output	The variable that is to contain the structure mapped according to the database file describing the input parameters anticipated by the CGI program.
Length of Response Available	Bindary(4) – Input	The total length of the buffer into which the CGI input parameters will be parsed.
Length of Response Variable	Binary(4) – Output	The length of the response. If the response variable is too small to contain the entire response, this parameter will be set to the size that is required to contain the entire response.
Response Code	Binary(4) – Output	A code that contains the status of the operation.
Error Parameter	Char(*) – Input/ Output	The standard API Error structure.

HTTP API REFERENCES

HTTP Server for AS/400 Webmaster's Guide V4R4:

```
http://publib.boulder.ibm.com/cgi-bin/bookmgr/BOOKS/QB3AE004/CCONTENTS
```

Web Programming Guide V4R4:

```
http://publib.boulder.ibm.com/cgi-bin/bookmgr/BOOKS/QB3AEQ03/CCONTENTS
```

Cool Title About the AS/400 and the Internet:

```
http://www.redbooks.ibm.com/abstracts/sg244815.html
```

APPENDIX F

Following is the all the source for the BVS-Computers example in chapter 8.

Index.html

```
<html>

<head>
<meta name="GENERATOR" content="Microsoft FrontPage 3.0">
<title>BVS-Computers</title>
<script language="JavaScript">
function Validate(form) {
    if (form.userid.value == "") {
        alert("Enter a user ID!");
        return false;
    } else {
        return true;
    }
}
</script>
</head>

<body>
```

Index.html (part 1 of 2).

```
<p align="center"><font color="#FF0000"><big><big>Welcome to BVS-
Computers!</big></big></font></p>

<form action="/cgi-bin/signin" method="post" onsubmit="return Vali-
date(this);">
  <div align="center"><center><table>
    <tr>
      <td>User ID:</td>
      <td><input type="text" name="userid" size="10"></td>
    </tr>
    <tr>
      <td>Password</td>
      <td><input type="password" name="password" size="10"></td>
    </tr>
  </table>
  </center></div><div align="center"><center><p><input type="submit"
value="Sign In"> </p>
  </center></div>
</form>

<p> </p>
</body>
</html>
```

Index.html (part 2 of 2).

Invoice Header (INVHDRPF)

```
A                                      UNIQUE
A           R RINVHDR                  TEXT('Invoice Header')
A             IHSTATUS      1          TEXT('Invoice Status')
A             IHINV         7S 0       TEXT('Invoice Number')
A             IHUSERID      10         TEXT('User ID')
A           K IHINV
```

Invoice Detail (INVDETPF)

```
A                                      UNIQUE
A           R RINVDET                  TEXT('Invoice Detail')
A             IDINV         7S 0       TEXT('Invoice Number')
A             IDSEQ         3S 0       TEXT('Sequence Number')
A             IDITEM        15         TEXT('Item Number')
A             IDQTY         7S 0       TEXT('Quantity')
A             IDPRC         7S 2       TEXT('Price')
A           K IDINV
A           K IDSEQ
```

Invoice Detail Logical (INVDET1LF)

```
A                                    UNIQUE
A         R RINVDET                  TEXT('Invoice Detail')
A                                    PFILE(INVDETPF)
A           K IDINV
A           K IDITEM
```

Item File (ITEMPF)

```
A                                    UNIQUE
A         R RITEM                    TEXT('User File')
A           ITITEM        15         TEXT('Item Number')
A           ITDESC        50         TEXT('Item Description')
A           ITIMG        100         TEXT('Image Path')
A           ITPRC          7S 2      TEXT('Item Price')
A           K ITITEM
```

User File (USERPF)

```
A                                    UNIQUE
A         R RUSER                    TEXT('User File')
A           USUSERID      10         TEXT('User ID')
A           USPASSWORD    10         TEXT('Password')
A           USFNAME       30         TEXT('First Name')
A           USLNAME       30         TEXT('Last Name')
A           USADDR1       30         TEXT('Address')
A           USCITY        30         TEXT('City')
A           USSTATE       30         TEXT('State')
A           USZIP         30         TEXT('Zip')
A           K USUSERID
```

Sign-in e-RPG Program (SIGNIN)

```
H DFTACTGRP(*NO) BNDDIR('CGIBNDDIR')
******************************************************************
FUSERPF    IF  E           K DISK
******************************************************************
/COPY QSRVSRC,P.CONVERT
******************************************************************
D RcvDS          E DS                    EXTNAME(BVSCOMP)
*
D RcvFile          DS
D  File                        1     10  INZ('BVSCOMP    ')
D  Lib                        11     20  INZ('AS400CGI   ')
*
D WPError          DS
D  EBytesP                     1      4B 0 INZ(40)
D  EBytesA                     5      8B 0
D  EMsgID                      9     15
D  EReserverd                 16     16
D  EData                      17     56
*
D HTTPHeader      C                       CONST('Content-type: text/html')
D Pragma          C                       CONST('Pragma: no-cache')
D Expires1        C                       CONST('Expires: Saturday, February')
D Expires2        C                       CONST('15, 1997 10:10:10 GMT')
D NewLine         C                       CONST(X'15')
*
D RcvRec          S           1024
D RcvLen          S              9B 0
D RcvRecLen       S              9B 0
*
D EnvRec          S           1024
D EnvLen          S              9B 0
D EnvRecLen       S              9B 0 INZ(%size(EnvRec))
D EnvName         S             14    INZ('CONTENT_LENGTH')
D EnvNameLen      S              9B 0 INZ(%size(EnvName))
*
D WrtDta          S           1024
D WrtDtaLen       S              9B 0
*
D CvtLen          S              9B 0 INZ(%size(RcvDS))
D CvtLenAv        S              9B 0
D CvtStat         S              9B 0
******************************************************************
C                   EXSR      $RdStin
C                   EXSR      $CvtDB
C                   EXSR      $Header
C                   EXSR      $Main
C                   EXSR      $Footer
C                   SETON                                        LR
******************************************************************
```

Sign-in e-RPG Program (SIGNIN) (part 1 of 4).

```
C       $Header      BEGSR
*
C                    eval      WrtDta = %trim(HTTPHeader) +
C                                     NewLine + Pragma +
C                                     NewLine +
C                                     Expires1 + Expires2 +
C                                     NewLine + NewLine
C                    EXSR      $WrStout
*
C                    eval      WrtDta = '<html><head>' +
C                                     '<title>' +
C                                     'BVS-Computers' +
C                                     '</title>' +
C                                     '</head>' +
C                                     '<body>' +
C                                     '<p align="center">' +
C                                     '<font color="#FF0000">' +
C                                     '<big><big>' +
C                                     'BVS-Computers' +
C                                     '</big></big></font></p>' +
C                                     NewLine
C                    EXSR      $WrStout
*
C                    ENDSR
*****************************************************************
C       $Main        BEGSR
*
C       USERID       CHAIN     USERPF
*
C                    if        (not %found) or (PASSWORD  USPASSWORD)
C                    eval      WrtDta = '<CENTER>' +
C                                     'Error!' +
C                                     '<BR>' +
C                                     'Invalid User ID or Password!' +
C                                     '</CENTER>' +
C                                     NewLine
C                    else
C                    eval      WrtDta = '<CENTER>' +
C                                     'Welcome ' +
C                                     %trim(USFNAME) + ' ' +
C                                     %trim(USLNAME) + '.' +
C                                     '<BR><BR>' +
C                                     '<a href="/cgi-bin/items?userid=' +
C                                     %trim(USERID) + '">' +
C                                     'Go Shopping!' +
C                                     '</CENTER>' +
C                                     NewLine
C                    endif
*
C                    EXSR      $WrStout
*
C                    ENDSR
```

Sign-in e-RPG Program (SIGNIN) (part 2 of 4).

277

```
**********************************************************
C       $Footer    BEGSR
 *
C                  eval      WrtDta = '</body></html>' +
C                                     NewLine
C                  EXSR      $WrStout
 *
C                  ENDSR
**********************************************************
C       $WrStout   BEGSR
 *
C                  eval      WrtDtaLen = %len(%trim(WrtDta))
 *
C                  CALLB     'QtmhWrStout'
C                  PARM                  WrtDta
C                  PARM                  WrtDtaLen
C                  PARM                  WPError
 *
C                  ENDSR
**********************************************************
C       $RdStin    BEGSR
 *
C                  CALLB     'QtmhGetEnv'
C                  PARM                  EnvRec
C                  PARM                  EnvRecLen
C                  PARM                  EnvLen
C                  PARM                  EnvName
C                  PARM                  EnvNameLen
C                  PARM                  WPError
 *
C                  eval      RcvLen = #CtoN(EnvRec)
 *
C                  if        (RcvLen > %size(RcvRec))
C                  eval      RcvLen = %size(RcvRec)
C                  endif
 *
C                  CALLB     'QtmhRdStin'
C                  PARM                  RcvRec
C                  PARM                  RcvLen
C                  PARM                  RcvRecLen
C                  PARM                  WPError
 *
C                  ENDSR
**********************************************************
C       $CvtDB     BEGSR
 *
C                  CALLB     'QtmhCvtDb'
C                  PARM                  RcvFile
C                  PARM                  RcvRec
C                  PARM                  RcvLen
C                  PARM                  RcvDS
C                  PARM                  CvtLen
```

Sign-in e-RPG Program (SIGNIN) (part 3 of 4).

```
C                   PARM                    CvtLenAv
C                   PARM                    CvtStat
C                   PARM                    WPError
 *
C                   ENDSR
```

Sign-in e-RPG Program (SIGNIN) (part 4 of 4).

Display Items e-RPG Program (ITEMS)

```
H DFTACTGRP(*NO) BNDDIR('CGIBNDDIR')
****************************************************************
FITEMPF    IF   E           K DISK
****************************************************************
D EnvDS          E DS                       EXTNAME(BVSCOMP)
 *
D EnvFile          DS
D  File                    1     10    INZ('BVSCOMP    ')
D  Lib                    11     20    INZ('AS400CGI  ')
 *
D WPError          DS
D  EBytesP                 1      4B 0 INZ(40)
D  EBytesA                 5      8B 0
D  EMsgID                  9     15
D  EReserverd             16     16
D  EData                  17     56
 *
D HTTPHeader      C                    CONST('Content-type: text/html')
D Pragma          C                    CONST('Pragma: no-cache')
D Expires1        C                    CONST('Expires: Saturday, February')
D Expires2        C                    CONST('15, 1997 10:10:10 GMT')
D NewLine         C                    CONST(X'15')
 *
D EnvRec          S           1024
D EnvLen          S              9B 0
D EnvRecLen       S              9B 0 INZ(%size(EnvRec))
D EnvName         S             12    INZ('QUERY_STRING')
D EnvNameLen      S              9B 0 INZ(%size(EnvName))
 *
D CvtLen          S              9B 0 INZ(%size(EnvDS))
D CvtLenAv        S              9B 0
D CvtStat         S              9B 0
 *
D WrtDta          S           1024
D WrtDtaLen       S              9B 0
****************************************************************
C                   EXSR      $GetQS
```

Display Items e-RPG Program (ITEMS) (part 1 of 4).

```
C                  EXSR      $CvtDB
C                  EXSR      $Header
C                  EXSR      $Main
C                  EXSR      $Footer
C                  SETON                                          LR
 **********************************************************************
C    $Header       BEGSR
 *
C                  eval      WrtDta = %trim(HTTPHeader) +
C                                     NewLine + Pragma +
C                                     NewLine +
C                                     Expires1 + Expires2 +
C                                     NewLine + NewLine
C                  EXSR      $WrStout
 *
C                  eval      WrtDta = '<html><head>' +
C                                     '<title>' +
C                                     '>BVS-Computers' +
C                                     '</title>' +
C                                     '</head><body>' +
C                                     '<p align="center">' +
C                                     '<font color="#FF0000">' +
C                                     '<big><big>' +
C                                     'BVS-Computers - List Items' +
C                                     '</big></big></font></p>' +
C                                     NewLine
C                  EXSR      $WrStout
 *
C                  ENDSR
 **********************************************************************
C    $Main         BEGSR
 *
C                  eval      WrtDta = '<center>' +
C                                     'Click on Item Description ' +
C                                     'to add to your cart.<br>' +
C                                     '<table border="1">' +
C                                     NewLine
C                  EXSR      $WrStout
 *
C                  eval      *IN66 = *OFF
C    *LOVAL        SETLL     ITEMPF
C                  READ      ITEMPF
 *
C                  dow       (not %eof)
 *
C                  if        (not *IN66)
C                  eval      WrtDta = '<tr>' +
C                                     NewLine
C                  EXSR      $WrStout
C                  endif
 *
```

Display Items e-RPG Program (ITEMS) (part 2 of 4).

```
C                   eval      WrtDta = '<td width="50%" align="center">' +
C                                      '<img src="' +
C                                      %trim(ITIMG) + '"><br>' +
C                                      NewLine
C                   EXSR      $WrStout
 *
C                   eval      WrtDta = '<a href=' +
C                                      '"/cgi-bin/buyitem?USERID=' +
C                                      %trim(USERID) +
C                                      '&ITEM=' +
C                                      %trim(ITITEM) + '">' +
C                                      %trim(ITDESC) + '</a><br>' +
C                                      NewLine
C                   EXSR      $WrStout
 *
C                   eval      WrtDta = 'Price: ' +
C                                      %trim(%editc(ITPRC:'3')) +
C                                      '</td>' +
C                                      NewLine
C                   EXSR      $WrStout
 *
C                   if        (*IN66)
C                   eval      WrtDta = '</tr>' +
C                                      NewLine
C                   EXSR      $WrStout
C                   endif
 *
C                   eval      *IN66 = (not *IN66)
C                   READ      ITEMPF
C                   enddo
 *
C                   if        (*IN66)
C                   eval      WrtDta = '<td></td></tr>' +
C                                      NewLine
C                   EXSR      $WrStout
C                   endif
 *
C                   eval      WrtDta = '</table></center>' +
C                                      NewLine
C                   EXSR      $WrStout
 *
C                   ENDSR
 ****************************************************************
C     $Footer       BEGSR
 *
C                   eval      WrtDta = '<br><center>' +
C                                      '<a href="/cgi-bin/checkout' +
C                                      '?userid=' +
C                                      %trim(USERID) +
C                                      '">Checkout</a>' +
C                                      '</center>' +
C                                      NewLine
```

Display Items e-RPG Program (ITEMS) (part 3 of 4).

```
C                      EXSR        $WrStout
  *
C                      eval        WrtDta = '</body></html>' +
C                                           NewLine
C                      EXSR        $WrStout
  *
C                      ENDSR
 ****************************************************************
C     $WrStout         BEGSR
  *
C                      eval        WrtDtaLen = %len(%trim(WrtDta))
  *
C                      CALLB       'QtmhWrStout'
C                      PARM                    WrtDta
C                      PARM                    WrtDtaLen
C                      PARM                    WPError
  *
C                      ENDSR
 ****************************************************************
C     $GetQS           BEGSR
  *
C                      CALLB       'QtmhGetEnv'
C                      PARM                    EnvRec
C                      PARM                    EnvRecLen
C                      PARM                    EnvLen
C                      PARM                    EnvName
C                      PARM                    EnvNameLen
C                      PARM                    WPError
  *
C                      ENDSR
 ****************************************************************
C     $CvtDB           BEGSR
  *
C                      if          (EnvLen = 0)
C                      eval        EnvLen = %size(EnvRec)
C                      endif
  *
C                      CALLB       'QtmhCvtDb'
C                      PARM                    EnvFile
C                      PARM                    EnvRec
C                      PARM                    EnvLen
C                      PARM                    EnvDS
C                      PARM                    CvtLen
C                      PARM                    CvtLenAv
C                      PARM                    CvtStat
C                      PARM                    WPError
  *
C                      ENDSR
```

Display Items e-RPG Program (ITEMS) (part 4 of 4).

Buy Item e-RPG Program (BUYITEM)

```
H DFTACTGRP(*NO) BNDDIR('CGIBNDDIR')
 **********************************************************************
FINVHDRPF  UF A E           K DISK
FINVDETPF  UF A E           K DISK
FINVDET1LF UF   E           K DISK    RENAME(RINVDET:RINVDET1)
FITEMPF    IF   E           K DISK
 **********************************************************************
D EnvDS        E DS                    EXTNAME(BVSCOMP)
 *
D EnvFile        DS
D  File                   1     10     INZ('BVSCOMP   ')
D  Lib                   11     20     INZ('AS400CGI  ')
 *
D WPError        DS
D  EBytesP                1      4B 0  INZ(40)
D  EBytesA                5      8B 0
D  EMsgID                 9     15
D  EReserverd            16     16
D  EData                 17     56
 *
D HTTPHeader    C                      CONST('Content-type: text/html')
D Pragma        C                      CONST('Pragma: no-cache')
D Expires1      C                      CONST('Expires: Saturday, February')
D Expires2      C                      CONST('15, 1997 10:10:10 GMT')
D NewLine       C                      CONST(X'15')
 *
D WrtDta        S              1024
D WrtDtaLen     S                 9B 0
 *
D EnvRec        S              1024
D EnvLen        S                 9B 0
D EnvRecLen     S                 9B 0  INZ(%size(EnvRec))
D EnvName       S                12     INZ('QUERY_STRING')
D EnvNameLen    S                 9B 0  INZ(%size(EnvName))
 *
D CvtLen        S                 9B 0  INZ(%size(EnvDS))
D CvtLenAv      S                 9B 0
D CvtStat       S                 9B 0
 *
D LastInv       S                      LIKE(IHINV)
D NextSeq       S                      LIKE(IDSEQ)
 **********************************************************************
C     InvItemKey    KLIST
C                   KFLD                     IHINV
C                   KFLD                     ITITEM
 *
C                   EXSR      $GetQS
C                   EXSR      $CvtDB
C                   EXSR      $Header
```

Buy Item e-RPG Program (BUYITEM) (part 1 of 5).

```
C                    EXSR      $Main
C                    EXSR      $Footer
C                    SETON                                              LR
 *****************************************************************
C     $Header        BEGSR
 *
C                    eval      WrtDta = %trim(HTTPHeader) +
C                                       NewLine + Pragma +
C                                       NewLine +
C                                       Expires1 + Expires2 +
C                                       NewLine + NewLine
C                    EXSR      $WrStout
 *
C                    eval      WrtDta = '<html><head>' +
C                                       '<title>' +
C                                       'BVS-Computers' +
C                                       '</title>' +
C                                       '</head><body>' +
C                                       '<p align="center">' +
C                                       '<font color="#FF0000">' +
C                                       '<big><big>' +
C                                       'BVS-Computers' +
C                                       '</big></big></font></p>' +
C                                       NewLine
C                    EXSR      $WrStout
 *
C                    ENDSR
 *****************************************************************
C     $Main          BEGSR
 *
C     ITEM           CHAIN     ITEMPF
 *
C                    if        (not %found)
C                    eval      WrtDta = '<center>' +
C                                       'Error - Item not found.<BR>' +
C                                       'Please call for assistance.' +
C                                       '</center>' +
C                                       NewLine
C                    else
C                    EXSR      $GetInv
C                    EXSR      $AddtoInv
C                    eval      WrtDta = '<center>' +
C                                       'The following item has been ' +
C                                       'to your shopping cart.<BR>' +
C                                       NewLine
C                    EXSR      $WrStout
C                    eval      WrtDta = '<table><tr>' +
C                                       NewLine +
C                                       '<td>Item Number:</td>' +
C                                       '<td>' + %trim(ITITEM) + '</td>' +
C                                       '</tr><tr>' +
C                                       '<td>Description:</td>' +
```

Buy Item e-RPG Program (BUYITEM) (part 2 of 5).

```
C                                  '<td>' + %trim(ITDESC) + '</td>' +
C                                  '</tr><tr>' +
C                                  '<td>Price:</td>' +
C                                  '<td>' +
C                                  %trim(%editc(ITPRC:'3')) +
C                                  '</td>' +
C                                  '</tr></table>' +
C                                  '</center>' +
C                                  NewLine
C                    EXSR     $WrStout
C                    endif
 *
C                    ENDSR
 ******************************************************************
C     $Footer        BEGSR
 *
C                    eval     WrtDta = '<br><br><center>' +
C                                  '<a href="/cgi-bin/items?userid=' +
C                                  %trim(USERID) +
C                                  '">Return to Shopping</a>' +
C                                  '<BR>' +
C                                  NewLine
C                    EXSR     $WrStout
 *
C                    eval     WrtDta = '<br><a href="/cgi-bin/checkout' +
C                                  '?userid=' +
C                                  %trim(USERID) +
C                                  '">Checkout</a>' +
C                                  '</center>' +
C                                  NewLine
C                    EXSR     $WrStout
 *
C                    eval     WrtDta = '</body></html>' +
C                                  NewLine
C                    EXSR     $WrStout
 *
C                    ENDSR
 ******************************************************************
C     $GetInv        BEGSR
 *
C                    eval     LastInv = 0
C     *HIVAL         SETGT    INVHDRPF
C                    READP(n) INVHDRPF
 *
C                    dow      (not %eof)
 *
C                    if       (IHUSERID = USERID) and (IHSTATUS = '0')
C                    LEAVE
C                    endif
 *
C                    if       (IHINV > LastInv)
C                    eval     LastInv = IHINV
```

Buy Item e-RPG Program (BUYITEM) (part 3 of 5).

```
C              endif
 *
C              READP(n)  INVHDRPF
C              enddo
 *
C              if        (%eof)
C              CLEAR     *ALL        RINVHDR
C              eval      IHINV = (LastInv + 1)
C              eval      IHSTATUS = '0'
C              eval      IHUSERID = USERID
C              WRITE     RINVHDR
C              endif
 *
C              ENDSR
 ****************************************************************
C   $AddtoInv  BEGSR
 *
C   InvItemKey CHAIN     INVDET1LF
 *
C              if        (%found)
C              eval      IDQTY = (IDQTY + 1)
C              UPDATE    RINVDET1
C              else
C              eval      NextSeq = 1
C   IHINV      SETGT     INVDETPF
C   IHINV      READPE(n) INVDETPF
 *
C              if        (not %eof)
C              eval      NextSeq = (IDSEQ + 1)
C              endif
 *
C              CLEAR     *ALL        RINVDET
C              eval      IDINV = IHINV
C              eval      IDSEQ = NextSeq
C              eval      IDITEM = ITITEM
C              eval      IDQTY = 1
C              eval      IDPRC = ITPRC
C              WRITE     RINVDET
C              endif
 *
C              ENDSR
 ****************************************************************
C   $WrStout   BEGSR
 *
C              eval      WrtDtaLen = %len(%trim(WrtDta))
 *
C              CALLB     'QtmhWrStout'
C              PARM                  WrtDta
C              PARM                  WrtDtaLen
C              PARM                  WPError
 *
C              ENDSR
```

Buy Item e-RPG Program (BUYITEM) (part 4 of 5).

```
*******************************************************************
C     $GetQS        BEGSR
 *
C                   CALLB     'QtmhGetEnv'
C                   PARM                    EnvRec
C                   PARM                    EnvRecLen
C                   PARM                    EnvLen
C                   PARM                    EnvName
C                   PARM                    EnvNameLen
C                   PARM                    WPError
 *
C                   ENDSR
*******************************************************************
C     $CvtDB        BEGSR
 *
C                   if        (EnvLen = 0)
C                   eval      EnvLen = %size(EnvRec)
C                   endif
 *
C                   CALLB     'QtmhCvtDb'
C                   PARM                    EnvFile
C                   PARM                    EnvRec
C                   PARM                    EnvLen
C                   PARM                    EnvDS
C                   PARM                    CvtLen
C                   PARM                    CvtLenAv
C                   PARM                    CvtStat
C                   PARM                    WPError
 *
C                   ENDSR
```

Buy Item e-RPG Program (BUYITEM) (part 5 of 5).

Remove Item e-RPG Program (RMVITEM)

```
H DFTACTGRP(*NO) BNDDIR('CGIBNDDIR')

****************************************************************
FINVDETPF  UF   E           K DISK
FITEMPF    IF   E           K DISK

****************************************************************
D EnvDS          E DS                    EXTNAME(BVSCOMP)
*
D EnvFile          DS
D  File                     1     10     INZ('BVSCOMP    ')
D  Lib                     11     20     INZ('AS400CGI   ')
*
D WPError          DS
D  EBytesP                  1      4B 0  INZ(40)
D  EBytesA                  5      8B 0
D  EMsgID                   9     15
D  EReserverd              16     16
D  EData                   17     56
*
D HTTPHeader      C                      CONST('Content-type:
text/html')
D Pragma          C                      CONST('Pragma: no-cache')
D Expires1        C                      CONST('Expires: Saturday,
February')
D Expires2        C                      CONST('15, 1997 10:10:10 GMT')
D NewLine         C                      CONST(X'15')
*
D WrtDta          S           1024
D WrtDtaLen       S              9B 0
*
D EnvRec          S           1024
D EnvLen          S              9B 0
D EnvRecLen       S              9B 0  INZ(%size(EnvRec))
D EnvName         S             12     INZ('QUERY_STRING')
D EnvNameLen      S              9B 0  INZ(%size(EnvName))
*
D CvtLen          S              9B 0  INZ(%size(EnvDS))
D CvtLenAv        S              9B 0
D CvtStat         S              9B 0

****************************************************************
C     InvSeqKey     KLIST
C                   KFLD                    Inv
C                   KFLD                    Seq
*
C                   EXSR      $GetQS
C                   EXSR      $CvtDB
C                   EXSR      $Header
C                   EXSR      $Main
```

Remove Item (RMVITEM) (part 1 of 4).

```
C                       EXSR      $Footer
C                       SETON                                           LR
 ****************************************************************
C       $Header         BEGSR
 *
C                       eval      WrtDta = %trim(HTTPHeader) +
C                                 NewLine + Pragma +
C                                 NewLine +
C                                 Expires1 + Expires2 +
C                                 NewLine + NewLine
C                       EXSR      $WrStout
 *
C                       eval      WrtDta = '<html><head>' +
C                                 '<title>' +
C                                 'BVS-Computers' +
C                                 '</title>' +
C                                 '</head><body>' +
C                                 '<p align="center">' +
C                                 '<font color="#FF0000">' +
C                                 '<big><big>' +
C                                 'BVS-Computers' +
C                                 '</big></big></font></p>' +
C                                 NewLine
C                       EXSR      $WrStout
 *
C                       ENDSR
 ****************************************************************
C       $Main           BEGSR
 *
C       InvSeqKey       CHAIN     INVDETPF
 *
C                       if        (not %found)
C                       eval      WrtDta = '<center>' +
C                                 'Error - Item not found.<BR>' +
C                                 'Please call for assistance.' +
C                                 '</center>' +
C                                 NewLine
C                       else
C                       DELETE    RINVDET
C                       eval      WrtDta = '<center>' +
C                                 'The following item has been ' +
C                                 'removed from your cart.<BR>' +
C                                 NewLine
C                       EXSR      $WrStout
C       IDITEM          CHAIN     ITEMPF
C                       eval      WrtDta = '<table><tr>' +
C                                 NewLine +
C                                 '<td>Item Number:</td>' +
C                                 '<td>' + %trim(ITITEM) + '</td>' +
C                                 '</tr><tr>' +
C                                 '<td>Quantity:</td>' +
C                                 '<td>' +
```

Remove Item (RMVITEM) (part 2 of 4).

```
C                                       %trim(%editc(IDQTY:'Z')) +
C                                       '</td>' +
C                                       '</tr><tr>' +
C                                       '<td>Description:</td>' +
C                                       '<td>' + %trim(ITDESC) + '</td>'
+
C                                       '</tr><tr>' +
C                                       '<td>Price:</td>' +
C                                       '<td>' +
C                                       %trim(%editc(ITPRC:'3')) +
C                                       '</td>' +
C                                       '</tr></Table>' +
C                                       '</center>' +
C                                       NewLine
C                    EXSR      $WrStout
C                    endif
*
C                    ENDSR
*****************************************************************
C     $Footer        BEGSR
*
C                    eval      WrtDta = '<br><br><center>' +
C                                       '<a
href="/cgi-bin/items?userid=' +
C                                       %trim(USERID) +
C                                       '">Return to Shopping</a>' +
C                                       NewLine
C                    EXSR      $WrStout
*
C                    eval      WrtDta = '<br><a href="/cgi-bin/checkout'
+
C                                       '?userid=' +
C                                       %trim(USERID) +
C                                       '">Checkout</a>' +
C                                       '</center>' +
C                                       NewLine
C                    EXSR      $WrStout
*
C                    eval      WrtDta = '</body></html>' +
C                                       NewLine
C                    EXSR      $WrStout
*
C                    ENDSR
*****************************************************************
C     $WrStout       BEGSR
*
C                    eval      WrtDtaLen = %len(%trim(WrtDta))
*
C                    CALLB     'QtmhWrStout'
C                    PARM                WrtDta
C                    PARM                WrtDtaLen
C                    PARM                WPError
```

Remove Item (RMVITEM) (part 3 of 4).

```
     *
C                    ENDSR
 **********************************************************************
C      $GetQS        BEGSR
     *
C                    CALLB     'QtmhGetEnv'
C                    PARM                      EnvRec
C                    PARM                      EnvRecLen
C                    PARM                      EnvLen
C                    PARM                      EnvName
C                    PARM                      EnvNameLen

C                    PARM                      WPError
     *
C                    ENDSR
 **********************************************************************
C      $CvtDB        BEGSR
     *
C                    if        (EnvLen = 0)
C                    eval      EnvLen = %size(EnvRec)
C                    endif
     *
C                    CALLB     'QtmhCvtDb'
C                    PARM                      EnvFile
C                    PARM                      EnvRec
C                    PARM                      EnvLen
C                    PARM                      EnvDS
C                    PARM                      CvtLen
C                    PARM                      CvtLenAv
C                    PARM                      CvtStat
C                    PARM                      WPError
     *
C                    ENDSR
```

Remove Item (RMVITEM) (part 4 of 4).

Check-Out e-RPG Program (CHECKOUT)

```
H DFTACTGRP(*NO) BNDDIR('CGIBNDDIR')
******************************************************************
FINVHDRPF  IF   E           K DISK
FINVDETPF  IF   E           K DISK
FITEMPF    IF   E           K DISK
FUSERPF    IF   E           K DISK
******************************************************************
D EnvDS         E DS                  EXTNAME(BVSCOMP)
*
D EnvFile         DS
D  File                   1     10    INZ('BVSCOMP   ')
D  Lib                   11     20    INZ('AS400CGI  ')
*
D WPError         DS
D  EBytesP                1      4B 0 INZ(40)
D  EBytesA                5      8B 0
D  EMsgID                 9     15
D  EReserverd            16     16
D  EData                 17     56
*
D HTTPHeader      C                   CONST('Content-type: text/html')
D Pragma          C                   CONST('Pragma: no-cache')
D Expires1        C                   CONST('Expires: Saturday, February')
D Expires2        C                   CONST('15, 1997 10:10:10 GMT')
D NewLine         C                   CONST(X'15')
*
D WrtDta          S           1024
D WrtDtaLen       S              9B 0
*
D EnvRec          S           1024
D EnvLen          S              9B 0
D EnvRecLen       S              9B 0 INZ(%size(EnvRec))
D EnvName         S             12    INZ('QUERY_STRING')
D EnvNameLen      S              9B 0 INZ(%size(EnvName))
*
D CvtLen          S              9B 0 INZ(%size(EnvDS))
D CvtLenAv        S              9B 0
D CvtStat         S              9B 0
*
D LastInv         S                   LIKE(IHINV)
D GRDTOT          S             11  2
D EXTPRICE        S              9  2
******************************************************************
C                   EXSR      $GetQS
C                   EXSR      $CvtDB
C                   EXSR      $Header
C                   EXSR      $Main
C                   EXSR      $Footer
C                   SETON                                        LR
******************************************************************
```

Check-out (CHECKOUT) (part 1 of 5).

```
C        $Header       BEGSR
C                      eval       WrtDta = %trim(HTTPHeader) +
C                                 NewLine + Pragma +
C                                 NewLine +
C                                 Expires1 + Expires2 +
C                                 NewLine + NewLine
C                      EXSR       $WrStout
C      *
C                      eval       WrtDta = '<html><head>' +
C                                 '<title>BVS-Computers</title>' +
C                                 '</head><body>' +
C                                 '<p align="center">' +
C                                 '<font color="#FF0000">' +
C                                 '<big><big>' +
C                                 'BVS-Computers' +
C                                 '</big></big></font></p>' +
C                                 NewLine
C                      EXSR       $WrStout
C      *
C                      ENDSR
C ****************************************************
C        $Main         BEGSR
C                      EXSR       $GetInv
C                      if         (LastInv = 0)
C                      eval       WrtDta = 'No open invoices found.<BR>' +
C                                 'Please call for assistance.' +
C                                 NewLine
C                      EXSR       $WrStout
C                      else
C                      EXSR       $Invoice
C                      endif
C                      ENDSR
C ****************************************************
C        $Footer       BEGSR
C                      eval       WrtDta = '<BR>' +
C                                 '<a href="/cgi-bin/items?userid=' +
C                                 %trim(USERID) +
C                                 '">Return to Shopping</a>' +
C                                 NewLine
C                      EXSR       $WrStout
C      *
C                      if         (LastInv  0)
C                      eval       WrtDta = '<BR>' +
C                                 '<a href="/cgi-bin/invship?inv=' +
C                                 %trim(%editc(IHINV:'Z')) +
C                                 '&userid=' +
C                                 %trim(USERID) +
C                                 '">Ship Order</a>' +
C                                 NewLine
C                      EXSR       $WrStout
C                      endif
C      *
```

Check-out (CHECKOUT) (part 2 of 5).

```
C                   eval      WrtDta = '</body></html>' +
C                                      NewLine
C                   EXSR      $WrStout
*
C                   ENDSR
****************************************************
C     $GetInv       BEGSR
*
C                   eval      LastInv = 0
C     *HIVAL        SETGT     INVHDRPF
C                   READP     INVHDRPF
*
C                   dow       (not %eof)
C                   if        (IHUSERID = USERID) and (IHSTATUS = '0')
C                   LEAVE
C                   endif
C                   READP     INVHDRPF
C                   enddo
*
C                   if        (not %eof)
C                   eval      LastInv = IHINV
C                   endif
*
C                   ENDSR
****************************************************
C     $Invoice      BEGSR
C                   eval      GRDTOT = 0
C                   EXSR      $HDG
C     IHINV         SETLL     INVDETPF
C     IHINV         READE     INVDETPF
*
C                   dow       (not %eof)
C                   eval      EXTPRICE = (IDQTY * IDPRC)
C                   eval      GRDTOT = (GRDTOT + EXTPRICE)
C                   EXSR      $DET
C     IHINV         READE     INVDETPF
C                   enddo
*
C                   EXSR      $BOT
*
C                   ENDSR
****************************************************
C     $HDG          BEGSR
C     IHUSERID      CHAIN     USERPF
C                   eval      WrtDta = '<TABLE width="25%"'  +
C                                      'bgcolor="#80FF80">' +
C                             '<TR><TD>' +
C                             'User ID:' + '</TD>' +
C                             '<TD>' + %trim(IHUSERID) +
C                             '</TD></TR><TR><TD>' +
C                             'Invoice:' + '</TD>' +
C                             '<TD>' + %editc(IHINV:'Z') +
```

Check-out (CHECKOUT) (part 3 of 5).

```
C                               '</TD></TR><TR>' +
C                               '<TD colspan="2">' +
C                               %trim(USFNAME) + ' ' +
C                               %trim(USLNAME) +
C                               '</TD></TR><TR>' +
C                               '<TD colspan="2">' +
C                               %trim(USADDR1) +
C                               '</TD></TR><TR>' +
C                               '<TD colspan="2">' +
C                               %trim(USCITY + USSTATE + USZIP) +
C                               '</TD></TR>' +
C                               '</TABLE>' + NewLine
C                     EXSR      $WrStout
C                     eval      WrtDta = '<TABLE width="100%"><TR>' +
C                               '<TD bgcolor="C0C0C0">Remove</TD>' +
C                               '<TD bgcolor="C0C0C0">Qty</TD>' +
C                               '<TD bgcolor="C0C0C0">Item</TD>' +
C                               '<TD bgcolor="C0C0C0">Description</TD>' +
C                               '<TD bgcolor="C0C0C0">Price</TD>' +
C                               '<TD bgcolor="C0C0C0">Total Due</TD></TR>' +
C                               NewLine
C                     EXSR      $WrStout
C                     ENDSR
C     ************************************************
C     $DET            BEGSR
C     IDITEM          CHAIN     ITEMPF
C                     eval      WrtDta = '<TR><TD align="center">' +
C                               '<a href="/cgi-bin/rmvitem?inv=' +
C                               %trim(%editc(IDINV:'Z')) +
C                               '&seq=' +
C                               %trim(%editc(IDSEQ:'Z')) +
C                               '&userid=' +
C                               %trim(USERID) +
C                               '">*</a>' +
C                               '</TD><TD>' +
C                               %editc(IDQTY:'3') + '</TD><TD>' +
C                               %trim(IDITEM) + '</TD><TD>' +
C                               %trim(ITDESC) + '</TD><TD>' +
C                               %editc(IDPRC:'3') + '</TD><TD>' +
C                               %editc(EXTPRICE:'3') + '</TD></TR>' +
C                               NewLine
C                     EXSR      $WrStout
C                     ENDSR
C     ************************************************
C     $BOT            BEGSR
C                     eval      WrtDta = '<TR>' +
C                               '<TD></TD><TD></TD><TD></TD><TD></TD>' +
C                               '<TD bgcolor="00FFFF">' +
C                               'Grand Total:' + '</TD>' +
C                               '<TD bgcolor="00FFFF">' +
C                               %editc(GRDTOT:'3') + '</TD></TR></TABLE>' +
C                               NewLine
```

Check-out (CHECKOUT) (part 4 of 5).

```
C                       EXSR      $WrStout
C                       ENDSR
 ****************************************************
C       $WrStout        BEGSR
C                       eval      WrtDtaLen = %len(%trim(WrtDta))
C                       CALLB     'QtmhWrStout'
C                       PARM                    WrtDta
C                       PARM                    WrtDtaLen
C                       PARM                    WPError
C                       ENDSR
 ****************************************************
C       $GetQS          BEGSR
C                       CALLB     'QtmhGetEnv'
C                       PARM                    EnvRec
C                       PARM                    EnvRecLen
C                       PARM                    EnvLen
C                       PARM                    EnvName
C                       PARM                    EnvNameLen
C                       PARM                    WPError
C                       ENDSR
 ****************************************************
C       $CvtDB          BEGSR
C                       if        (EnvLen = 0)
C                       eval      EnvLen = %size(EnvRec)
C                       endif
C                       CALLB     'QtmhCvtDb'
C                       PARM                    EnvFile
C                       PARM                    EnvRec
C                       PARM                    EnvLen
C                       PARM                    EnvDS
C                       PARM                    CvtLen
C                       PARM                    CvtLenAv
C                       PARM                    CvtStat
C                       PARM                    WPError
C                       ENDSR
```

Check-out (CHECKOUT) (part 5 of 5).

Invoice and Ship Order e-RPG Program (INVSHIP)

```
H DFTACTGRP(*NO) BNDDIR('CGIBNDDIR')
*******************************************************************
FINVHDRPF  UF   E           K DISK
*******************************************************************
D EnvDS          E DS                  EXTNAME(BVSCOMP)
 *
D EnvFile          DS
D  File                    1     10    INZ('BVSCOMP   ')
D  Lib                    11     20    INZ('AS400CGI  ')
 *
D WPError          DS
D  EBytesP                 1      4B 0 INZ(40)
D  EBytesA                 5      8B 0
D  EMsgID                  9     15
D  EReserverd             16     16
D  EData                  17     56
 *
D HTTPHeader      C                    CONST('Content-type: text/html')
D Pragma          C                    CONST('Pragma: no-cache')
D Expires1        C                    CONST('Expires: Saturday, February')
D Expires2        C                    CONST('15, 1997 10:10:10 GMT')
D NewLine         C                    CONST(X'15')
 *
D WrtDta          S           1024
D WrtDtaLen       S              9B 0
 *
D EnvRec          S           1024
D EnvLen          S              9B 0
D EnvRecLen       S              9B 0 INZ(%size(EnvRec))
D EnvName         S             12    INZ('QUERY_STRING')
D EnvNameLen      S              9B 0 INZ(%size(EnvName))
 *
D CvtLen          S              9B 0 INZ(%size(EnvDS))
D CvtLenAv        S              9B 0
D CvtStat         S              9B 0
*******************************************************************
C                   EXSR      $GetQS
C                   EXSR      $CvtDB
C                   EXSR      $Header
C                   EXSR      $Main
C                   EXSR      $Footer
C                   SETON                                        LR
*******************************************************************
C     $Header       BEGSR
 *
C                   eval      WrtDta = %trim(HTTPHeader) +
C                               NewLine + Pragma +
C                               NewLine +
C                               Expires1 + Expires2 +
C                               NewLine + NewLine
C                   EXSR      $WrStout
```

Invoice and Ship Order (INVSHIP) (part 1 of 3).

```
C                    eval      WrtDta = '<html><head>' +
C                                       '<title>' +
C                                       'BVS-Computers' +
C                                       '</title>' +
C                                       '</head><body>' +
C                                       '<p align="center">' +
C                                       '<font color="#FF0000">' +
C                                       '<big><big>' +
C                                       'BVS-Computers' +
C                                       '</big></big></font></p>' +
C                                       NewLine
C                    EXSR      $WrStout
C  *
C                    ENDSR
   *****************************************************************
C      $Main         BEGSR
C  *
C      Inv           CHAIN     INVHDRPF
C  *
C                    if        (not %found)
C                    eval      WrtDta = '<center>' +
C                                       'Error processing order.<BR>' +
C                                       'Please call for assistance.' +
C                                       '</center>' +
C                                       NewLine
C                    else
C                    eval      IHSTATUS = 'P'
C                    UPDATE    RINVHDR
C                    eval      WrtDta = '<center>'  +
C                                       'Invoice '  +
C                                       %trim(%editc(Inv:'Z')) +
C                                       ' has been processed.<BR>' +
C                                       'Thanks for shopping at ' +
C                                       'BVS-Computers! ' +
C                                       '</center>' +
C                                       NewLine
C                    endif
C  *
C                    EXSR      $WrStout
C  *
C                    ENDSR
   *****************************************************************
C      $Footer       BEGSR
C  *
C                    eval      WrtDta = '<br><br><center>' +
C                                       '<a href="/cgi-bin/items?userid=' +
C                                       %trim(USERID) +
C                                       '">Return to Shopping</a>' +
C                                       '</center>' +
C                                       NewLine
C                    EXSR      $WrStout
```

Invoice and Ship Order (INVSHIP) (part 2 of 3).

```
      *
C                      eval      WrtDta = '</body></html>' +
C                                   NewLine
C                      EXSR      $WrStout
      *
C                      ENDSR
      ***********************************************************
C     $WrStout         BEGSR
      *
C                      eval      WrtDtaLen = %len(%trim(WrtDta))
      *
C                      CALLB     'QtmhWrStout'
C                      PARM                    WrtDta
C                      PARM                    WrtDtaLen
C                      PARM                    WPError
      *
C                      ENDSR
      ***********************************************************
C     $GetQS           BEGSR
      *
C                      CALLB     'QtmhGetEnv'
C                      PARM                    EnvRec
C                      PARM                    EnvRecLen
C                      PARM                    EnvLen
C                      PARM                    EnvName
C                      PARM                    EnvNameLen
C                      PARM                    WPError
      *
C                      ENDSR
      ***********************************************************
C     $CvtDB           BEGSR
      *
C                      if        (EnvLen = 0)
C                      eval      EnvLen = %size(EnvRec)
C                      endif
      *
C                      CALLB     'QtmhCvtDb'
C                      PARM                    EnvFile
C                      PARM                    EnvRec
C                      PARM                    EnvLen
C                      PARM                    EnvDS
C                      PARM                    CvtLen
C                      PARM                    CvtLenAv
C                      PARM                    CvtStat
C                      PARM                    WPError
      *
C                      ENDSR
```

Invoice and Ship Order (INVSHIP) (part 3 of 3).

HTTP Configuration

```
Enable GET
Enable HEAD
Enable POST
Exec /cgi-bin/* /QSYS.LIB/AS400CGI.LIB/*.PGM %%EBCDIC%%
Pass /* /bvscomputers/* www.bvs-computers.com
Welcome index.html
```

APPENDIX G

This section contains service programs that I have found useful when writing CGI programs. Most of them, such as #WrtSout, #CvtDB, #GetEnv, and #RdStin, encapsulate the HTTP APIs used for CGI processing. Others are simple subprocedures that I have written to make coding easier and the programs more readable.

HTTP SERVICE PROGRAMS

The following HTTP Service programs make using the HTTP APIs available to us easier when writing CGI programs in any ILE language.

Write Standard Output (#WrStout)

The Write Standard Output (#WrtStout) subprocedure is used to write to standard output.

```
*//////////////////////////////////////////////////////////////////////*
 * (#WrStout) Write HTML to Web Page using the QtmhWrStout API   *
 *                                                               *
 * Use: #WrStout(HTML_string)                                    *
 *//////////////////////////////////////////////////////////////////////*
P #WrStout        B                     EXPORT
 *
D #WrStout        PI
D  WrtDta                       1024     VALUE
 *
D WrtDtaLen       S              9B 0
 *
C                   eval      WrtDtaLen = %len(%trim(WrtDta))
 *
C                   CALLB     'QtmhWrStout'
C                   PARM                    WrtDta
C                   PARM                    WrtDtaLen
C                   PARM                    WPError
 *
P #WrStout        E
```

Get Environment Variable (#GetEnv)

The Get Environment Variable (#GetEnv) subprocedure is used to retrieve an environment variable.

```
*//////////////////////////////////////////////////////////////////////*
 * (#GetEnv)  Get Environment Variables                          *
 *                                                               *
 * Use: #GetEnv(environment record :                             *
 *              environment record length :                      *
 *              environment variable name)                       *
 *                                                               *
 *//////////////////////////////////////////////////////////////////////*
P #GetEnv         B                     EXPORT
 *
D #GetEnv         PI
D  EnvRec                       1024
D  EnvLen                        9B 0
```

Get Environment Variable (#GetEnv) (part 1 of 2).

```
D  EnvName                        64     VALUE
   *
D  EnvRecLen        S             9B 0  INZ(%size(EnvRec))
D  EnvNameLen       S             9B 0
   *
C                   eval       EnvNameLen = %len(%trim(EnvName))
   *
C                   CALLB      'QtmhGetEnv'
C                   PARM                    EnvRec
C                   PARM                    EnvRecLen
C                   PARM                    EnvLen
C                   PARM                    EnvName
C                   PARM                    EnvNameLen
C                   PARM                    WPError
   *
P  #GetEnv          E
```

Get Environment Variable (#GetEnv) (part 2 of 2).

Read Standard Input (#RdStin)

Read Standard Input (#RdStin) is used to read from standard input.

```
*//////////////////////////////////////////////////////////////*
* (#RdStin) Read Standard Input using the QtmhRdStin API        *
*                                                               *
* Use: #RdStin(receive record : receive record length)         *
*//////////////////////////////////////////////////////////////*
P  #RdStin          B                      EXPORT
   *
D  #RdStin          PI
D  RcvRec                        1024
D  RcvLen                        9B 0
   *
D  RcvRecLen        S             9B 0
   *
C                   CALLB      'QtmhRdStin'
C                   PARM                    RcvRec
C                   PARM                    RcvLen
C                   PARM                    RcvRecLen
C                   PARM                    WPError
   *
P  #RdStin          E
```

Convert to Database (#CvtDB)

Convert to Database (#CvtDB) is used to convert data read from the query string environment variable or standard input into a data structure so the data is usable in your programs.

```
*//////////////////////////////////////////////////////////////*
* (#CvtDB) Convert to DB                                        *
*                                                              *
* Use: #CvtDb(receive record : receive record length :         *
*            convert status : data structure pointer)          *
*                                                              *
*//////////////////////////////////////////////////////////////*
P #CvtDB          B                    EXPORT
*--------------------------------------------------------------*
D #CvtDB          PI
D  RcvRec                     31000     VALUE
D  RcvLen                        9B 0
D  CvtStat                       9B 0
D  RcvDS@                         *
*
D File_DS        E DS                   EXTNAME(FILENAME)
*
D RcvFile          DS
D  File                    1     10     INZ('FILENAME ')
D  Lib                    11     20     INZ('FILELIB  ')
*
D RcvRecLen      S              9B 0 INZ(%size(RcvRec))
D CvtLen         S              9B 0 INZ(%size(File_DS))
*--------------------------------------------------------------*
C                    CALLB     'QtmhCvtDb'
C                    PARM                RcvFile
C                    PARM                RcvRec
C                    PARM                RcvRecLen
C                    PARM                File_DS
C                    PARM                CvtLen
C                    PARM                RcvLen
C                    PARM                CvtStat
C                    PARM                WPError
*
C                    eval      RcvDS@ = %addr(File_DS)
*--------------------------------------------------------------*
P #CvtDB          E
```

HTML SUBPROCEDURES

The following HTML subprocedures are used to make certain HTML codes easier, as well as to make your code more readable.

Create Hyperlink (#Link)

The Create Hyperlink (#Link) subprocedure returns formatted HTML text that will be used to create a standard hyperlink.

```
*//////////////////////////////////////////////////////////////*
* (#Link) Return HTML code for an href link                     *
*                                                               *
* Use: #Link(URL : Text {:onClick function})                    *
*                                                               *
*//////////////////////////////////////////////////////////////*
P #Link            B                       EXPORT
 *                                                              *
D #Link           PI          1024
D  Link                        512     VALUE
D  Text                        512     VALUE
D  onClick                     256     VALUE OPTIONS(*NOPASS)
 *
D RtnText         S           1024
 *                                                              *
C                   eval      RtnText = '<a href="' +
C                                       %trim(Link) + '"'
 *
C                   if        (%parms > 2) and (onClick ' ')
C                   eval      RtnText = %trim(RtnText) + ' ' +
C                                       'onClick="' +
C                                       %trim(onClick) + '"'
C                   endif
 *
C                   eval      RtnText = %trim(RtnText) +
C                                       '>' +
C                                       %trim(Text) +
C                                       '</a>'
 *
C                   RETURN    RtnText
 *                                                              *
P #Link            E
```

Create MailTo: Hyperlink (#MailTo)

The Create MailTo: Hyperlink (#MailTo) subprocedure returns formatted HTML text that is used to place a mailto hyperlink on your Web page.

```
*//////////////////////////////////////////////////////////////////*
* (#MailTo) Return HTML code for mailto tag                        *
*                                                                  *
* Use: #MailTo(E-Mail Address : Name)                              *
*                                                                  *
*//////////////////////////////////////////////////////////////////*
P #MailTo          B                   EXPORT
*
D #MailTo          PI          1024
D  EMail                         50    VALUE
D  User                          30    VALUE
*
C                  RETURN       '<a href=mailto:' +
C                               %trim(EMail) +
C                               '>' +
C                               %trim(User) +
C                               '</a>'
*
P #MailTo          E
```

Return Bold Text (#Bold)

The Return Bold Text (#Bold) subprocedure returns formatted HTML code to make the text appear in a bold typeface.

```
*//////////////////////////////////////////////////////////////////*
* (#Bold) Return bold text                                         *
*                                                                  *
* Use: #Bold(Text)                                                 *
*                                                                  *
*//////////////////////////////////////////////////////////////////*
P #Bold            B                   EXPORT
*
D #Bold            PI          1024
D  Text                       1024     VALUE
*
C                  RETURN       '' +
C                               %trim(Text) +
C                               '</B>'
*
P #Bold            E
```

Return Italics Text (#Italics)

The Return Italics Text (#Italics) returns formatted HTML code to make the text an italic typeface.

```
*//////////////////////////////////////////////////////////////*
* (#Italics) Return italics text                                *
*                                                               *
* Use: #Italics(Text)                                           *
*                                                               *
*//////////////////////////////////////////////////////////////*
P #Italics        B                       EXPORT
*---------------------------------------------------------------*
D #Italics        PI             1024
D   Text                         1024     VALUE
*---------------------------------------------------------------*
C                 RETURN         '' +
C                                %trim(Text) +
C                                '</I>'

*---------------------------------------------------------------*
P #Italics        E
```

Return Centered Text (#Center)

The Return Centered Text (#Center) subprocedure returns formatted HTML to center text on the Web page.

```
*//////////////////////////////////////////////////////////////*
* (#Center) Return centered text                                *
*                                                               *
* Use: #Center(Text)                                            *
*                                                               *
*//////////////////////////////////////////////////////////////*
P #Center         B                       EXPORT
*---------------------------------------------------------------*
D #Center         PI             1024
D   Text                         1024     VALUE
*---------------------------------------------------------------*
C                 RETURN         '<CENTER>' +
C                                %trim(Text) +
C                                '</CENTER>'
*---------------------------------------------------------------*
P #Center         E
```

Return Input Field (#Input)

The Return Input Field (#Input) subprocedure returns the formatted HTML code for an input field.

```
*////////////////////////////////////////////////////////////////*
* (#Input) Return Input                                           *
*                                                                 *
* Use: #Input(Input Type : {Name : Size : Value :                 *
*             onClick function})                                  *
*                                                                 *
*////////////////////////////////////////////////////////////////*
P #Input          B                        EXPORT
*----------------------------------------------------------------*
D #Input          PI          1024
D  Type                        256    VALUE
D  Name                        256    VALUE OPTIONS(*NOPASS)
D  Size                        256    VALUE OPTIONS(*NOPASS)
D  VALUE                       256    VALUE OPTIONS(*NOPASS)
D  onClick                     256    VALUE OPTIONS(*NOPASS)
*
D RtnText          S          1024
*----------------------------------------------------------------*
C                   eval      RtnText = '<INPUT TYPE=' +
C                                       %trim(Type)
*
C                   if        (%parms > 1) and (Name  '< >')
C                   eval      RtnText = %trim(RtnText) + ' ' +
C                                       'NAME=' +
C                                       %trim(Name)
C                   endif
*
C                   if        (%parms > 2) and (Size  '< >')
C                   eval      RtnText = %trim(RtnText) + ' ' +
C                                       'SIZE=' +
C                                       %trim(Size)
C                   endif
*
C                   if        (%parms > 3) and (VALUE  '< >')
C                   eval      RtnText = %trim(RtnText) + ' ' +
C                                       'VALUE=' +
C                                       %trim(VALUE)
C                   endif
*
C                   if        (%parms > 4) and (onClick  '< >')
C                   eval      RtnText = %trim(RtnText) + ' ' +
C                                       'onClick="' +
C                                       %trim(onClick) + '"'
C                   endif
*
C                   eval      RtnText = %trim(RtnText) + '>'
*
C                   RETURN    RtnText
*----------------------------------------------------------------*
P #Input          E
```

Write Source Member (#WrtSrcMbr)

The Write Source Member (#WrtSrcMbr) subprocedure is used to write the
HTML or JavaScript source that is located in the given source member. The
subprocedure is useful in cases where you wish to write a large portion of static
HTML to the browser.

```
FQHTMLSRC  IF   E            DISK    USROPN
RENAME(QHTMLSRC:HTMLSRC)
*//////////////////////////////////////////////////////////////*
* (#WrtSrcMbr) Write JavaScript Member to HTML Form            *
*                                                              *
* Use: #WrtSrcMbr(Library : File : Member)                     *
*                                                              *
*//////////////////////////////////////////////////////////////*
P #WrtSrcMbr     B                      EXPORT
*                                                              *
D #WrtSrcMbr     PI
D Lib                           10    VALUE
D File                          10    VALUE
D SrcMbr                        10    VALUE
*
D NewLine        C                     CONST(X'15')
*
D WrtDta         S             1024
D QCmdCmd        S              512    INZ
D QCmdLength     S               15  5 INZ(%size(QCmdCmd))
*                                                              *
C                    if        (Lib = ' ')
C                    eval      Lib = '*LIBL'
C                    endif
*
C                    eval      QCmdCmd = 'OVRDBF FILE' +
C                                        '(QHTMLSRC) ' +
C                                        'TOFILE(' +
C                                        %trim(Lib) + '/' +
C                                        %trim(File) +
C                                        ') MBR(' +
C                                        %trim(SrcMbr) + ')'
*
C                    CALL      'QCMDEXC'
C 99
C                    PARM                QCmdCmd
C                    PARM                QCmdLength
*
C                    OPEN      QHTMLSRC
C                    READ      QHTMLSRC
C 69
*
```

Write Source Member (#WrtSrcMbr) (part 1 of 2).

```
C                    dow       (not *IN69)
C                    eval      WrtDta = SRCDTA + NewLine
C                    CALLP     #WrStout(WrtDta)
C                    READ      QHTMLSRC
69
C                    enddo
 *
C                    CLOSE     QHTMLSRC
 *
P #WrtSrcMbr       E
```

Write Source Member (#WrtSrcMbr) (part 2 of 2).

MISCELLANEOUS SUPROCEDURES

The following subprocedures are useful in day-to-day CGI programming.

Convert Character to Numeric (#CtoN)

The Convert Character to Numeric (#CtoN) subprocedure will return the numeric representation of the character value passed into it. This is useful when converting the values returned from the CONTENT_LENGTH environment variable for use with the Read Standard Input API.

```
*//////////////////////////////////////////////////////////////////*
* (#CtoN) Character to Numeric                                      *
*                                                                   *
* Use: #CtoN(Character String)                                      *
*                                                                   *
*                                                                   *
*//////////////////////////////////////////////////////////////////*
P #CtoN            B                        EXPORT
 *
D #CtoN            PI            30P 9
D  Char                         32     VALUE
 *
D                  DS
D Char1                          1
D Num1                           1  0 OVERLAY(Char1) INZ
 *
D Num              S             30P 9
D WrkNum           S             30P 0
```

Convert Character to Numeric (#CtoN) (part 1 of 2).

```
D Sign            S              1  0 INZ(1)
D DecPos          S              3  0
D Decimal         S              1    INZ('N')
D i               S              4  0
D j               S              4  0
 *----------------------------------------------------------------*
C                 eval      Char = %triml(Char)
C        ' '      CHECKR    Char            j                        99
 *
C                 if        (not *IN99)
C                 eval      j = %size(Char)
C                 endif
 *
C        1        do        j               i
C                 eval      Char1 = %subst(Char:i:1)
 *
C                 select
C                 when      (Char1 = '-')
C                 eval      Sign = -1
C                 when      (Char1 = '.')
C                 eval      Decimal = 'Y'
C                 when      (Char1 >= '0') and (Char1 <= '9')
C                 eval      WrkNum = (WrkNum * 10 + Num1)
 *
C                 if        (Decimal = 'Y')
C                 eval      DecPos = (DecPos + 1)
C                 endif
 *
C                 endsl
 *
C                 enddo
 *
C                 eval(h)   Num = (WrkNum * Sign / (10 ** DecPos))
C                 RETURN    Num
 *----------------------------------------------------------------*
C        *PSSR    BEGSR
C                 RETURN    0
C                 ENDSR
 *----------------------------------------------------------------*
P #CtoN           E
```

Convert Character to Numeric (#CtoN) (part 2 of 2).

Replace Characters (#Replace)

The Replace Characters (#Replace) subprocedure is useful to replace one character with another when writing HTML code. For example, replacing quotation
marks (") with ".

```
*//////////////////////////////////////////////////////////////////*
* (#Replace) Replace Characters to Numeric                         *
*                                                                  *
* Use: #Replace(String : Replace_This : With_This)                 *
*                                                                  *
*//////////////////////////////////////////////////////////////////*
D #Replace        PR            1024
D  InString                     1024    VALUE
D  From                           56    VALUE
D  To                             56    VALUE
*//////////////////////////////////////////////////////////////////*
* (#Replace) Replace character(s) with new character(s)            *
*                                                                  *
* Use: #Replace(String : Replace_This : With_This)                 *
*                                                                  *
*//////////////////////////////////////////////////////////////////*
P #Replace        B                     EXPORT
*------------------------------------------------------------------*
D #Replace        PI            1024
D  InString                     1024    VALUE
D  From                           56    VALUE
D  To                             56    VALUE
*
D String          S             1024
D Temp            S             1024
D i               S                4 0
D j               S                4 0
D len             S                4 0
D lenTo           S                4 0
*------------------------------------------------------------------*
C                 eval          String = InString
C                 eval          i = 1
C        ' '      CHECKR        From              len
99
*
C                 if            (not *IN99)
C                 eval          len = %size(From)
C                 endif
*
C        ' '      CHECKR        To                lenTo
99
*
C                 if            (not *IN99)
C                 eval          lenTo = %size(To)
```

Replace Characters (#Replace) (part 1 of 2).

```
C                    endif
*
C      From:len      SCAN      String:i     j
*
C                    dow       (j  0)
C                    eval      Temp = %trim(To) +
%subst(String:j+len)
*
C                    if        (j = 1)
C                    eval      String = Temp
C                    else
C                    eval      String = %subst(String:1:j-1) + Temp
C                    endif
*
C                    eval      i = (j + lenTo)
C      From:len      SCAN      String:i     j
C                    enddo
*
C                    RETURN    String
*                                                              *
C      *PSSR         BEGSR
C                    RETURN    InString
C                    ENDSR
*                                                              *
P #Replace        E
```

Replace Characters (#Replace) (part 2 of 2).

APPENDIX H

The following sections include the full source for the examples given in chapter 10. The ITEMLIST example is used to read through an item file and display the items on the browser. The BVS-Cars example is used to show how to set up an interactive e-commerce site which allows the user to browse a list of used cars.

LIST ITEMS (ITEMLIST)

The following source is for the ITEMLIST example in chapter 10.

Item Master File (ITEMSPF)

```
A               R RITEMS
A                 ITTYPE         3          TEXT('Item TYPE')
A                 ITITEM        15          TEXT('Item Number')
A                 ITDESC        50          TEXT('Item Description')
A                 ITPRC         7S 2        TEXT('Item Price')
A                 ITONH         7S 0        TEXT('ONHAND')
```

Item Master Logical File (ITEMS1LF)

```
     A           R RITEMS
     A                                           PFILE(ITEMSPF)
     A           K ITTYPE
     A           K ITITEM
```

Item Listing Modules (F.ITEMLIST)

```
     ****************************************************************
     * Item Listing Functions                                      *
     ****************************************************************
     H NOMAIN
     ****************************************************************
     * Global Definitions                                          *
     ****************************************************************
     D File_DS         E DS                  EXTNAME(ITEMSPF)
     *
     D WPError           DS
     D  EBytesP                 1      4B 0 INZ(40)
     D  EBytesA                 5      8B 0
     D  EMsgID                  9     15
     D  EReserverd             16     16
     D  EData                  17     56
     ****************************************************************
     * Prototypes                                                  *
     ****************************************************************
     D #WrStout          PR
     D   PR_WrStout             1024     VALUE
     *
     D #GetEnvQS         PR
     D   PR_EnvRec              1024
     D   PR_EnvLen                9B 0
     *
     D #CvtDB            PR
     D   PR_RcvRec              1024     VALUE
     D   PR_RcvLen                9B 0
     D   PR_CvtStat               9B 0
     D   PR_RcvDS@                 *
     *//////////////////////////////////////////////////////////////*
     * (#WrStout) Write HTML to Web Page                           *
     *//////////////////////////////////////////////////////////////*
     P #WrStout          B                  EXPORT
     *------------------------------------------------------------------*
     D #WrStout          PI
     D  WrtDta                  1024     VALUE
     *
     D WrtDtaLen         S          9B 0
     *------------------------------------------------------------------*
     C     ' '           CHECKR    WrtDta:1024    WrtDtaLen
     *
     C                   CALLB     'QtmhWrStout'
```

Item Listing Modules (F.ITEMLIST) (part 1 of 2).

```
C                       PARM                WrtDta
C                       PARM                WrtDtaLen
C                       PARM                WPError
 *------------------------------------------------------------------*
P #WrStout           E
 *////////////////////////////////////////////////////////////////*
 * (#GetEnvQS) Get QUERY_STRING Environment Variables              *
 *////////////////////////////////////////////////////////////////*
P #GetEnvQS          B                      EXPORT
 *------------------------------------------------------------------*
D #GetEnvQS          PI
D  EnvRec                          1024
D  EnvLen                             9B 0
 *
D EnvRecLen          S               9B 0 INZ(%size(EnvRec))
D EnvName            S              12    INZ('QUERY_STRING')
D EnvNameLen         S               9B 0 INZ(%size(EnvName))
 *------------------------------------------------------------------*
C                       CALLB     'QtmhGetEnv'
C                       PARM                EnvRec
C                       PARM                EnvRecLen
C                       PARM                EnvLen
C                       PARM                EnvName
C                       PARM                EnvNameLen
C                       PARM                WPError
 *------------------------------------------------------------------*
P #GetEnvQS          E
 *////////////////////////////////////////////////////////////////*
 * (#CvtDB) Convert to DB                                          *
 *////////////////////////////////////////////////////////////////*
P #CvtDB             B                      EXPORT
 *------------------------------------------------------------------*
D #CvtDB             PI
D  RcvRec                          1024     VALUE
D  RcvLen                             9B 0
D  CvtStat                            9B 0
D  RcvDS@                              *
 *
D RcvFile            DS
D  File                      1      10     INZ('ITEMSPF   ')
D  Lib                      11      20     INZ('AS400CGI  ')
 *
D RcvRecLen          S               9B 0 INZ(%size(RcvRec))
D CvtLen             S               9B 0 INZ(%size(File_DS))
 *------------------------------------------------------------------*
C                       CALLB     'QtmhCvtDb'
C                       PARM                RcvFile
C                       PARM                RcvRec
C                       PARM                RcvRecLen
C                       PARM                File_DS
C                       PARM                CvtLen
C                       PARM                RcvLen
C                       PARM                CvtStat
C                       PARM                WPError
 *
C                       eval      RcvDS@ = %addr(File_DS)
 *------------------------------------------------------------------*
P #CvtDB             E
```

Item Listing Modules (F.ITEMLIST) (part 2 of 2).

Item Listing e-RPG Program (ITEMLIST)

```
H DFTACTGRP(*NO) BNDDIR('CGIBNDDIR')
****************************************************************
FITEMS1LF   IF   E            K DISK
****************************************************************
D #WrStout        PR
D   PR_WrStout                    1024    VALUE
 *
D #GetEnvQS        PR
D   PR_EnvRec                     1024
D   PR_EnvLen                        9B 0
 *
D #CvtDB           PR
D   PR_RcvRec                     1024    VALUE
D   PR_RcvLen                        9B 0
D   PR_CvtStat                      9B 0
D   PR_RcvDS@                        *
 *
D EnvDS           E DS                    EXTNAME(ITEMSPF) BASED(EnvDS@)
D HTTPHeader        C                     CONST('Content-type: text/html')
D NewLine           C                     CONST(X'15')
 *
D WrtDta            S             1024
 *
D EnvDS@            S                *
D EnvRec            S             1024
D EnvLen            S                9B 0
D CvtLen            S                9B 0 INZ(%size(EnvDS))
D LastType          S                     LIKE(ITTYPE)
D LastItem          S                     LIKE(ITITEM)
D Count             S                4S 0
****************************************************************
C     ItemKey        KLIST
C                    KFLD                          ITTYPE
C                    KFLD                          ITITEM
C                    CALLP     #GetEnvQS(EnvRec:EnvLen)
C                    CALLP     #CvtDB(EnvRec:EnvLen:CvtLen:EnvDS@)
C                    EXSR      $Header
C                    EXSR      $Main
C                    EXSR      $Footer
C                    SETON                                       LR
****************************************************************
C     $Header        BEGSR
 *
C                    eval      WrtDta = %trim(HTTPHeader) +
C                                       NewLine + NewLine
C                    CALLP     #WrStout(WrtDta)
 *
C                    eval      WrtDta = '<html><head>' +
```

Item Listing (ITEMLIST) (part 1 of 3).

```
C                                       '<title>' +
C                                       'Item List' +
C                                       '</title>' +
C                                       '</head><body>' +
C                                       '<p align="center">' +
C                                       '<big><big>' +
C                                       'Item List' +
C                                       '</big></big></p>' +
C                                       NewLine
C                         CALLP     #WrStout(WrtDta)
 *
C                         ENDSR
 ***********************************************************************
C       $Main             BEGSR
 *
C                         eval      WrtDta = '<table border="1"><tr>' +
C                                       NewLine +
C                                       '<td>Item Type</td>' +
C                                       '<td>Item Number</td>' +
C                                       '<td>Description</td>' +
C                                       '<td>On-Hand</td>' +
C                                       NewLine
C                         CALLP     #WrStout(WrtDta)
C                         eval      Count = 0
C       ItemKey           SETGT     ITEMS1LF
C                         READ      ITEMS1LF
 *
C                         dow       (not %eof) and (Count < 2)
C                         eval      WrtDta = '<tr><td>' +
C                                       %trim(ITTYPE) +
C                                       '</td><td>' +
C                                       %trim(ITITEM) +
C                                       '</td><td>' +
C                                       %trim(ITDESC) +
C                                       '</td><td>' +
C                                       %trim(%editc(ITONH:'3')) +
C                                       '</td></tr>' +
C                                       NewLine
C                         CALLP     #WrStout(WrtDta)
C                         eval      Count = (Count + 1)
C                         eval      LastType = ITTYPE
C                         eval      LastItem = ITITEM
C                         READ      ITEMS1LF
C                         enddo
 *
C                         eval      WrtDta = '</tr></table>' +
C                                       '</center>' +
C                                       NewLine
C                         CALLP     #WrStout(WrtDta)
 *
C                         ENDSR
 ***********************************************************************
```

Item Listing (ITEMLIST) (part 2 of 3).

```
C     $Footer      BEGSR
 *
C                  if        (not %eof)
C                  eval      WrtDta = '<a href="/cgi-bin/ITEMLIST?' +
C                                     'ITTYPE=' +
C                                     %trim(LastType) +
C                                     '&ITITEM=' +
C                                     %trim(LastItem) +
C                                     '">Next Page</a>' +
C                                     NewLine
C                  CALLP     #WrStout(WrtDta)
C                  endif
 *
C                  eval      WrtDta = '</body></html>' +
C                                     NewLine
C                  CALLP     #WrStout(WrtDta)
 *
C                  ENDSR
```

IItem Listing (ITEMLIST) (part 3 of 3).

BVS-CARS

BVS-Cars HTML Starting Page (bvscars.html)

```html
<html>

<head>
<title>BVS-Cars</title>
</head>

<Body>
<p><font color="#FF0000"><strong>Welcome to BVS-Cars!</strong></font></p>

<p>Please select from the following and press <em><strong>View
Cars!</strong></em> to view
vehicles that meet the criteria.</p>

<form method="GET" action="/cgi-bin/ListCars" method="GET">
  <p>Make: <select name="MAKE" size="1">
    <option value="ALL">All Makes</option>
    <option value="Ford">Ford</option>
    <option value="Cheverolet">Cheverolet</option>
    <option value="Honda">Honda</option>
    <option value="Toyota">Toyota</option>
```

BVS-Cars HTML Starting Page (bvscars.html) (part 1 of 2).

```
    </select>Year:<select name="YEAR" size="1">
      <option value="ALL">All Years</option>
      <option value="1999">1999</option>
      <option value="1998">1998</option>
      <option value="1997">1997</option>
      <option value="1996">1996</option>
      <option value="Pre1996">Pre 1996</option>
    </select>Price:<select name="PRICE" size="1">
      <option value="ALL">All Prices</option>
      <option value="0002000">Up to 2000</option>
      <option value="0005000">Up to 5000</option>
      <option value="0010000">Up to 10,000</option>
      <option value="0020000">Up to 20,000</option>
    </select></p>
    <p><input type="submit" value="View Cars!"> </p>
  </form>

  <p> </p>
  </body>
  </html>
```

BVS-Cars HTML Starting Page (bvscars.html) (part 2 of 2).

Car Database (CARSPF)

```
     A              R RCARS
     A                CMAKE         30         TEXT('Make')
     A                CMODEL        30         TEXT('Model')
     A                CYEAR         4S 0       TEXT('Year')
     A                CPRICE        7S 0       TEXT('Price')
```

External Data Structure for LISTCARS (LISTCARSDS)

```
     A              R RLISTCARS
     A                MAKE          30         TEXT('Make of car')
     A                YEAR          4          TEXT('Year')
     A                PRICE         10         TEXT('Price Range')
     A                SORTBY        10         TEXT('Sort By')
     A                LRRN          9S 0       TEXT('Last RRN')
```

List Cars Subprocedures (F.LISTCARS)

```
H NOMAIN
 *****************************************************************
 * Global Definitions                                           *
 *****************************************************************
D File_DS         E DS                     EXTNAME(LISTCARSDS)
 *
D WPError           DS
D  EBytesP                    1      4B 0 INZ(40)
D  EBytesA                    5      8B 0
D  EMsgID                     9     15
D  EReserverd                16     16
D  EData                     17     56
 *****************************************************************
 * Prototypes                                                   *
 *****************************************************************
D #CvtDB          PR
D  PR_RcvRec                       1024     VALUE
D  PR_RcvLen                        9B 0
D  PR_CvtStat                       9B 0
D  PR_RcvDS@                          *
 *////////////////////////////////////////////////////////////////*
 * (#CvtDB) Convert to DB                                        *
 *////////////////////////////////////////////////////////////////*
P #CvtDB          B                     EXPORT
 *------------------------------------------------------------------*
D #CvtDB          PI
D  RcvRec                          1024     VALUE
D  RcvLen                           9B 0
D  CvtStat                          9B 0
D  RcvDS@                             *
 *
D RcvFile           DS
D  File                       1     10     INZ('LISTCARSDS')
D  Lib                       11     20     INZ('STONEBOOK ')
 *
D RcvRecLen       S                  9B 0 INZ(%size(RcvRec))
D CvtLen          S                  9B 0 INZ(%size(File_DS))
 *------------------------------------------------------------------*
C                   CALLB     'QtmhCvtDb'
C                   PARM                    RcvFile
C                   PARM                    RcvRec
C                   PARM                    RcvRecLen
C                   PARM                    File_DS
C                   PARM                    CvtLen
C                   PARM                    RcvLen
C                   PARM                    CvtStat
C                   PARM                    WPError
 *
C                   eval      RcvDS@ = %addr(File_DS)
 *------------------------------------------------------------------*
P #CvtDB          E
```

List Cars e-RPG Program (LISTCARS)

```
H DFTACTGRP(*NO) BNDDIR('CGIBNDDIR')
 ***********************************************************
FCARSPF    IF  E            DISK      USROPN
F                                     INFDS(INFDS)
 ***********************************************************
 * Prototypes                                            *
 ***********************************************************
/COPY QSRVSRC,P.HTTPSTD
 *
D #CvtDB         PR
D  PR_RcvRec                    1024    VALUE
D  PR_RcvLen                      9B 0
D  PR_CvtStat                     9B 0
D  PR_RcvDS@                       *
 ***********************************************************
D                SDS
D  W$PGM                   1    10
 *
D INFDS          DS
D  F$RRN                  397   400B 0
 *
D EnvDS          E DS                  EXTNAME(LISTCARSDS)
D                                      BASED(EnvDS@)
 *
D HTTPHeader     C                     CONST('Content-type: text/html')
D NewLine        C                     CONST(X'15')
D Apos           C                     CONST(X'7D')
 *
D EnvDS@         S               *
D EnvRec         S            1024
D EnvLen         S               9B 0
D EnvName        S              64
D CvtStat        S               9B 0
 *
D WrtDta         S            1024
 *
D QryNam         S            1024
D QrySlt         S            1024
D KeyFld         S            1024
D QCmdCmd        S            1024
D QCmdLength     S              15  5 INZ(%size(QCmdCmd))
 *
D InLink         S             256
D OutLink        S             256
D Count          S               7  0
 ***********************************************************
C                    EXSR      $LoadHTML
C                    eval      *INLR = *On
 ***********************************************************
```

List Cars (LISTCARS) (part 1 of 7).

```
C      $LoadHTML      BEGSR
 *
C                     EXSR      $Header
C                     EXSR      $Main
C                     EXSR      $Footer
 *
C                     ENDSR
 ******************************************************************
C      $Header        BEGSR
 *
C                     eval      WrtDta = %trim(HTTPHeader) +
C                                         NewLine + NewLine
C                     CALLP     #WrStout(WrtDta)
 *
C                     eval      WrtDta = '<HEAD>' +
C                                        '<TITLE>BVS-Cars</TITLE>' +
C                                        '</HEAD><BODY>' +
C                                        NewLine
C                     CALLP     #WrStout(WrtDta)
 *
C                     ENDSR
 ******************************************************************
C      $Main          BEGSR
 *
C                     eval      WrtDta = '<table border="1" width="100%">' +
C                                        NewLine
C                     CALLP     #WrStout(WrtDta)
 *
C                     eval      WrtDta = '<tr>' +
C                                        '<td align="right">' +
C                                        '<a href="' + %trim(InLink) +
C                                        '&sortby=YEAR">' +
C                                        'Year</a>' +
C                                        '</td>' +
C                                        '<td>' +
C                                        '<a href="' + %trim(InLink) +
C                                        '&sortby=MAKE">' +
C                                        'Make</a>' +
C                                        '</td>' +
C                                        '<td>' +
C                                        '<a href="' + %trim(InLink) +
C                                        '&sortby=MODEL">' +
C                                        'Model</a>' +
C                                        '</td>' +
C                                        '<td align="right">' +
C                                        '<a href="' + %trim(InLink) +
C                                        '&sortby=PRICE">' +
C                                        'Price</a>' +
C                                        '</td>' +
C                                        NewLine
C                     CALLP     #WrStout(WrtDta)
 *
```

List Cars (LISTCARS) (part 2 of 7).

```
C                   EXSR      $Detail
C *
C                   eval      WrtDta = '</table>' +
C                                     NewLine
C                   CALLP     #WrStout(WrtDta)
C *
C                   ENDSR
*****************************************************************
C     $Detail       BEGSR                     .
C *
C                   EXSR      $OPNQRYF
C                   OPEN      CARSPF
C *
C                   eval      Count = 0
C                   eval      *IN69 = *OFF
C *
C                   if        (LRRN > 0)
C     LRRN          CHAIN     CARSPF                                99
C                   endif
C *
C                   dow       (not *IN69) and (Count < 5)
C                   READ      CARSPF                                69
C *
C                   if        (*IN69)
C                   ITER
C                   endif
C *
C                   eval      WrtDta = '<tr>' +
C                                     '<td align="right">' +
C                                     %trim(%editc(CYEAR:'Z')) +
C                                     '</td>' +
C                                     '<td>' +
C                                     %trim(CMAKE) +
C                                     '</td>' +
C                                     '<td>' +
C                                     %trim(CMODEL) +
C                                     '</td>' +
C                                     '<td align="right">' +
C                                     %trim(%editc(CPRICE:'3')) +
C                                     '</td>' +
C                                     '</tr>' +
C                                     NewLine
C                   CALLP     #WrStout(WrtDta)
C *
C                   eval      Count = (Count + 1)
C                   enddo
C *
C * LRRN is filled here for the Next Page Link.  The next read could
C   mess it up if
C * I used F$RRN.
C                   if        (not *IN69)
C                   eval      LRRN = F$RRN
```

List Cars (LISTCARS) (part 3 of 7).

```
     *
     * This read is simply to flip on 69 if the last record read was the last
     * record in the file.  This way they Next Page link won't show up if
     * this is the last record.
C                        READ      CARSPF                                      69
C                        endif
     *
C                        CLOSE     CARSPF
C                        EXSR      $DLTOVR
     *
C                        ENDSR
     ***********************************************************************
C    $OPNQRYF            BEGSR
     *
C                        eval      QCmdCmd = 'OVRDBF FILE(CARSPF) ' +
C                                            'SHARE(*YES) '
     *
C                        CALL      'QCMDEXC'                                    99
C                        PARM                QCmdCmd
C                        PARM                QCmdLength
     *
C                        EXSR      $QRYSLT
C                        EXSR      $KEYFLD
     *
C                        if        (QrySlt  '< >')
C                        eval      QCmdCmd = 'OPNQRYF FILE(CARSPF) ' +
C                                            'OPTION(*INP)' + ' QRYSLT(' +
C                                            '''' + %trim(QrySlt) + ''') ' +
C                                            %trim(KeyFld)
C                        else
C                        eval      QCmdCmd = 'OPNQRYF FILE(CARSPF) ' +
C                                            'OPTION(*INP)' + ' ' +
C                                            %trim(KeyFld)
C                        endif
     *
C                        CALL      'QCMDEXC'                                    99
C                        PARM                QCmdCmd
C                        PARM                QCmdLength
     *
C                        ENDSR
     ***********************************************************************
C    $QRYSLT             BEGSR
     *
C                        if        (MAKE < > 'ALL')
C                        EXSR      $AND
C                        eval      QrySlt = %trim(QrySlt) +
C                                  ' (CMAKE *EQ "' +
C                                  %trim(MAKE) + '")'
C                        endif
     *
C                        if        (YEAR < > 'ALL')
C                        EXSR      $AND
```

List Cars (LISTCARS)(part 4 of 7).

```
     *
C                  if       (YEAR = 'Pre1996')
C                  eval     QrySlt = %trim(QrySlt) +
C                           ' (%digits(CYEAR) *LT ("1996")'
C                  else
C                  eval     QrySlt = %trim(QrySlt) +
C                           ' (%digits(CYEAR) *EQ "' +
C                           %trim(YEAR) + '")'
C                  endif
     *
C                  endif
     *
C                  if       (PRICE < > 'ALL')
C                  EXSR     $AND
C                  eval     QrySlt = %trim(QrySlt) +
C                           ' (%digits(CPRICE) *LE "' +
C                           %trim(PRICE) + '")'
C                  endif
     *
C                  ENDSR
 ********************************************************************
C     $AND         BEGSR
     *
C                  if       (QrySlt < > ' ')
C                  eval     QrySlt = %trim(QrySlt) +
C                           ' *AND'
C                  endif
     *
C                  ENDSR
 ********************************************************************
C     $KEYFLD      BEGSR
     *
C                  eval     KeyFld = ' '
     *
C                  select
C                  when     (SORTBY = 'YEAR')
C                  eval     KeyFld = %trim(KeyFld) +
C                           ' (CYEAR)'
C                  when     (SORTBY = 'MAKE')
C                  eval     KeyFld = %trim(KeyFld) +
C                           ' (CMAKE)'
C                  when     (SORTBY = 'MODEL')
C                  eval     KeyFld = %trim(KeyFld) +
C                           ' (CMODEL)'
C                  when     (SORTBY = 'PRICE')
C                  eval     KeyFld = %trim(KeyFld) +
C                           ' (CPRICE)'
C                  other
C                  eval     KeyFld = %trim(KeyFld) +
C                           ' (CYEAR)'
C                  endsl
```

List Cars (LISTCARS) (part 5 of 7).

```
 *
C                     eval      KeyFld = 'KEYFLD(' +
C                                 %trim(KeyFld) + ')'
 *
C                     ENDSR
 **************************************************************
C     $DLTOVR         BEGSR
 *
C                     eval      QCmdCmd = 'DLTOVR FILE(CARSPF)'
 *
C                     CALL      'QCMDEXC'                          99
C                     PARM                QCmdCmd
C                     PARM                QCmdLength
 *
C                     eval      QCmdCmd = 'CLOF OPNID(CARSPF)'
 *
C                     CALL      'QCMDEXC'                          99
C                     PARM                QCmdCmd
C                     PARM                QCmdLength
 *
C                     ENDSR
 **************************************************************
C     $Footer         BEGSR
 *
C                     if        (*IN69)
C                     CALLP     #WrStout('End of Listing' +
C                                 NewLine)
C                     else
C                     eval      OutLink = %trim(InLink) +
C                                 '&lrrn=' +
C                                 %trim(%editc(LRRN:'L'))
 *
C                     eval      WrtDta = '<a href="' + %trim(OutLink) +
C                                 '&SORTBY=' + %trim(SORTBY) +
C                                 '">Next Page</a>' +
C                                 NewLine
C                     CALLP     #WrStout(WrtDta)
C                     endif
 *
C                     eval      WrtDta = '</BODY></HTML>' +
C                                 NewLine
C                     CALLP     #WrStout(WrtDta)
 *
C                     ENDSR
 **************************************************************
C     $GetEnv         BEGSR
 *
C                     eval      EnvName = 'QUERY_STRING'
C                     CALLP     #GetEnv(EnvRec:EnvLen:EnvName)
C                     CALLP     #CvtDB(EnvRec:EnvLen:CvtStat:EnvDS@)
 *
C                     ENDSR
```

List Cars (LISTCARS) (part 6 of 7).

```
*****************************************************************
C     *INZSR         BEGSR
 *
C                    EXSR      $GetEnv
 *
C                    if        (SORTBY = ' ')
C                    eval      SORTBY = 'MAKE'
C                    endif
 *
C                    eval      InLink = %trim(W$PGM) +
C                                       '?MAKE=' + %trim(MAKE) +
C                                       '&YEAR=' + %trim(YEAR) +
C                                       '&PRICE=' + %trim(PRICE)
 *
C                    ENDSR
```

List Cars (LISTCARS) (part 7 of 7).

APPENDIX I

The CD-ROM you receive with *e-RPG: Building Web Applications in RPG* contains all the source code presented in this book as examples. To use this code on an AS/400, you'll need a PC with file transfer capability attached to your AS/400. You can use a PC that's running a product such as IBM's PC Support or Client Access. Or you could use a PC connected to your AS/400 through TCP/IP and use FTP.

The source code included in this book is meant to serve as an example only and not as a working application. You may find that it does not perform exactly the same on your machine as described in the text. However, you may find the code helpful when used as modules to be copied into your own applications.

When you upload a file, you should transfer it to a source physical file, such as QRPGSRC, from which it can be compiled if necessary. Not all illustrations found in the book are included on this CD. The code on the CD-ROM is organized in folders as follows:

Binder Language. The binder language folder contains binder language used when creating service programs for this book (in ASCII text files).

COPY Source. The COPY source folder contains /COPY prototype source for the programs and modules used in this book (in ASCII text files).

DDS Source. The DDS Source folder contains the DDS for physical file, logical file, and external-data structures for program examples used in this book (in ASCII text files).

HTML Source. The HTML Source folder contains the HTML source for examples given in this book (Microsoft HTML document files).

Module Source. The Module Source folder contains the source for modules used as examples in this book (in ASCII text files).

RPG Source. The RPG Source folder contains the RPG source for programs used in the book (in ASCII text files).

All source members are named with the same name used in the book.

The code should be aligned properly on the AS/400. For example, the form type in an RPG program should be in column 6. If any alignments are incorrect after you have uploaded the code, please adjust as necessary.

INDEX

A

\<A\> (Anchor) tag, 12
access logs, CGI programming and, 61-62
ACTION, 105
ADD, 26
Add Binding Directory Entry (ADDBNDDIRE),
   CGI programming and, 57
Add Library List Entry (ADDLIBLE), CGI
   programming and, 59
ADMIN server instance, HTTP server and,
   87-88
aligning HTML fields using tables, 15-16, **15,
   16**
Application Program Interfaces (APIs), 99-118,
   239, 269
   adding QTMHCGI to binding directory for,
     117
   binding directories for, 101, 116-117
   calling, CALLB, 101
   CGI programming and, 50, 52, 100, 116-117
   Convert to DB (QthmCvtDB) as, 112-116,
     162, 190-192, 271

copying QTMHCGI before modifications to,
   102
Create Bound RPG (CRTBNDRBG) for, 101
Create Program (CRTPGM) for, 101
Display Service Program (DSPSRVPGM)
   for, 100
e-RPG programs and, 120, 122
error data structure in, 125
Get Environment Variable (QtmGetEnv) as,
   108-112, 156-160, 186-188, 189, 192, 270
Integrated Language Environment and, 100
location of, 100-102
modularizing of, 140-144
preparing for use of, 116-117
QTMHCGI service program containing, 100,
   101, 116
query string environment variables and, 109
Read from Standard Input (QtmhRdStin) as,
   105-108, 162-163, 188-189, 270
receiver variables in, 106-107, 110
reference sources for, 271
referencing of, 101

Note: Boldface numbers indicate illustrations

APIs, *continued*
  required parameters for, 269-271
  service programs and, 100, 184
  subprocedures to modularize, 140-141
  uses for, 100-102
  Write to Standard Output (QtmhWrstout) as, 102-105, 125, 130, 140-144, 185-186, 269
application-specific service programs, 207
AS/400 and e-business applications (*See also* e-RPG business programs), xvi-xvii
assignment vs. conditional operator, JavaScript and, 27
authorities
  CGI programming and, 58
  HTTP server and, 93-97
  Integrated File System (IFS) and, 268

B

BASIC, 50-51
Batch (BCH) job, HTTP server and, 84, 210-213, **212**
Batch Immediate (BCI), HTTP server and, 84, 210-213, **212**
binder language, companion CD-ROM, 332
binding by reference, CGI programming and, 56
binding directories
  APIs and, 101
  CGI programming and, 56-58, 116-117
  for e-RPG programs, 179-180
  QTMHCGI added to, 117
<BODY> tag, 11-12, 13-14, **13**, **14**
bold text
  #Bold (Return Bold Text) for, 196, 306
  <BOLD> tag for, 12

 (Line break) tag, 12
browsers, reading input from (*See* input from browsers)
built in functions (BIF), e-RPG programs and, 120, 136
Buttons, 147
buy item e-RPG application (BUYITEM), 179, 282-287
BVS-Cars HTML starting page (BVSCARS.HTML), 320-321
BVS-Cars program, 320-329

BVS-Computer example (*See* e-RPG programs)
BVS-Reprints source code, 42-44, **42**, 249-254

C

C language, 49
Call Bound Procedure (CALLB)
  APIs and, 101
  CGI programming and, 55
Car database (CARSPF), 321
case sensitivity, HTTP server and, 73
CD-ROM companion disk to book, 331-332
centered text
  #Center (Return Centered Text), 197-198, 307
  <CENTER> tag, 12
CGI (*See* Common Gateway Interface (CGI) programming)
CHAIN operations, CGI programming and, 59
Change Authority (CHGAUT), HTTP server and, 95-96
Change HTTP Attributes (CHGHTTPA), HTTP server and, 67
character data, #CtoN subprocedure to convert, 189, 203-204, 310-311
Checkboxes, 147
checkout application (CHECKOUT), 172-174, 173, 174, 179, 292-296
client/server processes
  CGI programming and, 45-46
  HTTP server and, 64-66
COBOL, 6-7, 49
Cold Fusion, 49
commands, JavaScript and, 32
Common Gateway Interface (CGI)
  programming, xvii, 6, 45-62, 209, 239-240
  access logs and, 61-62
  Add Binding Directory Entry (ADDBNDDIRE) in, 57
  Add Library List Entry (ADDLIBLE) in, 59
  APIs and, 50, 52, 99, 100, 116-117
  AS/400 configuration for, 52-53
  AS/400 programming with, 49-52
  BASIC programming as an example of, 50-51
  binding by reference in, 56

binding directories and, 56-58, 116-117

Call Bound Procedure (CALLB) for, 55

CHAIN operations and, 59

client/server process and, 45-46

Convert to DB (QthmCvtDB) and, 112-116, 162, 271

Create Binding Directory (CRTBNDDIR) for, 56-58

Create Bound RPG (CRTBNDRPG) vs., 56

Create Module (CRTMOD) for, 56

Create Program (CRTPGM) for, 55-56

creation of, 53, 55-58

debugging, 212

directives in, 53-54

dynamic query strings and, 152-160, **153**

dynamic web pages and, 6-7

ENABLE directive in, 53-54

environment variables and, 112-116

for e-RPG programs, 120, 121, 178

errors in, 60

EXEC directive in, 54, 59

GET method in, 53, 160-163

HTML and JavaScript combined with, 165-181

HTTP configuration for, 53-54, 75

input and output applications using, 50-51

Integrated Language Environment (ILE) and, 53

interfaces and, 46-48

interpreter use of, 48-49

JavaScript and vs., 21

job library list for, 59-60

keyed file paging in, 219-222

languages used in, 49

Message Wait (MSGW) status reported in, 60

multithreaded, 212

Open Query File (OPNQRYF) and, 218

paging, 217-222

passwords and, 165, **168**

physical files in, 177

POST method in, 53, 160-163

QCMDEXEC API and, 59

QDFTJOBD default job description for, 59

QHTTPSVR subsystem location of, 59

QTMHCGI service program for, 54-55

QTMHHTP1 user profile for, 58, 59

QTMHHTTP user profile for, 58, 59

query string environment variables in, 53, 150-160

READ operations and, 59

references for, 259

Relative Record Number (RRN) and paging in, 218-222

Remove Library List Entry (RMVLIBLE) in, 59

RPG used in, 239-240

sequential file paging in, 218-219

Server Side Includes (SSIs), 213-217, **214**, **216**

service programs and, 53, 54-55, 57-58, 207

shopping cart applications and, 47-48

special considerations for, 58-62

standard input using, 149-150, 160-163

standard output using, 52

static query strings and, 150-152, **151**

storage of, 76

TCP/IP configuration and, 52-53

user IDs and, 165, **168**

user profiles/authorities for, 58, 59

Work with Active Jobs (WRKACTJOB) for, 60

CONFIG configuration file, HTTP server and, 69, 70, 262-267

Configure TCP/IP HTTP (CFGTCPHTTP), HTTP server and, 66

constraints, 26

constructs, JavaScript and, 28-29

Content Length environment variables, 111, 112

Convert to DB (QthmCvtDB), 112-116, 162, 190-192, 271

#CvtDb subprocedure vs., 190-192, 304

Cookie Basket source code, 245-249

cookies

Cookie Basket source code, 245-249

JavaScript and, 24-25, 37-42, 40, 41

COPY source, companion CD-ROM, 332

Create Binding Directory (CRTBNDDIR), CGI programming and, 56-58

Create Bound RPG (CRTBNDRBG)
APIs and, 101
CGI programming and, 56
Create Directory (CRTDIR), HTTP server and, 89
Create Hyperlink (#Link) 193-194, 305
Create MailTo hyperlink (#MailTo), 195-196, 306
Create Module (CRTMOD), CGI programming and, 56
Create Physical File (CRTPF), 177
Create Program (CRTPGM)
APIs and, 101
CGI programming and, 55-56
#CtoN subprocedure, 189, 203-204, 310-311
Customer Credit Data e-RPG example, 132-135, **135**
CvtDb#CvtDb subprocedure, 190-192, 304

D
DDS
HTML compared to, 8
source code for, on companion CD-ROM, 332
debugging e-RPG programs, 209-213
Batch (BCH) vs. Batch Immediate (BCI) jobs in HTTP server, 210-213, **212**
CGI programs, 212
HTTP Server Instance and, 209-213
multithreaded programs and, 212
Start Debug (STRDBG) for, 213
Work with Active Jobs (WRKACTJOB) in, 210, 211
DEFAULT server instance, HTTP server and, 87, 88
delimiters, JavaScript and, 28-29
dialog boxes, JavaScript and, 25-26
directives, HTTP server and, 72
Display Authority (DSPAUT), HTTP server and, 94-95
display items (ITEMS) program, 279-282
DO, 26
dynamic query strings for, 152-160, **153**
dynamic web pages, 6-7
CGI programming and, 6-7

e-RPG programs and, 130-140
JavaScript and, 42-44, **42**
subfile programs vs., 6-7

E
e-business statistics, xv
Edit Code (%EDITC built-in function), 136-140
Edit Word (%EDITW built-in function) in, 137-140
e-mail services, xvii
EMBEDS directive, HTTP server, 215
ENABLE directive, CGI programming and, 53-54
End TCP Server (ENDTCPSVR), HTTP server and, 84-85
End TCP/IP HTTP Server (ENDDTCPSVR SERVER HTTP), HTTP server and, 67
environment variables
#CtoN subprocedure to convert, 189, 203-204, 310-311
#CvtDb subprocedure, 190-192, 304
#GetEnv subprocedure in, 186-188, 189, 192, 302-303
CGI programming and, 112-116
Content Length environment variables, 111, 112
Convert to DB (QthmCvtDB) for, 112-116, 162, 271, 190
Get Environment Variable (QtmGetEnv) as, 108-112, 156-160, 186-188, 189, 192, 270
GET operation for, 109
list of, 111-112
query string type, 109, 111, 112
Remote Address environment variables, 111
Remote Host environment variables, 111
Request Method environment variables, 111, 112
e-RPG business programming, 119-144, 165-181, 209-222, 273-300, 315-329
Application Programming Interfaces (APIs) and, 120, 122
binding directories and, 179-180
built in functions (BIF) and, 120, 136
buy item (BUYITEM) application in, 179, 282-287

BVS-Cars HTML starting page (BVSCARS.HTML) in, 320-321

BVS-Cars program in, 320-329

BVS-Reprints source code in, 249-254

Car database (CARSPF) in, 321

CGI programming and, 120, 121, 178

checkout application (CHECKOUT) in, 172-174, 173, 174, 179, 292-296

compiling and running programs in, 127-129

Customer Credit Data example using, 132-135, **135**

debugging, 209-213

display items (ITEMS) in, 279-282

dynamic output using, 130-140

Edit Code (%EDITC built-in function) in, 136-140

Edit Word (%EDITW built-in function) in, 137-140

error data structure for, in APIs, 125-126

EXEC directives in, 175-176

external data structure for, 177-178, 321

Go Shopping page example in, 169-175, **170**

Hello World sample application in, 122-125, **129**

HTML file in, 180

HTML, JavaScript, and CGI combined in, 165-181

HTTP configuration for, 122, 128, 175-176, 300

HTTP header information in, 126

hyperlinks in, 168-169

index.html documents in, 176, 180, 273-274

invoice and ship order (INVSHIP), 173-174, **173**, 178, 179, 274-275, 297-299

invoice detail (INVDETPF) source code for, 274

invoice detail logical (INVDET1LF) source code for, 275

invoice header (INVHDRPF) source code for, 274

item file (ITEMSPF) in, 169-171, **170**, 178, 179, 275, 315

item listing program (ITEMLIST) in, 315-320

item listing modules (F.ITEMLIST) in, 316-317

item master logical file (ITEMS1LF) in, 316

list cars program (LISTCARS) in, 323-329

list cars subprocedures (F.LISTCARS) in, 322

modularizing APIs in, 140-144

new-line character use in, 126-127

numeric data converted to characters (%EDITC) in, 136-140

numeric data displayed using, 135-136, **139**

PASS directives in, 175-176

passwords in, 165-168, **168**, 178

physical files for, 177

pseudocode for, 131

QTMHCGI service program and, 179

record selection in, 130-131

remove item (RMVITEM) application in, 173, 173, 179, 288-291

sequence numbers in, 178

Server Side Includes (SSIs), 213-217, **214**, **216**

shopping cart applications in, 171-172, **172**

sign in screen for, 165-168, **167**, **168**, 179, 276-279

subprocedures to modularize APIs for, 140-141

uniform resource locators (URLs) in, 178

user ID file (USERPF) source code in, 165-168, **168**, 178, 275

using RPG to relate to, 130-131

viewing HTML source in, 129-130, **129**

WELCOME directive in, 176

Write to Standard Output (QtmhWrstout) in, 125, 130, 140-144

error data structure in APIs, 125

error messages in HTML, 242-243

EVAL, 26

events, JavaScript and, 31-32

EXEC directive
   CGI programming and, 54, 59
   HTTP server and, 72, 76-78, 92, 175-176, 215, 262

EXECUTE authority, HTTP server and, 93

Note: Boldface numbers indicate illustrations

EXFMT operation, 149
external data structure for LISTCARS
(LISTCARSDS), 321

F

FAIL directive, HTTP server and, 72, 81, 262
fields, JavaScript and, 26
file transfer protocol (FTP), xvii
FOR, JavaScript and, 28-29
<FORM> tag, 12
forms, JavaScript and, 23
functions, JavaScript and, 32

G

Get Environment Variable (QtmhGetEnv),
108-112, 156-160, 270
#GetEnv subprocedure vs., 186-188, 189,
192, 302-303
GET method, 109, 160-163
CGI programming and, 53
query strings using, 154-156
#GetEnv subprocedure, 186-188, 189, 192,
302-303
Go Shopping page example, 169-175, **170**

H

<HEAD> tag in, 10-11, **10**, **11**, 13-14, **13**, **14**
Hello World sample e-RPG application,
122-125, **129**
hiding directory structure of server, MAP, 74-76
hit, 23
<Hn> (Header text) tag, 12
home page sample, IBM-provided, 88, **89**
hostname name property, HTTP server and, 91
HTML (*See* Hypertext Markup Language)
<HTML> tag, 9-10, **9**
HTTP Configuration, 128
HTTP Header, 126
HTTP server, 63-97, 239
ADMIN server instance in, 87-88
Application Programming Interfaces (APIs)
for, 99-118, 269-271
AS/400 as, 63

authority to IFS objects on, 93-97, 268
Batch (BCH) job for, 84, 210-213, **212**
Batch Immediate (BCI) jobs in, 84, 210-213,
212
case sensitivity in, 73
CGI program storage in, 75
Change Authority (CHGAUT) for, 95-96
Change HTTP Attributes (CHGHTTPA) for,
67
client/server processes in, 64-66
combining directives for, 77, 78, 79-80
combining instance and configuration for,
89-90
CONFIG (default configuration) 69, **70**,
262-267
configuration of, 66-67, 175-176, 262
Configure TCP/IP HTTP (CFGTCPHTTP)
for, 66
Create Directory (CRTDIR) for, 89
creating Server Instance, 85-87, **86**
default (CONFIG) configuration for, 262-267
DEFAULT server instance in, 87, 88
directives for, 72
Display Authority (DSPAUT) for, 94-95
EMBEDS directive for, 215
End TCP Server (ENDTCPSVR) for, 84-85
End TCP/IP HTTP Server (ENDDTCPSVR
SERVER HTTP) for, 67
e-RPG program configuration of, 122, 128,
300
errors in, 90
EXEC directive for, 72, 76-78, 92, 175-176,
215, 262
EXECUTE authority in, 93
explicit PASS directive in, 83
FAIL directive in, 72, 81, 262
file types for, 65-66
header, HTTP Header information in, 126
hiding directory structure of, using MAP,
74-76
home page sample for, IBM-provided, 88, **89**
hostname name property for, 91
HTML and, 63
HTTP Server Configuration in, 67, 68-84,
128

HTTP Server Instance and debugging programs in, 209-213
HTTP Server Instance for, 67, 84-89, 128
index.html documents in, 176, 180
Integrated File System (IFS) and, 93-97, 268
library list subprocedures for, 257-259
machines compatible as, 63
MAP directive in, 72, 73-76, 92, 262
naming server instances in, 87
order of directives in, 80, 83-84
PASS directive in, 72, 78-80, 89, 92, 175-176, 262
passwords for, 69
paths and filenames for, 65-66
PORT directive for, 91
port numbers and, 64, 68, 91-92
potential of, 97
properties for server instances in, 91
QHTTPSVR subsystem for, 84, 88, 90
READ authority in, 93, 94
Read Standard Input (QtmhRdStin) and, 105-108, 270
REDIRECT directive in, 72, 81-82, 262
reference sources for, 268
reserved port numbers, 91, 92
sample configuration file, 267
Secure Sockets Layer (SSL) and, 68
Server Side Includes (SSIs), 213-217, **214**, **216**
service programs and subprocedures for, 184-192, 207, 301-304
sign in screen for, 165-168, **167**, **168**
Start TCP Server (STRTCPSVR) for, 84
Start TCP/IP HTTP Server (STRTCPSVR SERVER HTTP) for, 67
storing files on, 65-66
Tasks page of AS/400 and, accessing, 261
Tasks page of AS/400 for configuration of, 67, 69-71, **69**, 85
TCP/IP configuration and, 66-67
Uniform Resource Locators (URLs) and, 64
user IDs for, 69
virtual hosting on, 92-93
WELCOME directive for, 72, 82-83, 176, 262

Work with Active Job (WRKACTJOB) for, 88, 90, 210, 211
Work with Authority (WRKAUT) for, 96-97, **96**
Work with HTTP Configuration (WRKHTTPCFG) for, 67, 72-73, 90
WRITE authority in, 93
Write to Standard Output (QtmhWrStout) for, 102-105, 269
HTTP Server Configuration, 53-54, 67, 68-84
HTTP Server Instance, 67, 84-89, 128
hyperlinks, 168-169
HTML and, 2-3
#Link (Create Hyperlink) subprocedure in, 193-194, 305
#MailTo (Create MailTo Hyperlink), 195-196, 306
mail=to hyperlinks and, 2-3, 195-196
hypertext markup language (HTML), xvii, xviii, 1-20, 52, 238
(Anchor) tag in, 12
<BODY> tag in, 11-12, 13-14, **13**, **14**
#Bold (Return Bold Text), 196, 306
bold text, 12, 196, 306
tag in, 12

 (Line break) tag in, 12
Buttons in, 147
#Center (Return Centered Text), 197-198, 307
<CENTER> tag in, 12
centered text, 197, 307
Checkboxes in, 147
Customer Credit Data example using, 132-135, **135**
DDS compared to, 8
dynamic query strings and, 152-160, 153
dynamic web pages and, 6-7, 130-140
error messages in, 242-243
<FORM> tag in, 12
GET method query strings in, 154-156
<HEAD> tag in, 10-11, **10**, **11**, 13-14, **13**, **14**
header, HTTP Header information in, 126
Hello World sample e-RPG application, 122-125, **129**
<Hn> (Header text) tag in, 12

HTML, *continued*
  <HTML> tag in, 9-10, **9**
  HTTP server and, 63
  hyperlinks and, 2-3
  index.html file in, 180
  #Input (Return Input Field), 198-201, 308
  input fields in, 147-148, 198, 308
  input from browsers using, 146-148
   tag in, 12
  italic text, 197, 307
  #Italics (Return Italic Text), 197, 307
  JavaScript and CGI combined with, 165-181
  JavaScript and, 21-23, 32-33
  #Link (Create Hyperlink) subprocedure in, 193-194, 305
  mail=to hyperlinks and, 2-3
  #MailTo (Create MailTo Hyperlink), 195-196, 306
  new-line character use in, 126-127
  numeric data displayed using, 135-136, **139**
  query strings and, 150-160
  Radio buttons in, 147
  Read Standard Input (QtmhRdStin) and, 105-108, 270
  references for, 243-244
  #Replace (Replace Characters), 204-207, 312-313
  Select Boxes in, 147
  Server Side Includes (SSIs), 213-217, **214, 216**
  service programs and subprocedures for, 193-202, 207, 305-310
  source folder on companion CD-ROM for, 332
  standard input in, 160-163
  static query strings and, 150-152, **151**
  static web pages using, 4-6
  structures in, 7-8
  subprocedures for, 193-202, 207, 305-310
  <TABLE> tag in, 12, 17-19
  tables to align fields in, 15-16, **15, 16**
  tables to format output from, 14-15
  tables to report data in, 17-19
  tags in, 7-8, 9-10
  <TD> (Table cell data) tag in, 12, 18

Text Area fields in, 147
Text fields in, 147
<TEXTAREA> tag in, 12
<TITLE> tag in, 10-11, **10, 11**
<TR> (Table row) tag in, 12, 18
uses for, 4, 8, 19-20
viewing HTML source in, 129-130, **129**
world wide web (WWW) use of, 1-2
Write to Standard Output (QtmhWrStout) and, 102-105, 125, 130, 140-144, 269
WrtSrcMbr (Write Source Member), 201-202, 309-310
hypertext transfer protocol (HTTP) (*See also* HTTP server), xvii, xviii

I
IF, 26
  JavaScript and, 28-29
index.html documents, 176, 180, 273-274
input fields, #Input (Return Input Field), 198-201, 308
input from browsers, 145-163
  Buttons for, 147
  Checkboxes for, 147
  Convert to DB (QthmCvtDB) for, 162
  dynamic query strings for, 152-160, **153**
  dynamic query strings using JavaScript for, 152-154
  Get Environment Variable (QtmhGetEnv) to read, 156-160
  GET method for, 160-163
  GET method query strings for, 154-156
  HTML tools for, 146-148
  input fields in HTML for, 147-148
  POST method for, 160-163
  query strings for, 148-149, 150-160
  Radio buttons for, 147
  Read Standard Input (QtmhRdStin) for, 162-163
  reading query string input with e-RPG and, 156-160
  reading standard input with e-RPG and, 162-163
  Select Boxes for, 147
  standard input for, 148, 149-150, 160-163

static query strings for, 150-152, **151**

Text Area fields for, 147

Text fields for, 147

#Input (Return Input Field), 198-201, 308

<INPUT> tag, 12

Integrated File System (IFS)

    authorities and, 268

    HTTP server and, 93-97

Integrated Language Environment (ILE)

    APIs and, 100

    CGI programming and, 53

    service programs and, 183-184

interactive error processing, JavaScript and, 34-37, **36**

interfaces, CGI programming and, 46-48

Internet usage statistics, xv

invoice application, 173-174, **173**, 178, 179, 274-275

invoice detail (INVDETPF) source code, 274

invoice detail logical (INVDET1LF) source code, 275

invoice header (INVHDRPF) source code, 274

italic text

    #Italics (Return Italic Text), 197, 307

item file (ITEMPF) in e-RPG program/web page, 169-171, 170, 178, 179, 275, 315

item listing e-RPG program (ITEMLIST), 318-320

item listing modules (F.ITEMLIST), 316-317

item master logical file (ITEMS1LF), 316

J

Java, xvii, 120

    CGI programming and, 49

    vs. JavaScript, 21

JavaScript, xvii, xviii, 21-44, 238

    assignment vs. conditional operator in, 27

    CGI vs., 21

    commands in, 32

    constructs in, 28-29

    cookies and, 24-25, 37-42, **40**, **41**

    delimiters used in, 28-29

    development history of, 22-23

    dynamic query strings using, 152-154

    dynamic web pages using, 42-44, **42**

    events in, 31-32,

    examples of, 32-33

    field validation using, 25, 34-37, **36**

    fields in, 26

    FOR in, 28-29

    forms using, 23

    functions in, 32

    hit counter using, 23

    HTML and, 21-23, 32-33

    HTML and CGI combined with, 165-181

    IF in, 28-29

    interactive error processing using, 34-37, **36**

    Java vs., 21

    looping in, 28-29

    methods in, 31

    multiple cookies and multiple elements in, 38-42

    objects in, 30-31

    OnBlur event in, 32

    OnClick event in, 31

    OnFocus event in, 32

    OnLoad event in, 32

    OnMouseOut event in, 32

    OnMouseOver event in, 31

    OnUnload event in, 32

    operators in, 27-28

    precedence of operators in, 28

    properties in, 30-31

    pseudoarrays in, 39

    quoting system using, 42-44, **42**, 249-254

    redirecting browsers using, 33-34

    reference sources for, 255

    shopping carts using, 24-25, 37-42, **40**, **41**

    terminology of, 29-30

    two-dimensional arrays in, 43-44

    uses for, 21, 23-24

    variables in, 26

    viewing HTML source in, 129-130, **129**

    WHILE in, 28-29

    window relocation/creation using, 25-26

    Write to Standard Output (QtmhWrStout) and, 102-105, 269

#WrtSrcMbr (Write Source Member), 201-202, 309-310

Note: Boldface numbers indicate illustrations

K

keyed file paging, CGI programs, 219-222

L

library lists
  CGI programming and, 59-60
  #PopLib subprocedure for, 257-259
  #PushLib subprocedure for, 257-259
#Link (Create Hyperlink) subprocedure in,
  193-194, 305
list cars e-RPG program (LISTCARS), 323-329
list cars subprocedures (F.LISTCARS), 322
list items (ITEMLIST) code, 315-320
LOOKUP, 26
looping, JavaScript and, 28-29
Lotus Notes, 49

M

mail=to hyperlinks, 2-3
  #MailTo (Create MailTo Hyperlink),
    195-196, 306
MAP directive, HTTP server and, 72, 73-76, 92,
  262
menus, static web pages as, 5-6, **5**, **6**
Message Wait (MSGW) status reported, CGI
  programming and, 60
methods, JavaScript and, 31
Module source, companion CD-ROM, 332
multithreaded CGI programs, 212

N

Net.Data, 49, 120
new-line character use, e-RPG programs and,
  126-127
numeric data
  #CtoN subprocedure to convert, 189,
    203-204, 310-311
  convert to characters (%EDITC), 136-140
  e-RPG programs and, 135-136

O

objects, JavaScript and, 30-31
OnBlur event, JavaScript and, 32
OnClick event, JavaScript and, 31
OnFocus event, JavaScript and, 32
OnLoad event, JavaScript and, 32
OnMouseOut event, JavaScript and, 32
OnMouseOver event, JavaScript and, 31
OnUnload event, JavaScript and, 32
Open Query File (OPNQRYF), 209, 218
operators, JavaScript and, 26, 27-28
Override Database File (OVRDBF), 202

P

paging in CGI, 217-222
  keyed file routine for, 219-222
  Open Query File (OPNQRYF) and, 218
  Relative Record Number (RRN) and,
    218-222
  sequential file routine for, 218-219
PASS directive, HTTP server and, 72, 78-80,
  89, 90, 92, 175-176, 262
passwords, 165-168, **168**
  CGI programming and, 165, **168**
  for e-RPG programs, 178
  HTTP server and, 69
Perl, xvii, 49, 99, 120
physical files, for e-RPG programs, 177
#PopLib subprocedure, 257-259
PORT directive, HTTP server and, 91
port numbers, HTTP server and, 64, 68, 91-92
POST method, 105, 109, 160-163
  CGI programming and, 53
precedence of operators, JavaScript and, 28
properties, JavaScript and, 30-31
properties for server instances, HTTP server
  and, 91
pseudoarrays in JavaScript cookies, 39
pseudocoding e-RPG programs, 131
#PushLib subprocedure, 257-259

Q

QCMDEXEC API, CGI programming and, 59
QDFTJOBD default job description, CGI
  programming and, 59
QHTTPSVR subsystem
  CGI programming and, 59
  HTTP server and, 84, 88, 90
QRPGLESRC source physical file, xvii

QthmCvtDB, 112-116, 162, 190-192, 271
QTMHCGI service program
  APIs and, 100, **101**
  CGI programming and, 54-55
  for e-RPG programs, 179
QtmhGetEnv, 108-112, 156-160, 270
  #GetEnv subprocedure vs., 186-188, 189,
    192, 302-303
QTMHHTP1 user profile, CGI programming
  and, 58, 59
QTMHHTTP user profile, CGI programming
  and, 58, 59
QtmhRdStin, 105-108, 162-163, 188-189, 270
QtmhWrstout, 102-105, 125, 130, 140-144, 269
  #WrStout subprocedure and, 185-186, 302
query string environment variables, 109, 111,
  112
  CGI programming and, 53
  #CvtDb subprocedure, 190-192, 304
  Convert to DB (QtmhCvtDB), 190
  dynamic query strings for, 152-160, **153**
  GET method in, 154-156
  input from browsers and, 148-149, 150-160
  JavaScript and, 152-154
  static, 150-152, **151**
quoting system using JavaScript and, 42-44, 42,
  249-254

R

Radio buttons, 147
#RdStin subprocedure, 188-189, 303
READ authority, HTTP server and, 93, 94
Read from Standard Input (QtmhRdStin),
  105-108, 162-163, 188-189, 270
  #RdStin subprocedure vs., 188-189, 303
READ operation, 149
  CGI programming and, 59
receiver variables, APIs and, 106-107, 110
record selection, e-RPG programs and, 130-131
REDIRECT directive, HTTP server and, 72,
  81-82, 262
redirecting browsers, JavaScript and, 33-34
Relative Record Number (RRN) and paging,
  218-222
Remote Address environment variables, 111

Remote Host environment variables, 111
remove item (RMVITEM) application, 173,
  173, 179, 288-291
Remove Library List Entry (RMVLIBLE), CGI
  programming and, 59
Replace Characters (#Replace), 204-207,
  312-313
Report Program Generator (*See* RPG; e-RPG
  business programming)
Request Method environment variables, 111,
  112
reserved port numbers, 91, 92
Return Bold Text (#Bold), 196, 306
Return Centered Text (#Center), 197-198, 307
Return Input Field (#Input), 198-201, 308
Return Italic Text (#Italics), 197, 307
RPG and e-business applicatios, xvi-xvii, xviii
  CGI programming and, 49, 239-240
  source folder on companion CD-ROM for,
    332

S

Secure Sockets Layer (SSL), HTTP server and,
  68
Select Boxes, 147
sequence numbers for e-RPG programs, 178
sequential file paging, CGI programs, 218-219
Server Side Includes (SSI), 209, 213-217, **214**,
  216
service programs and subprocedures, 183-208
  Application Programming Interfaces (APIs)
    and, 100, 184
  application-specific, 207
  #Bold (Return Bold Text), 196, 306
  #Center (Return Centered Text), 197-198,
    307
  CGI programming and, 53, 54-55, 57-58, 207
  #CtoN subprocedure, 189, 203-204, 310-311
  #CvtDb subprocedure, 190-192, 304
  Display Service Program (DSPSRVPGM)
    for, 100
  #GetEnv subprocedure in, 186-188, 189, 192,
    302-303
  HTML and, 193-202, 207, 305-310
  HTTP and, 207, 301-304

Note: Boldface numbers indicate illustrations

service programs and subprocedures, *continued*
 #Input (Return Input Field), 198-201, 308
 Integrated Language Environment (ILE) and, 183-184
 #Italics (Return Italic Text), 197, 307
 #Link (Create Hyperlink) subprocedure in, 193-194, 305
 #MailTo (Create MailTo Hyperlink), 195-196, 306
 pound sign to identify, 184-185
 QTMHCGI, 179
 #RdStin subprocedure in, 188-189, 303
 #Replace (Replace Characters), 204-207, 312-313
 standard HTTP subprocedures in, 184-192
 #WrStout subprocedure in, 185-186, 302
 #WrtSrcMbr (Write Source Member), 201-202, 309-310
shopping cart applications, 171-172, **172**
 CGI programming and, 47-48
 Cookie Basket source code, 245-249
 JavaScript and, 24-25, 37-42, **40**, **41**
sign in program, 165-168, **167**, **168**, 179, 276-279
source members, #WrtSrcMbr (Write Source Member), 201-202, 309-310
standard input, 148-150, 160-163
 CGI programming and, 149-150
 Convert to DB (QthmCvtDB) for, 162
 #RdStin subprocedure, 188-189, 303
 Read from Standard Input (QtmhRdStin), 162-163, 188-189
standard output
 CGI programming and, 52
 Read Standard Input (QtmhRdStin) and, 105-108, 270
 Write to Standard Output (QtmhWrStout) API for, 102-105, 125, 130, 140-144, 185-186, 269
 #WrStout subprocedure for, 185-186, 302
Start Debug (STRDBG), 213
Start TCP Server (STRTCPSVR), HTTP server and, 84
Start TCP/IP HTTP Server (STRTCPSVR SERVER HTTP), HTTP server and, 67

static query strings, 150-152, **151**
static web pages, 4-6
 menu=like appearance of, 5-6, **5**, **6**
Status Data Structures (SDS), 108
structures in HTML (*See* hypertext markup language)
subfile programs, 6-7
Submit buttons, 105
subprocedures to modularize APIs (*See also* service programs and subprocedures), 140-141

T

<TABLE> tag, 12, 17-19
tables
 aligning HTML fields using, 15-16, **15**, **16**
 formatting HTML output with, 14-15
 reporting data using, 17-19
 <TABLE> tag in, 12, 17-19
 <TD> tag in, 12, 18
 <TR> tag in, 12, 18
tags in HTML (*See* hypertext markup language)
Tasks page of AS/400
 accessing of, 261
 HTTP server and, 67, 69-71, **69**, 85
TCP/IP
 CGI programming and, 52-53, 52
 HTTP server and, 66-67, **66**
<TD> (Table cell data) tag, 12, 18
Text Area fields, 147
Text fields, 147
<TEXTAREA> tag, 12
tips and techniques (*See* e-RPG business programming)
<TITLE> tag in, 10-11, **10**, **11**
<TR> (Table row) tag, 12, 18
two-dimensional arrays, JavaScript and, 43-44

U

Uniform Resource Locators (URLs)
 for e-RPG programs, 178
 HTTP server and, 64
user ID file (USERPF) source code, 165-168, **168**, 275

CGI programming and, 165, **168**
for e-RPG programs, 178
HTTP server and, 69
user profiles, authorities, CGI programming and, 58, 59

V

validation, JavaScript and, 25, 34-37, **36**
variables, JavaScript and, 26
viewing HTML source, 129-130, **129**
virtual hosting, 92-93
Visual Basic, 49, 120

W

Webmasters, 3-4
WELCOME directive, HTTP server and, 72, 82-83, 176, 262

WHEN, 26
WHILE, JavaScript and, 28-29
Work with Active Job (WRKACTJOB), 210-211
CGI programming and, 60
HTTP server and, 88, 90
Work with Authority (WRKAUT), HTTP server and, 96-97, **96**
Work with HTTP Configuration (WRKHTTPCFG), 67, 72-73, 90
WRITE authority, HTTP server and, 93
Write Source Member (#WrtSrcMbr), 201-202, 309-310
Write to Standard Output (QtmhWrstout), 102-105, 125, 130, 140-144, 269
#WrStout subprocedure vs., 185-186, 302
#WrtSrcMbr (Write Source Member), 201-202, 309-310

Note: Boldface numbers indicate illustrations

Other Best-sellers of Related Interest

Getting Down to e-business with AS/400

by Bob Cancilla

Gain an understanding of the issues, concepts, and technologies necessary to implement an AS/400-based e-business solution with the help of this new book from Bob Cancilla. From planning for e-business to selecting an ISP, you'll learn through examples from those companies that have successfully deployed mission-critical e-business applications with the IBM AS/400. You'll also learn about the many products that work together to make the AS/400 a Web server, how to develop a project plan, and how to design and build an e-business Web site. While many other books touch on individual Internet-related technologies, Getting Down to e-business with AS/400 puts all the pieces together! 448 pages. Level: Novice, Intermediate, and Advanced.

BOOK 5014 ....$89
ISBN 1-58347-010-7

Re-engineering RPG Legacy Applications

by Paul Tuohy

Now you can use IBM's recent enhancements to the AS/400, OS/400, and RPG to immediately increase the reliability of your legacy applications, improve programmer productivity, and build a firm basis for the future of your business. This book and companion CD-ROM provide a tutorial aimed at showing you how to modernize your applications by taking you through a re-engineering of a sample application step-by-step. Author Paul Tuohy covers conversion of RPG IV programs as well as re-engineering them to take full advantage of RPG IV and ILE. He also covers triggers, referential integrity, and APIs so that your applications can take advantage of all the new technology that is available today. This book will be a valuable aid as you evaluate your legacy applications and then move into re-engineering.

Putting your company's IT resources in a condition of stasis while technology moves on may be a costly business mistake. It is possible and profitable to derive some of the benefits of new technology from within a legacy application. Best of all, re-engineering gives you the opportunity to learn new programming concepts and acquire new skills. 528 pages. Level: Intermediate to Advanced.

BOOK 5009 ....$99
ISBN 1-58347-006-9

AS/400 Primer—Third Edition

by Ernie Malaga, Doug Pence, and Ron Hawkins

Increase understanding of the AS/400 and boost productivity with AS/400 Primer—Third Edition, the new book from Midrange Computing. A must for every AS/400 professional, this comprehensive, newly revised, 30-chapter volume is perfect for novice and intermediate programmers as well as for system administrators and operators. In simple, straightforward style, the authors not only explain core AS/400 concepts but also show you—step-by-step—how to perform 30 essential AS/400 functions, including installation, troubleshooting, administration, operations, programming, and 25 other tasks!

Updated by Doug Pence and Ron Hawkins, this third edition of the Primer contains page after page of enhanced information covering programming in RPG IV, new system values, ILE concepts, important new system security information, running the AS/400 as an Internet server, and much more! You'll definitely find AS/400 Primer—Third Edition to be a learning tool and valuable reference for years to come. 560 pages. Level: Novice, Intermediate, and Advanced.

BOOK 5012 ....$99
ISBN 1-883884-59-4

5 Easy Ways to Order!

FAX
this order form to 760-931-9935,
24 hours a day, 365 days a year.

MAIL
your order to 5650 El Camino Real,
Suite 225, Carlsbad, CA 92008.

EMAIL
your order to *custsvc@*
midrangecomputing.com.

PHONE
toll-free 1-800-477-5665
(Mon. to Fri., 6 a.m. to 5 p.m. PST).

ONLINE
ordering is available at *www.*
mc-store.com.

For a complete list of titles, call 1-800-477-5665 or visit our Web site at www.midrangecomputing.com.

Other Bestsellers of Related Interest

Complete CL

The Definitive Control Language Programming Guide—Third Edition
by Ernie Malaga and Ted Holt
This new and updated version of the classic 1992 book brings together the solid basics of CL and the newest innovations to this mainstay programming language.

When you have completed this book, you will be able to write simple and advanced CL programs, understand the strengths and limitations of the CL language, develop a good CL coding style, and avoid common mistakes when writing CL. You will learn to manipulate strings with built-in functions and operators, code looping, and decision structures; make procedures communicate with one another via messages; make CL procedures communicate with users; and use data queues and data areas. You also will learn to understand and use overrides effectively, process display and database files, use APIs, and effectively use the QTEMP library. You will be able to avoid the pitfalls of adopted authorities, understand security issues, convert S/36 OCL and S/38 CL to native CL, and much more. If you are responsible for AS/400 application development or if you are an operator or programmer responsible for AS/400 operations, you won't want to be without this book. 496 pages. Level: Novice to Intermediate.

❏ BOOK C5001 .... $79
ISBN 1-883884-58-6

The AS/400 Owner's Manual for V4

by Mike Dawson
Midrange Computing's all-time best-selling manual is now V4R2-ready! Designed for AS/400 professionals at all levels, *The AS/400 Owner's Manual for V4* walks you through hundreds of AS/400 tasks from the perspective of how most shops actually work. Cutting through the dozens of parameters and options of AS/400 commands, *The AS/400 Owner's Manual for V4* takes you directly to the results you need. Offering much more than brief, to-the-point instructions, it also includes valuable descriptions that examine why AS/400 managers, administrators, operators, and programmers do certain things on the machine and how the AS/400 works internally. This edition is completely up-to-date for Version 4 of OS/400 and contains a new chapter about the Internet and TCP/IP. Wire-bound and concise, *The AS/400 Owner's Manual for V4* is the perfect workstation tool for anyone who does AS/400 operations, administration, or management. 464 pages. Level: Intermediate to Advanced.

❏ BOOK C5000 .... $59
ISBN 1-58347-001-8

The AS/400 & Microsoft® Office Integration Handbook

by Brian Singleton with Colleen Garton
This book takes a detailed look at how you can integrate applications in the Microsoft Office 97 product suite with data from your AS/400. Unravel secrets such as how to use your AS/400's output with your PC's data formatting tools or how to make attractive, professional reports with AS/400 data the easy way. Learn the secret of using visual query tools to point and click the creation of sophisticated information output and how to analyze and summarize the detailed (and often cumbersome) reports from your AS/400. Discover how you can combine the presentation capabilities of Microsoft Office with the database capabilities of the AS/400 to provide your company with the best of both worlds.

In the first sections of the book, Singleton introduces you to the essential knowledge you need to use Client Access as you integrate AS/400 data with the Microsoft Office applications. He covers installing and configuring Client Access, how to provide a seamless method of AS/400 integration with Microsoft Office using ODBC, the network drive functionality of Client Access, and the Client Access data transfer function. He also covers TCP/IP's FTP file transfer function and how to use it to bring data from the AS/400 to your PC.

The remaining sections of the book cover the veritable Swiss Army knife functions of Microsoft Office. 320 pages. Level: Novice, Intermediate, and Advanced.

❏ BOOK 587 .... $79
ISBN 1-883884-49-7

The Modern RPG [III] Language with Structured Programming

by Bob Cozzi
Whether you're a new programmer or an old hand, this best-selling book will help you write the kind of code that sets you apart from the crowd—powerful RPG code that's easy to use, enhance, and expand. You'll increase your professional value as you apply the principles and ready-to-use solutions that have made *The Modern RPG [III] Language with Structured Programming* the world's most popular RPG III book.

You'll learn about structured programming concepts—from design to implementation—so that you can easily write, debug, and maintain truly modern modular programs. He explains how to code and implement traditional RPG database file processing so that you will no longer be constricted by the RPG cycle. He even includes information on database file processing with embedded SQL. 458 pages. Level: Novice, Intermediate, and Advanced.

BOOK 531 .... $69
ISBN 0-9621825-0-8